# Dis/ability in Media, Law and History



This book explores how being "disabled" originates in the physical world, social representations and rules, and historical power relations—the interplay of which render bodies "normal" or not.

Do parking signs that represent people in wheelchairs as self-propelling influence how we view dis/ability? How do wheelchair users understand their own bodies and an environment not built for them? By asking questions like these the authors reveal how normalization has informed people's experiences of their bodies and their fight for substantive equality. Understanding these processes requires acknowledging the tension between social construction and embodiment as well as centering the intersection of dis/abilities with other identities, such as race, class, gender, sex orientation, citizen status, and so on.

Scholars and researchers will find that this book provides new avenues for thinking about dis/ability. A wider audience will find it accessible and informative.

**Micky Lee** is a Professor of Media Studies at Suffolk University, Boston. She has published in the areas of feminist political economy; information, technologies, and finance. Her latest books are *Media Technologies for Work and Play in East Asia: Critical Perspectives on Japan and the Two Koreas* (Bristol University Press, 2021; co-edited with Peichi Chung, Chinese University of Hong Kong), *Information* (Routledge, 2021), *Alphabet: The Becoming of Google* (Routledge, 2019), and *Bubbles and Machines: Gender, Information, and Financial Crises* (University of Westminster Press, 2019).

**Frank Rudy Cooper** is William S. Boyd Professor of Law and Director of the Program on Race, Gender & Policing at the University of Nevada, Las Vegas, William S. Boyd School of Law. He is co-editor of *Masculinities and Law: A Multidimensional Approach* (with Ann C. McGinley, 2012). He has published 30 articles on racial profiling, cultural studies, policing, masculinities studies, and intersectionality theory in venues such as the *Boston University Law Review*, the *University of California – Davis Law Review*, the *University of Illinois Law Review*, and the *Arizona State Law Journal*. His most recent publication is *Fight the Power!: Law and Policy Through Hip-hop Songs* (Cambridge University Press, 2022) (co-edited with Gregory S. Parks).

**Patricia Reeve** is an Associate Professor of U.S. History at Suffolk University. Her scholarship focuses on 19th-century workers in the United States and their reimagining of citizenship as an embodied status in response to unprecedented and disabling industrial accidents. Currently, she is researching Suffolk County Coroners' Inquests conducted from 1775 through 1860 which provide an important lens on Bostonians' public lives, occupations, and health. Patricia also co-directs the annual American Studies Institute co-sponsored by the Graduate Program in American Studies at University of Massachusetts Boston and the John F. Kennedy Presidential Library and Museum.

## Interdisciplinary Disability Studies

Series editor: Mark Sherry

*The University of Toledo, USA*

Dis/ability studies has made great strides in exploring power and the body. This series extends the interdisciplinary dialogue between dis/ability studies and other fields by asking how dis/ability studies can influence a particular field. It will show how a deep engagement with dis/ability studies changes our understanding of the following fields: sociology, literary studies, gender studies, bioethics, social work, law, education, or history. This ground-breaking series identifies both the practical and theoretical implications of such an interdisciplinary dialogue and challenges people in dis/ability studies as well as other disciplinary fields to critically reflect on their professional praxis in terms of theory, practice, and methods.

**Dis/ability Representation in Film, TV, and Print Media**
*Edited by Michael S. Jeffress*

**Accessibility Denied. Understanding Inaccessibility and Everyday Resistance to Inclusion for Persons with Dis/abilities**
*Hanna Egard, Kristofer Hansson and David Wästerfors*

**Understanding Dis/ability Throughout History**
Interdisciplinary Perspectives in Iceland from Settlement to 1936
*Edited by Hanna Björg Sigurjónsdóttir and James G. Rice*

**Dis/ability and Art History from Antiquity to the Twenty-First Century**
*Edited by Ann Millett-Gallant and Elizabeth Howie*

**Dis/ability in Media, Law and History: Intersectional, Embodied AND Socially Constructed?**
*Edited by Micky Lee, Frank Rudy Cooper and Patricia Reeve*

For a full list of titles in this series, please visit: www.routledge.com/series/ASHSER1401

# Dis/ability in Media, Law and History

## Intersectional, Embodied AND Socially Constructed?

**Edited by Micky Lee, Frank Rudy Cooper, and Patricia Reeve**

Routledge
Taylor & Francis Group
LONDON AND NEW YORK

First published 2022
by Routledge
4 Park Square, Milton Park, Abingdon, Oxon OX14 4RN

and by Routledge
605 Third Avenue, New York, NY 10158

*Routledge is an imprint of the Taylor & Francis Group, an informa business*



*British Library Cataloguing-in-Publication Data*
A catalogue record for this book is available from the British Library

*Library of Congress Cataloging-in-Publication Data*
A catalog record has been requested for this book

ISBN: 978-1-032-18976-5 (hbk)
ISBN: 978-1-032-18980-2 (pbk)
ISBN: 978-1-003-25719-6 (ebk)

DOI: 10.4324/9781003257196

Typeset in Goudy
by MPS Limited, Dehradun

Micky Lee: *To the people in Hong Kong.*

Frank Rudy Cooper: *To all who suffer beneath the surface and await the day their struggles can be acknowledged.*

Patricia Reeve: *To all who challenge ableism and whose experiences and ideas inform this collection.*

# Contents

# Figures

# Contributors

**Jenifer L. Barclay** is an assistant professor in the Department of History at the University at Buffalo and an associate editor for *Review of Disability Studies*. Her first book, *The Mark of Slavery: Disability, Race, and Gender in Antebellum America* (2021), was supported by fellowships in African American Studies at the University of Virginia's Carter G. Woodson Institute and Case Western Reserve University.

**Mary Crossley** is a professor of Law, John E. Murray Faculty Scholar, and Director of the Health Law Program at the University of Pittsburgh School of Law. Widely recognized for her scholarship in disability and health law, Professor Crossley has written broadly on issues of inequality in health care financing and delivery and has published articles in numerous law journals, including *Columbia Law Review*, *Iowa Law Review*, and *Notre Dame Law Review*.

**Radu-Harald Dinu** is a Senior Lecturer in History at the School of Education and Communication, Jönköping University (Sweden). He received his Ph.D. in history from The Max Weber Center for Advanced Cultural and Social Studies, Erfurt University and an M.A. degree in East European History from Leipzig University (Germany).

**Kim Carina Hebben** is a doctoral researcher in media studies at Ruhr University of Bochum. She graduated from Ruhr University of Bochum with a master's degree in media studies and German studies in 2014. Furthermore, she is a research assistant and student council at the Department of Diversity Studies at TU Dortmund University since 2017.

**Tom Lininger** is the Orlando J. and Marian H. Hollis Professor at the University of Oregon School of Law. He graduated from Harvard Law School and Yale College. His scholarship focuses on evidence and ethics. The US Supreme Court has cited Lininger's scholarship on evidence law, and Justice Elena Kagan has described a treatise co-authored by Lininger as "the principal modern treatise on evidence."

**Eric J. Miller** is a professor and Leo J. O'Brien Fellow at Loyola Law School in Los Angeles, where he teaches and writes in the areas of criminal procedure, jurisprudence, critical race theory, reparations, and problem-solving courts. Professor Miller is a former Chair of the AALS Section on Criminal Justice, and a co-editor of the *Cambridge Handbook on Policing in America* (2019), as well as co-founder of the Policing Los Angeles Forum.

**Anne-Lise Mithout** is an assistant professor of Japanese studies at Université de Paris. Her research deals with disability in Japanese society, from a sociological and historical perspective. She has conducted research on education for disabled children, the Disability Rights Movement, disabled people's employment, and representations of people with disabilities in the media.

**Pam Mullins, LMHC**, is a psychotherapist in private practice in the Boston area. With over 30 years of experience, she has worked in a variety of settings including detox, residential programs, college counseling, and outpatient mental health programs. In addition, Pam was a site supervisor for Lesley interns as well as a Clinical Practice and Supervision Instructor at Lesley University for 20 years. Her diagnosis of multiple sclerosis 20 years ago leads her to reflect on her particular way of being in the world using these perspectives.

**Madeleine M. Plasencia** earned tenure in 2003 at the University of Tulsa College of Law. Broadly published in constitutional law, tort law, redlining, and inequality, Professor Plasencia's published books include *Privacy and the Constitution* (Routledge) as well as numerous law review articles, including *No Right to Lie, Cheat, or Steal: Public Good v. Private Order*, 68 U. MIA L. Rev. 677 (2014). She teaches at the University of Miami School of Law, and is the Chair of the Civil Rights Law Section of the Hispanic National Bar Association.

**Lauren Rouse** is a doctoral candidate in Texts and Technology at the University of Central Florida. Their dissertation research focuses on representations of cognitive disabilities, neurodiversity, and mental health in fan works.

**Sebastian Schlund** is a research assistant at the Department of History, Kiel University, Germany. His main research interests focus on 19th- and 20th-century Disability History, Global History, Migration History, and the Theory of Intersectionality. In 2017, his Ph.D. thesis on the History of Disabled Sports in the Federal Republic of Germany was awarded with the prestigious Deutscher Studienpreis by the Körber Foundation.

**Raphaela Tkotzyk** is an assistant professor at the Institute of Diversity Studies at the Technological University of Dortmund, Germany. Dr. Tkotzyk completed her Ph.D. at the Ruhr-University Bochum, Germany with a thesis on Gender- and Media Studies. She also holds two M.A.s, one in

History and the other one in German Literature and Languages. Much of her research deals with reading literacy and early literacy education and its effects, for example, on political attitudes.

**Lauri Umansky** serves as professor of history and Director of the Heritage Studies Ph.D. Program at Arkansas State University. She holds a Ph.D. in American Civilization from Brown University. With Paul K. Longmore, she edited *The New Disability History: American Perspectives* and The History of Disability book series at New York University Press.

**Anna-Viktoria Vittinghoff** is a Ph.D. candidate in Japanese Studies at the University of Edinburgh, UK. Her research uses theories of bio-power to examine the intersection of radical feminism and the disability movement in Japan from the 1970s to the present day. She is supported by the Great Britain Sasakawa Foundation and the Japan Foundation Endowment Committee.

**Jennifer Way** is an art historian who studies the social meanings and uses that people make of art, craft, design, and exhibitions. Her current monograph book project, *Craft, Wellness, and Healing in Contexts of War* examines craft deployed as a therapeutic modality and an aesthetics of care for Americans coping, healing, and rehabilitating from traumas and injuries of war, including COVID-19.

# Acknowledgments

We are grateful to the authors, each of whom contributed outstanding new ideas and was a pleasure to work with. Thanks to Lauri Umansky who consulted on the book proposal and symposium design and wrote the foreword. We appreciate our Editor at Routledge Press, Claire Jarvis, Senior Editor for Health and Social Care, whose support and guidance was indispensable. We are indebted to our Project Manager, Urvi Sharma, and the Copy Editor Rakhi Sharma, whose attention to detail and clear communication brought this project to fruition. Much to her chagrin, Frank and Patricia acknowledge Micky's extra efforts in creating the website and keeping us organized and deadline focused.

Special thanks to James Walsh, research assistant for the symposium. Thanks to our Writing Buddy, Suffolk University Professor Monika Raesch of the Communication, Journalism and Media Department, who supported us throughout the project with friendship and reads of drafts and edited the author video for the book. Thanks to Patrick Lys, Daniel Weidknecht, and Hunter Berube for filming the author video. We also thank Melissa Gately, former Assistant Dean, Suffolk's College of Arts and Sciences (CAS); Susan Keefe, Administrative Services Manager, CAS; Madelyn Soto, Administrative Coordinator, CAS; Alison Tejeda, Director of Conferences Events; Jeff Rind, Director of University Media Services; and Josh Cornell, Classroom Technology & Media Specialist, for helping organize the symposium.

This project benefitted from strong institutional support from Suffolk University and the University of Nevada, Las Vegas William S. Boyd School of Law. Suffolk's College of Arts and Sciences, under the leadership of Deans Maria Toyoda and Krisanne Bursik, provided project funding to Micky and a research assistant to Patricia. UNLV Boyd Dean Dan Hamilton and Assistant Dean of Finance Angie Doran provided a grant that helped produce the book.

Micky also acknowledges her husband, Gary Bartos, for inspiring her to think about visual impairment differently. Frank also acknowledges the support of his wife, Daniella Etel Courban, who has made these the best 20 years of his life. Patricia also thanks her wife, Debby Briggs; their daughter, Lauri McLaughlin; and friends who encouraged Patricia's work on this project.

# Foreword

## Doing Disability: The Case for Social Construction AND Embodiment Approaches

*Lauri Umansky*

Twenty years ago, when Paul Longmore and I curated the 15 essays that make up *The New Disability History: American Perspectives* (2001b), we held a few principles to be self-evident.

First, we rejected the so-called "medical model" of dis/ability as both deficient and misleading. Dis/ability neither originates nor persists in the supposedly deviant or defective bodies of individuals nor does bodily (or sensory or intellectual) impairment in itself constitute dis/ability. Whereas a medical model of dis/ability posits difference as pathology, putting the onus of "disablement" on the individual divergent body itself, we recognized dis/ability as socially constructed. To understand dis/ability, to understand the history and experiences of people with dis/abilities, one must trace the processes of discrimination, exclusion, and oppression that have defined and delimited disabled people's lives in specific eras and locations. One must unravel and expose the damaging labeling, the pernicious representation, the harmful treatment of disabled people by disparate, pervasive forces of power and institutional authority in society. One must call out and dismantle the constructed barriers—be they physical, architectural, legal, educational, occupational, or attitudinal—to the equal participation of every "dis/abled" person in every aspect of life. Dis/ability rights are civil rights and human rights. And like all other human beings on the planet, disabled people possess agency, possess the innate right to self-determination.

In other words, Longmore and I subscribed strongly to a social constructionist view of dis/ability. In doing so, we situated ourselves squarely in the critical mainstream of the new Dis/ability Studies scholarship that had been emerging over the preceding decade or so across the humanities and social sciences. That literature, in addition to rejecting a medical model of dis/ability, located itself in the intellectual embrace of the contemporary Disability Rights Movement, with the overarching goal of making the conditions of everyday life, in all dimensions, better for dis/abled people. We viewed ourselves and our scholarship as "activist," broadly speaking, as we endeavored to bring the principles and perspectives of a newly forming

Critical Dis/ability Studies movement into the humanities, and into the field of History in particular.

At the same time, we recognized the contingencies, complexities, and even contradictions inherent in a deep analysis of dis/ability. A strictly social constructionist approach stopped short of answering all of our questions. As we wrote in the introduction to *The New Dis/ability History* (Longmore & Umansky 2001):

> Just as bodies are mediated and interpreted by their surroundings, so, too, does the social construction of dis/ability manifest in part through felt and perceived embodiment. Some of the history of dis/ability has to do simply with differences in appearance or modes of functioning. Some of it has to do with bodily limitation. Further, as many dis/ability activists acknowledge, impairment can bring pain, and loss, and difficulty in its own right. Using a social model of dis/ability ought not mean negating the significance of physiological, cosmetic, or functional differences, or of impairment, injury, or illness in disabled people's lives. At its best, the new dis/ability history recognizes the corporeal dimension of human experience and its consequences for daily functioning, while striving continually to understand the contingencies that shape, reflect, express, and result from that dimension. By probing this tension rather than ignoring the role of difference, historians can reveal dis/ability's complexity (p. 20).

In the two decades since *The New Dis/ability History*'s publication, Critical Dis/ability Studies scholars across the humanities and social sciences have rigorously taken up the matter of "embodiment" in dis/ability, and they have done so in ways that seek to incorporate the insights of prior Dis/ability Rights Movement activism and Dis/ability Studies scholarship. As the editors point out in the introduction of *Dis/ability in Media, Law, and History: Embodied AND Socially Constructed*, social constructionist and embodiment approaches to dis/ability contain points of commonality, as well as points of tension. Both scholarly approaches to dis/ability reject the "medical model" as too wedded to normative views of the body, too invested in hierarchical and externalized attempts to control or eliminate departures from medically determined norms. As Mark Jeffreys (2002) writes, and editors Micky Lee, Patricia Reeve, and Frank Rudy Cooper quote, "At the seam where the body joins culture, every construction of the body begins and ends. On the efforts of cultures to hide that seam, every oppression depends" (p. 33).

Indeed, this volume pokes at the seam where body and culture/society meet, unravels it, shines light into it—and not just any light, but the powerful, full-spectrum light of intersectional analysis, which peers into entire systems, not mere instances, of power and oppression.

And look what emerges from obscurity into clarity from this examination! In the essays collected here, scholars from the disparate disciplines of media studies, history, and critical legal studies point us toward understandings of dis/ability that could not have been illuminated by analysis skewed too precipitously toward social constructionism or embodiment, respectively, or from within a single academic discipline. None suffices alone.

This volume leaves us better informed about particular topics, particular examples of how dis/ability plays out, materially and discursively, in a wide range of settings. Few Dis/ability Studies sources rival *Dis/ability in Media, Law, and History* for the sheer scope of material examined through a common analytical lens. From the United States to Japan and both Eastern and Western Europe, from the realms of medical discourse, political activism, policing and public policy, cultural representation, popular culture, and beyond, from personal narrative to historical analysis to critical legal application, these essays model the fruitful breadth and applicability of a conjoint social constructionist and embodied approach to dis/ability. Each essay on its own, as all *en ensemble*, provides a strong case for a hybrid and intersectional approach to dis/ability scholarship.

This volume, these authors, do not simply explode the social construction versus embodiment binary that so confounded earlier Dis/ability Studies scholars, leaving the pieces scattered and separate. *Dis/ability in Media, Law, and History: Embodied AND Socially Constructed* unpacks the social construction/embodiment relationship carefully and with a sense of futurity, providing us with ways to ask a host of implicit and underlying questions, as well. The "seam where body joins culture," where social construction and embodiment meet, and where intersectional and multidisciplinary interrogation occurs, is a place where a host of putative opposites, closed binaries, can be opened for examination. Here, inner, subjective, personal, or individual experience and outer, objective, societal, or community forces or phenomena can be viewed as mutually constitutive rather than mutually exclusive. Dis/ability can be seen as a process, and not a strictly linear one.

Mutable, historically contingent, materially relevant, and intersectionally rich, dis/ability appears in these pages in multidirectional motion, never static. Dis/ability is a verb! Modeling it in the present tense in these pages, this volume presages its use in future tenses as well. Let us all continue to "do dis/ability" in the fullest ways we can imagine.

## References

Jeffreys, M., (2002). The visible cripple (scars and other disfiguring displays included). In: S. L. Snyder, B. J. Brueggemann and R. Garland-Thomson, eds. *Dis/ability studies: enabling the humanities*. New York: Modern Language Association of America. pp. 31–33.

Longmore, P. K. and Umansky, L., (2001a). Introduction: dis/ability history: from the margins to the mainstream. In: P. K. Longmore and L. Umanksy, eds. *The new dis/ability history: American perspectives*. New York: New York University Press. pp. 1–32.

Longmore, P. K. and Umansky, L., eds. (2001b). *The new dis/ability history: American perspectives*. New York: New York University Press.

# 1 Introduction: Dis/abilities at the Intersections

*Micky Lee, Frank Rudy Cooper, and Patricia Reeve*

We three authors are old enough to remember when you rarely saw "handicapped" parking signs. Our memory goes back before the Americans with Disabilities Act (ADA) changed the legal landscape for people with dis/abilities in the United states of America.[1] Most of the 30 years since the passage of the ADA have seen "handicapped" parking signs with a figure sitting up straight in a stationary wheelchair. The provision of such "easily recognizable" signs is part of municipal compliance with the ADA. Today, though, the trend in signage is toward a new image: a self-propelled figure tilted forward in a chair that is in motion (Figure 1.1). Such signs reconfigure the meanings of agency, mobility, and dis/ability by depicting dis/abled people as active participants in their environments. They represent dis/abled drivers as self-moving corporeal subjects who are also objects of legal discourse.[2] The new signs are a simple symbol that "dis/ability" is both embodied— constituted by the configuration of a body in a physical world—and socially constructed—made meaningful through historical representations of the body in society and law.

It is important to explain how embodiment and social constructionist perspectives have theorized dis/abilities before suggesting what interventions this volume offers. Theories of embodiment are multifaceted. Some dis/ability scholars privilege the body as a medium for sensory experiences including pleasure and its opposites: psychological and chronic illnesses that cause pain and discomfort. Others conceive of the body as a medium "for self-understanding and self-definition" and for interactions "with others and with the world more generally." Additionally, some theorize that embodiment is a "mode of material/cultural analysis that illuminates the 'political economy of difference'" created by the material and geographic specificities of globalization, labor markets, and the like (Wilkerson 2015, pp. 68–69). Running through each of these perspectives is the rejection of a medical model of dis/abilities. That model views the body as an object for scientific inquiry that is measured against a norm and seeks to correct its "impairments." Instead, the embodiment approach rejects the premise that people sharing the same attributes would all subjectively experience their bodies in the same way. Given the manifold dimensions of what it means to be embodied, there is no objective means to distinguish an abled from a dis/abled body. Moreover, the body is fluid and

DOI: 10.4324/9781003257196-1

*Figure 1.1* A parking sign for persons with dis/abilities outside Cambridge City Hall, Massachusetts (photo credit: Micky Lee).

subject to change. For example, our bodies change when we age, so all of us will experience different forms of dis/abilities. Dis/ability is always a process of being and becoming, it is not a fixed condition for anybody (Annamma et al. 2018). The embodiment approach thus questions what bodily normalcy is: at which point is the body normal, at which point abnormal? Would a normal body be made abnormal in another social context?

Embodiment theorists also ask how the body mediates daily activities and how the resulting experiences shape our self-identities in society (Silvers 2019). This approach also asks us to pay attention to how "major life functions such as mobilizing, hearing, seeing, communicating and understanding" (para. 46) shape our social experience and help us navigate the world on which we project our ambitions. From this perspective, dis/ability is about how individuals make dis/ability arises from an individual's understanding of how the body conditions social experience and the ability to act in the world.

Now we turn our attention to a social constructionist approach. The main social constructionist argument about dis/abilities is that they are socially produced. Ideologies engender hierarchies of normative and non-normative bodies. Likewise, these ideas give rise to a built environment that fails to take different bodily abilities into account, as illustrated by the absence of designated spots for dis/abled drivers prior to the passing of the ADA.

The social constructionist approach was first proposed by the Union of the Physically Impaired Against Segregation (UPIAS) based in the UK in the 1970s, and it has been known as the social model of dis/abilities. The UPIAS advocated for dis/ability rights, arguing that society is organized in a way that excludes populations with dis/abilities. Therefore, the UPIAS aimed to empower populations with dis/abilities through political actions. It rejected a definition of dis/ability as bodily impairments and refused to see populations with dis/abilities as recipients of charitable benefits. Instead, it proposed that dis/abilities result from social and physical environments that neglect the needs of populations with physical dis/abilities. The UPIAS also rejected medical and psychological solutions to dis/abilities that purport to understand and "cure" them.[3] One goal of social constructionist advocates, then, is to change how society organizes itself such that populations with dis/abilities enjoy full citizenship and substantively equal rights and privileges (Hall 2019).

Going back to the wheelchairs example, we can argue that bodily mobility and immobility themselves are socially constructed. Humans are not born with a dis/ability, they are made dis/abled by the normalization of unmarked parking spots, lack of a ramp, and so on. Equally, people are made abled because architects and city planners designed parking lots with an abled-bodied bias, creating spaces that accommodate abled bodies and afford them mobility.

In this edited collection, we problematize dis/ability by examining the strengths and shortcomings of both embodiment and social constructionist approaches while contending that each approach can challenge, complicate, and compensate for the other. We have reservations about a strong version of embodiment theory, which, while not ignoring ideology, grounds its analysis in the bodily senses. Accordingly, we examine the agency of the body in its navigation of material landscapes and in the upholding and challenging of power relations. As was shown, whether a body is abled or dis/abled is made and unmade by society. However, we are not among those who suggest that dis/ability is meaningful only through its construction in language, for there is a body in the wheelchair image we are discussing. We acknowledge that bodily experiences of pain are not simply discursive. We then recognize that an embodiment approach excels at pointing out how the body's existence changes the social world, which in turn changes the meaning and movement of the body. Further, how we describe the world influences how we act in it and upon it. A strong social constructionist approach holds that language distinguishes people with different bodies, resulting in the unsurprising (but not inevitable) hierarchization of those differences. These constructed differences in turn create ableism or the normalization of certain bodily and mental configurations over others. Ableism guides the configuration of material life, making some bodies abled and others dis/abled.

To illustrate how "abled" bodies are normalized, recall that most parking spots are unmarked. The "regular" spot is like the "flesh" in flesh-colored emojis (white or a strange yellow that obviously stands in for white) or the "man" in "woman." The "normal" is signaled unquestioningly and accepted as given. But the normalization of "abled" bodies does not stop at discursive imaginings of physical dis/ability. Think of what happens when one rolls or walks into a grocery store and the environment contains loud noises, flashing lights, and food samples. People who are "on the spectrum" or diagnosed as Attention deficit disorder-hyperactivity disorder (ADD-HD) are easily affected by such distractions, and their dis/abilities are thus triggered in some environments and not others. The cultural norms of treatment of those considered dis/abled ameliorate or exacerbate that dis/ability. Even though the ADA requires buildings to provide access to the people with bodily dis/abilities, it has not yet required every public place to have quiet hours to accommodate patrons who fall onto the spectrum or to have less colorful displays and quieter environments for patrons with ADD-HD.

In search of a hybrid perspective on embodiment and social construction of dis/abilities, we proceed as follows. First, we will explore the tension and interplay between embodiment and social constructionist approaches to dis/abilities. That section will examine how these methods complement and contradict one another. Next, we will discuss the two contributions offered by the volume. We begin by centering intersectionality theory's consideration of multiple aspects of identity at once. We then discuss how our own disciplines—media studies, critical legal studies (CLS), and the cultural and social histories of embodiments—have interrogated and applied these theoretical frameworks and accounted for the tensions between them. We conclude with an overview of contributors' chapters.

## From medical model to synthesis

This volume is the product of our individual inquiries into the interaction between the embodied experiences of dis/ability and social experiences of it. We recognize that the acting of one upon the other is historically conditioned and, consequently, that the social and civic status of people with dis/abilities has waxed and waned through time. In short, the embodied and social experiences of dis/ability are mutable and historically contingent. It follows that the liberation of people with dis/abilities is impossible unless we undertake both rigorous analysis and the dismantling of the ableist ideas that delimit their individual and bodily autonomy.

Despite their shared rejection of the medical model, proponents of embodiment and social construction theories have frequently disagreed on how to understand the co-constitutive relationship between bodies and social discourse. This volume, therefore, seeks to understand whether one approach can complement the other, and how.

### *Rejection of a medical model by both approaches*

We assert that there is a fundamental but potentially solvable conflict between embodiment and constructionist theories. Likewise, there is the potential for productive exchange between these approaches. For example, the two approaches coincide in their rejection of an older medical model that saw people with dis/abilities as physically, mentally, or otherwise lacking in ways that could be calculated as deficits. As we have argued, the medical model may appear to be a scientific, empirical lens on the human body, but it actually posits normative and non-normative bodies in binary terms. Prior to the age of science, ancient societies blamed dis/abilities on the work of evil spirits and later peoples interpreted dis/abilities as divine punishment for sin. The Enlightenment Era and modernity ushered in a new understanding of the body by externalizing the body from the person, making it a "thing" that could be examined, diagnosed, and fixed. Today, a medical model believes that the body can be seen and known by professionals and that the nature of the body remains unchanged over time and place (Loeser et al. 2017). This medical model sees abled and dis/abled bodies as dichotomous: one either has an abled body or a dis/abled body. Thus, the dis/abled body is a negation that needs to be corrected (Haegele & Hodge 2016).

Both embodiment and social constructionist theorists reject a medical model of dis/abilities for similar and dissimilar reasons. On the one hand, they agree that the medicalizing of dis/abilities has three deleterious effects. First, and as we have seen, it normalizes the abled body. Second, it assumes that a normal body exists and is attainable. The differentiation between a normal and an abnormal body legitimates the disproportionate allocation of resources to abled bodies (Garland-Thomson 2002). Third, the medical model sees a body with dis/ability as inferior to one without.

Both approaches also have differing reasons for rejecting the medical model. An embodiment approach rejects this paradigm because it does not take into account the subjective experiences of one's own body. Social constructionists reject the medical model primarily because it does not take into account the social factors that constitute how the body is understood and labeled.

### *The embodiment critique of social construction*

Despite embodiment theorists and social constructionists' mutual distrust of the medical model, they do not always agree with each other. Some embodiment scholars have found both medical and social constructionist models to be inadequate for understanding dis/abilities for several reasons. First, both approaches homogenize individuals (Haegele & Hodge 2016) by conceiving of bodily experience as a universal rather than a particularized phenomenon.

Embodiment scholars thus reject both medical and constructionist models as under privileging the diversity of embodiment.

Second, embodiment scholars also reject the strong constructionist idea that "the body does not determine its own representation in any way because the sign [or cultural imprint] precedes" it. Thus, Siebers (2006) argues that constructivist representations of bodily pain fail to account meaningfully for the manifold dimensions of physical suffering and their implications for individuals experiencing it. He argues,

> Physical pain is highly individualistic, unpredictable, and raw as reality. It pits the mind against the body in ways that make the opposition between thought and ideology in most current body theory seem trivial. ... Theories that encourage these interpretations are not only unrealistic about pain; they contribute to an ideology of ability that marginalizes people with disabilities and makes their stories of suffering and victimization both politically impotent and difficult to believe (Siebers 2006, p. 178).

It would seem, then, that bodily pain is too gritty a subject for scholars inclined to represent dis/abilities in disembodied terms.

Third, embodiment scholars, such as Leanne McRae (2019), further claim that the social constructionist model reinforces binaries by characterizing people with dis/abilities as a minority in relation to the able-bodied. Rather than seeing the dis/abled as a minority group, reducible to statistics, she characterizes them as a possibility of humanity. This is made obvious by the fact that everyone who lives long enough will have their body change with age. Equally, the dis/abled body is more than just a site where Foucauldian power operates. The dis/abled body itself serves as a foundation of how meaning is built, made, and understood because the body is the place where the self and society interact. In this way, an embodiment approach seeks to "consider what it means to be human and understands dis/ability not only as an environmental obstruction or impasse, but as an ontological question of self, agency, consciousness, representation, and being" (p. 224).

### *Reconciliation of embodiment theory and social constructivism*

Scholars have attempted to draw on the strengths of both approaches to understand the body. For example, Loeser et al. (2017) seek to establish a linkage between social and biological needs. On the one hand, dis/ability scholars believe that even if the body is affected by social factors, it can't be reduced to them alone. On the other hand, they do not agree with "anti-essentialist" embodiment theorists who believe that there is no correspondence between symbolic representation and material practices. They therefore advocate for a post-essentialist model that, for instance, "allows the disabled masculine subject to be heard as a materiality that is (re)constructed in and through changing historical, social and discursive condition" (p. xxvi). In this sense, a male body with dis/abilities cannot be reduced to qualities that justify whether it is masculine or not. At the same time, this body uses tools and devices created in society to re-negotiate its masculinity through discourses.

In another example, scholars such as Mark Jeffreys and Rosemarie Garland-Thomson (2002) advocate for an embodiment model that also takes into account the social environment that confers meaning on the body. By considering discursive practices, Jeffreys argues, scholars may engage in a "humanities-based inquiry into disability," which was "previously the exclusive domain of the biological, medical, and rehabilitative professions" (Jeffreys 2002, p. 32). Cultural analyses of dis/abilities have proven to be a potent corrective to "empiricist objectification of the body" (Jeffreys 2002, p. 32). Constructivism not only has established dis/ability as "a new field of cultural studies" (Jeffreys 2002, p. 32), but has also fostered greater understanding of the political consequences for the dis/abled of ableism. Jeffreys (2002) explains, "At the seam where body joins culture, every construction of the body begins and ends. On the efforts of cultures to hide that seam, every oppression depends" (p. 33). Jeffreys thus advocates for a point of entry where the body meets culture. Similarly, Garland-Thomson (2001) believes that dis/ability is constituted by the relationship between bodies and their environments. Specifically, dis/ability is "not so much a property of bodies as a product of cultural rules about what bodies should be or do" (Garland-Thomson 2002, p. 6).

Lastly, O'Connor (2016) has asked constructionists to reconsider the body by seeing its social representation as a byproduct of the interaction between an individual's personal bodily experience and an external, "common-sense" social knowledge of everyday life. Although constructionists show that the social world acts on the body by guiding one's own and others' experiences of that body, experiences of the body are necessarily made possible only through sensorimotor processes such as seeing and hearing.

The aforementioned scholars all acknowledge that social and material environments give meanings to the body; yet bodily experiences alter how these environments are understood and used. This volume aims to explore the tensions and interplay between and possible reconciliation of both approaches. As we have suggested earlier, it does so by offering two contributions: situating intersectionality theory in critical dis/abilities studies (CDS) framework; and locating both approaches in one or more of three disciplines—media studies, CLS, and the cultural and social histories of embodiment.

## This volume's intersectional approach to CDS

The first contribution of this volume is to build upon a CDS framework using intersectionality theory. We suggest that intersectional analysis remains necessary for CDS. CDS is a method and site of theorizing about dis/ability that incorporates the analytical insights and political agendas associated with postcolonial, queer and feminist theories. CDS is, in the words of Julie Avril Minich, a "mode of analysis" rather than the study of dis/abilities. It focuses "on the social norms that define particular attributes as impairments, as well as the social conditions that concentrate stigmatized attributes in particular populations" (Minich 2016). Further, it problematizes the lived experiences of people with dis/abilities and aims to transform the power relations under which oppressed subjects live through critical, intersectional analysis. CDS is self-critical and reflexive. Its goal is to promote a more distributed, collectivist, and ensembled form of human capacity (Goodley et al. 2019). Gender, race, and class are not simply additive lenses, but the means to highlight how power constructs abnormality and hierarchy.

CDS is well suited to the task of tackling the complexity and scope of the phenomena of dis/ability because no one single theory, be it the critical race theory (CRT) or feminist theory, can successfully do so. Its explanatory power derives from its interdisciplinary interrogation of power—whether exerted through discourse or the political economy of medicine, law, religion, and so on.

In thinking intersectionally, we center Iris Marian Young's concept of the "scaling" of bodies (Young 1990). Young argues that Western Enlightenment epistemology ranked bodies within classifications such as race, gender, and able-bodiedness. The interaction of those rankings creates and reinforces a hierarchy of bodies, and the hierarchy not only normalizes the body but also dictates how the body should be experienced and felt. Once bodies are ranked, ideals and deficiencies can be established. For example, in his writings on biopolitics, Foucault asserts that medical knowledge establishes "truths" that set up norms for the body. That is, the medical discourse frames the dis/abled as having an observable impairment which in turn is labeled a deficit, making the dis/abled those who are lacking. Medical professions thus tell people with dis/abilities how they and others should feel about their bodies: that they are impaired and in need of remediation through rehabilitation or surgery.

The singlular insight that came out of the CRT, and maybe all of the humanities in the last 30 years, is intersectionality theory. As formulated by legal scholar Kimberlé Crenshaw (1989), intersectionality is the idea that where multiple identities intersect, unique subjective experiences of the world and distinct forms of treatment come into being. Crenshaw demonstrated this by showing that employment discrimination law treated black women as though they could not be subject to racial or gender bias when some black men were hired or some white women were hired. In fact, employers do sometimes accept black men based on gender affinity and white women based on racial affinity and still discriminate against black women. Similarly, Asch (2001) has suggested that CRT informs dis/ability studies by showing how discrimination against people with dis/abilities, like non-white minorities, is made to appear natural and ordinary in Western cultures. Likewise, anti-racist and feminist groups have tended to ignore the particular interests of black women by using a lowest common denominator understanding of the group's interests that devolved into those of black men and white women. Such thinking ignores that black women are *both* raced *and* gendered. Sociologists Patricia Hill Collins and Sirma Bilge thus summarize intersectionality as the understanding that "people's lives and the organization of power in a given society are better understood as being shaped not by a single axis of social division but by many axes that work together and influence each other" (Collins & Bilge 2016, p. 2). As proponents of intersectionality theory, we are eager to integrate this framework with CDS to better understand the interaction between ableism, gender, race, and other factors that shape our experience with the world. While previous volumes have explained how identities of gender, race, class, and sexuality are shaped by dis/ability and vice versa, we are also overlaying an interdisciplinary exploration of the interplay between embodiment and social construction of the body.[4]

An effective way to examine intersectionality theory's relation to CDS is to pay attention to the lived experiences of oppressed persons, including the dis/abled (Hall 2019).[5] Based on this, we identify four key premises of intersectionality that may inform inquiries by CDS scholars.

First, the norms created by the scaling of bodies construct power relations. Racial hierarchy begets racism, gender hierarchy begets sexism, and so on. Intersectionality theory demonstrates that it is not sufficient to compare social categories, such as asking if a person with dis/abilities experiences life like a person of color. Such a comparison is limiting for two reasons. First, it effaces the differing statuses accorded to the dis/abled and people of color in a capitalist democracy. Second, it ignores the interdependence of the social ideologies and relations that constitute the statuses accorded individuals in one or both of these populations. In other words, dis/ability is made and unmade through gender, race, class, and other relations (Gerschick 2000; Moser 2006). To give an example, there are societal expectations of how people with dis/abilities should act to be deemed appropriately gendered. Case in point, a white male veteran with a visible dis/ability is often deemed to be feminized and, therefore, he might demonstrate and reinscribe his manliness by undertaking physically demanding activities such as triathlon competitions. These processes of making and unmaking identity are interrelated with science, medicine, and technologies because each brings to bear the institutional practices and materialities that constitute us as subjects of dis/ability, gender, race, and class (Moser, 2006).

The second premise is that the social location of individuals and groups within intersecting power relations shapes their experiences within and perspectives on the social world (Hall 2019). This states the idea that being dis/abled and, say, a female of color, affects how others see us as a matter of the characteristics they attribute to us and also how we see ourselves, subjectively.

Third, these systems of power are "interdependent and mutually construct one another" (Collins 2019, p. 48). In brief, that means that systems of power based upon categories of identity, such as ableism, always intersect with other categories of social identity, and both constitute and are constituted by them. Ableism systematically interacts with other power structures and together they produce the co-constitutive social relations of race, gender, sex, and dis/ability (Goodley et al. 2019; Hall 2019).

Lastly, an intersectional approach reveals the existence of hierarchies among individuals with a shared dis/ability but having differently privileged identities of gender, race, and class. Therefore, solving social problems "requires intersectional analyses" (Collins 2019, p. 48). For the dis/abled, the creation of greater social liberation will require attending to the ways both systems of power and the specific identities of those who are dis/abled intersect with other systems of power and identities.

In sum, an intersectional approach to CDS reveals human beings as multidimensional persons grounded in multiple and intersecting identities and prone to privileging one or more identities over others. This privileging occurs because society and the material world may make a particular identity more salient or because an individual is drawn to one self-identity rather than another. Needed then is theorizing about why and how individuals privilege particular identities in particular contexts and with what social and historical effects.

## The figuring of dis/abilities in media studies, critical legal theory, and the cultural and social histories of embodiment

The second contribution of this volume is to assess how media studies, critical legal theory, and the cultural and social histories of embodiment could provide analytical frameworks and methods for examining and resolving the tensions between embodiment and social construction approaches. As scholars who are trained and have published in these three areas, we recognize that these fields have been at the vanguard in exploring the intersectionality of race, gender, class, etc., but, with notable exceptions, they have not significantly theorized dis/ability. In addition, we acknowledge that our training problematizes some objects of study while neglecting others. For example, media studies scholars may analyze representations of dis/abilities but tend not to interrogate the nature of historical knowledge about dis/abilities or the contingency of the laws affecting the dis/abled. Legal theorists tend to focus on who and what the law does and does not protect, rather than on broader questions of how dis/abilities interact with other identities. Similarly, historians research and interpret the lived experiences of dis/ability, broadly defined, and the social production of dis/ability in society and at law. They also tease out the implications for the dis/abled of this meaning making and the ways in which it sustains and undercuts structures of power. However, few historians have deployed embodiment theory "to explore how social, economic, and political forces [are] expressed in [and by] bodies" and with what consequences for historical change (Walters et al. 2011, p. 183).

In the following, we will summarize how these three areas have studied dis/abilities from the vantage point of the tension between embodiment and social constructionism.

### *Media studies*

Critical cultural theories have been informing media studies since the 1970s when scholars began to wonder how media embed gender, race, and class ideologies. The Contemporary Centre of Cultural Studies based in the University of Birmingham has been instrumental in drawing attention to the dominant ideology in mainstream media. This dominant ideology overwhelmingly represents middle-class interests but disguises its interest by representing it as universal. In addition, the dominant ideology naturalizes culture, explaining the inferior social positions of women and non-whites as biologically determined (Hall 1997). Though media studies scholars have critiqued media representations of gender, race, class, and sexual orientations, they have generally neglected dis/abilities.

Media studies scholars may have neglected dis/abilities based on an assumption that they are merely medical matters, thus falling outside their research interest. Subscribing to a medical model of dis/abilities necessarily limits media studies scholars' examination of how power is exercised through the exclusion of people with dis/abilities as a social group. Nevertheless, in the past decade, there has been a sudden surge of studies of dis/abilities in the field. While it is unclear why dis/abilities became a research focus, it is plausible that digital media technologies have prompted scholars to examine the possibilities that technologies would afford people with dis/abilities.

Media studies of dis/abilities have the following genealogy. Some of the earliest studies that examined media representations (Jackson et al. 2015; Smit & Enns 2001) tend to employ a social constructionist framework to examine how people with dis/abilities are portrayed in film and television. Characters with physical dis/abilities are frequently stereotyped as asexual beings or "super crips" (Ellis 2019): while dis/abilities annihilate sexual desire for the former, they inspire the latter to overcome bodily limitations and become superhumans.

The advancement of digital technologies has allowed media companies to offer captioning and audio description even if the laws do not require them to do so. This prompted media studies scholars to look at telecommunications policies (Goggin & Newell 2002; Goggin et al. 2019) and media accessibility (Ellis 2019; Ellis et al. 2017). These studies tend to adopt a social constructionist model of dis/abilities because they assume that policy loopholes and companies' economic considerations explain why media technologies and media content do not always cater to populations with dis/abilities.

Other scholars examine how subjectivity is fostered in a digital environment. They argue that the interactivity and sociality of Internet-enabled computing devices and video games create subjectivity in an online space for users with varying abilities (Boellstorff 2019; Goggin & Newell 2002). Digital technologies are believed to enable people to form different experiences with others, regardless of their varying bodily configurations (Alper 2017). As such, technologies neither amend nor normalize the body, they enable people with dis/abilities to experience a new form of subjectivity, including as a productive economic being or a creative artist (Davis & Boellstorff 2016). These studies advance an embodiment approach to dis/abilities because bodily experiences are believed to be enabled by digital technologies, which in turn shape how subjectivity is experienced through human-technology interaction. One good example is that GPS on the smartphone orients the user as the center of the map, so places become relative to the body rather than the body relative to places.

To bridge the social constructionist and embodiment approaches to dis/abilities in media studies, techno feminist thought may be applied to understand how gender and technology are co-constructed in media. Work by feminist science and technology scholars such as Judy Wajcman (1991) and Donna Haraway (2016), in particular, have modeled approaches to analyzing and affirming the malleability of the body in human-machine interaction. For them, technologies create new forms and meanings of the body. For example, smartphone apps that keep track of health data are not just an external tool that helps users monitor their health; they have become part of the reflexive self, a validation of one's attitude toward health. If the phone is not charged or the app is not working, then users may feel that their health is at risk. The body is, then, an unfinished process that is shaped and molded through interactions with the material and social world.

To fully embrace embodiment in media studies would require scholars to see the body as a multi-modal construct that is simultaneously biological, informational, metaphorical, aesthetic, political, and social. In other words, technologies are not external to the body, but part of the assemblage of this multi-modal construct (Galis 2011). In this sense, media is not just representations or policies or technologies, it encompasses the digital interface between humans and machines, DNA and genomes that decode life, language and symbols that describe and create the human form, and social political forms that define how humans must relate to other humans and be governed (Mills & Sterne 2017). Consequently, media studies scholars must attend to the materiality of human bodies and technologies as well as to how discourses have power in the material world to enable or limit human actions through their bodies.

### *Critical legal theory*

At rock bottom, what makes a critical legal study critical is its commitment to seeing the law from outside its own closed system for explaining the world. Historical roots of CLS are seen in the legal realism movement within law in the early 20th century. Paradigmatically, revered jurisprudential scholar and judge Oliver Wendell Holmes said that "the life of the law has not been logic, it has been experience" (Holmes 1880, pp. 233–234). That is, judges bring their experiences and viewpoints to their supposedly neutral and objective interpretations of the law. In fact, there is no "view from nowhere" that could be a vantage point for an objective analysis of law (Nagel 1986).

The CLS movement of the 1970s picked up on legal realism's critique of objectivity and ran with it in legal scholarship. CLS scholars were steeped in the poststructuralist theories coming from Europe in the 1960s and 1970s. For our purposes, poststructuralist, or postmodern, scholars did not believe in the Enlightenment project of finding Truth with a capital "T." CLS scholars showed how legal rules, and especially rights, had no fixed content but were subject to political contestation over their meaning. However, many CLSers went so far as to say that since race, gender, and so on did not exist, it did not make sense to organize around identity-based social groups.

By the late 1980s, feminists among CLSers were rebelling against theoretical and personal marginalization within CLS, and that helped spawn the CRT critique of CLS (Crenshaw et al. 1995). Critical race theorists said that while phenotypical race was not objectively true in the sense of being a scientifically valid means of differentiating people, it was materially significant. CRT created the insight that race is "socially constructed but materially crucial" (Cooper 2009). That paradox is a basis for carefully studying how race is made to mean particular things, especially in the law. Likewise, CRT studies how the law is made to mean certain things based upon cultural meanings of identities. As the legal realists said, law is not separate from culture, so law and culture mutually construct one another.

As mentioned, intersectionality theory has influenced CRT. Furthermore, CRT's intersectionality theory is the insight that drives an important movement within dis/abilities studies (DS), CDS, or DisCrit. Leaders of this movement describe DS as "focus[ed] on ableism as an organizing principle in personal, societal, educational, and historical structures" (Annamma et al. 2018, p. 46, 48). For those authors, CRT adds value because it can show how "racism and ableism are interconnected and collusive normalizing processes" (p. 47). For example, dis/abilities such as ADD-HD can simultaneously "leverage access [to support services] for wealthy white students, while serving as a barrier for Black students" (p. 49). Wealthy families turn their kids' ADD-HD into a claim for accommodations; black kids with ADD-HD are often marginalized as unable to learn.

Recent developments in critical legal scholarship on dis/abilities are mentioned here. As a general insight, legal scholar Katie Eyer's application of the metaphor of the closet to dis/abilities is significant. She contends that biases against people with dis/abilities have remained in large part because "many of the disability rights movements' constituents do not self-identify as dis/abled—i.e., do not 'claim disability' as an identity" (Eyer 2021, p. 551). While Eyer is aware of the intersectional nature of identities, we encourage claiming dis/ability as an identity but with the understanding that identities are compound. Critical disabilities scholars should continue to explore how race, gender, class, and dis/ability influence law's construction and enforcement. We thus applaud legal scholar Ann C. McGinley's recent pursuit of an intersectional approach to how police deal with people having mental health episodes (McGinley 2021). In this volume, Eric Miller's chapter on police officers' fear of disablement and use of disabling force moves that conversation forward.

### *Cultural and social histories of embodiment*

Dis/ability history, a sub-field of history, emerged out of 20th-century movements for dis/ability rights in North America and the UK and the related growth of dis/ability studies (Rembis et al. 2018). Though organizations by and for the deaf coalesced at the turn of the 20th century in the United States, widespread and broad-based dis/ability activism accelerated markedly during the 1920s and through the 1980s. Late 20th century mobilizations for individual autonomy and equal access in the United States culminated in passage of the Americans with Disability Act in 1990 and assertions of dis/ability pride (Nielsen 2012). Similar mobilizations were afoot in other countries, as we see in this book's chapters about Japan, Germany, and the former Soviet bloc. Over the course of the 1970s through the 1990s, claims-making by people with dis/abilities in combination with arguments advanced by civil rights and women's rights activists sparked the establishment within the academy of "rights-based, social-justice-influenced knowledge building and disseminating initiatives" (Garland-Thomson 2013, pp. 915–916). The result was the proliferation of new subject areas such as women's studies, Black studies, and dis/ability studies.

Like dis/ability activism, the fields of dis/ability studies and its offshoot dis/ability history reject the medical model of dis/ability that imagines the body as natural, fixed across time and place, and normative or deficient. As we have seen, scholars of dis/ability have long argued that standard and non-standard bodies are "constructed cultural categor[ies] and representational system[s]" (Garland-Thomson 2013, p. 916). Furthermore, these ideas and practices have either denied or conferred bodily agency and equality of persons.

The emergence of dis/ability history from dis/ability studies occurred during the 1990s as the second wave of dis/ability studies crested. Whereas the first wave had swelled during the 1980s in the social sciences, the second arose from the humanities (Longmore & Umansky 2001). Especially influential were semiotic studies, post-structural literary criticism, and Foucauldian and feminist interrogations of the body, including historians' explorations of "monstrous" or non-normative bodies. This multi-disciplinary scholarship not only interested historians, but it demonstrated the utility of critical theory for problematizing dis/ability (Kudlick 2003). Still, not until after 2000 did dis/ability establish a foothold in the discipline of history (Longmore & Umansky 2001).

American historians began to engage intensively with dis/ability as a critical lens after 2000 and through 2012, and two pathbreaking publications bookend this development. The first is the anthology *The New Disability History: American Perspectives* (2001), edited by Paul Longmore and Lauri Umansky, and the second is *A Disability History of the United States* (2012), written by Kim Nielsen. The former provides us with a snapshot of the development of dis/ability history in 2001. Longmore and Umansky endeavor to reverse the neglect of dis/ability by historians, an oversight which they attribute to "the 'existential anxiety' that disability often evokes" and to the medical model, which marginalizes people with dis/abilities (Nielsen 2012, pp. 6–7). However, recently,

Michael Rembis, Catherine Kudlick, and Kim E. Nielsen have identified other possible causes for this gap in the scholarship. These are "a perceived lack of sources"—a perennial supposition about the alleged difficulties of writing social history, and resistance from within the history discipline to unconventional analyses and methods. They write,

> With its intellectual and political roots in the disability rights movement and in disability studies, disability history struggles with a double identity—one linked to the careful, sometimes stodgy discipline of history, and the other characterized by the unconventional, sometimes controversial, and occasionally shocking ideas and behavior of a movement and a feisty interdisciplinary field committed to systemic change and social justice (Rembis et al. 2018, p. 3, 9).

Though the increasing number of publications in dis/ability history belies this assertion, it is true that traditionalists have resisted and continue to resist critical theorizing, as will be discussed later.

Longmore and Umansky (2001) also contend that historians must investigate the interaction of dis/ability with race, gender, and class and the co-constitution of these identities and ideologies. They advise scholars to "join the social constructionist insights and interdisciplinarity of cultural studies with sold empirical research as we analyze disability's past" (p. 15). The fourteen contributors to their anthology, *The New Disability History*, accomplish the editors' goals in two ways. First, several chapters demonstrate the value of reading oft-cited sources against the grain to document the lives and status of the dis/abled. For example, Douglas Baynton's penetrating rereading of immigration records enables him to delineate how discriminatory immigration policies and practices penalized emigres deemed defective. Second, many of the contributors establish the efficacy of intersectionality as a tool for investigating the co-construction of gender, race, class, and dis/ability. To that end, John Williams Searle demonstrates that Gilded Age railroaders understood that they were susceptible to industrial accidents, yet they turned their backs on dis/abled counterparts. According to the era's definitions of manly social and economic independence which railway men held dear, dis/abled railroaders were anomalous and unfit for the fraternity of sovereign men.

Published 11 years later, Nielsen's chronicling of the American history of dis/ability capped a decade of increasing historical scholarship focused on dis/ability. Nielsen's study is the first narrative survey of its kind, and her purposes are twofold: to use dis/ability as a lens on US history, presumably to decenter traditional narratives that overlook dis/ability, and to understand how dis/ability and "race, gender, class, and sexuality" are mutually constructed (Nielsen 2012, pp. xvii–xviii). As others have noted, Nielsen could not have written her study had sufficient scholarship not existed (Rembis et al. 2018). That it did attests to the increase of publication in the decade after Longmore and Umansky (2001) issued their call for historians to engage with dis/ability.

Focusing on these two works is not to minimize the important contributions made by other dis/ability historians before and during the first decade of the 20th century (Baynton 1996; Bogdan 1988; Garland-Thomson 1997; Pernick 1999; Stiker 1999; Trent 1995). Indeed, a bumper crop of book chapters and articles have cataloged and evaluated this literature, and these historiographic writings are available to anyone wishing to trek the byways of dis/ability history (Burch 2005; Wilson 2018).

Despite the advances in dis/ability history discussed earlier, some in the discipline expressed skepticism about the merits of the field. In 2006, Douglas Baynton remarked that skeptics dismissed dis/ability history as a dubious attempt to create "a new Other" because, or so they argued, the "possibilities for race, class, and gender" had been depleted. Nonetheless, dis/ability historians found an increasingly receptive audience for their writings among editors of academic journals and members of conference program committees (Baynton 2008 cited in Martínez-Pére & Del Cura 2016; Martínez-Pére & Del Cura 2016). It is noteworthy that dis/ability history has also begun to reach "a broader public" as evidenced by the 2013 virtual exhibit "EveryBody: An Artifact History of Disability in America" hosted by the Smithsonian National Museum of American History (Rembis et al. 2018). Websites such as the Disability History Museum[6] also educate popular audiences.

Presently, dis/ability historians have established themselves in the discipline of history and are both pursuing earlier lines of inquiry and exploring the interactions of dis/ability with sexuality, critical race studies, and globalization. In the first case, "two broad strands of inquiry—one focused on the oppression and marginalization of disabled people and the other on the pathologization of human difference—have persisted" (Rembis et al. 2018, p. 4).

Examples of works that have broadened the scope of dis/ability history include Whitney Womack Smith's "'Blind Tom' abroad: race, disability, and transatlantic representations of Thomas Wiggins" (2016); Regina Kunzel's "The rise of gay rights and the disavowal of disability in the United States" (2018); and Stefanie Hunt-Kennedy's "Between fitness and death: disability and slavery in the Caribbean" (2020).

As this discussion has shown, though dis/ability historians approach their projects from diverse standpoints, all must reckon with a set of analytical challenges identified by Burch and Rembis (2014). These are that:

> Disability is ubiquitous, yet it is also irreducible. Lived experiences of disability defy universalized or essentialized interpretations. They do not conform to common historical narratives of unilinear progress. Although historians find commonalities among individuals and groups and trace continuities over time, it would be unfair and inaccurate to say that there has been a singular "disabled experience" (p. 1).

Given these facts, impulses to synthesize scholarship in the field are likely doomed to failure. Nonetheless, more than 30 years of scholarship has created a mosaic (albeit incomplete) of the aspirations and lives of people with dis/abilities, the cultural and institutional phenomena that impinge on their agency and equality, and their modes of resistance to objectification and marginalization. Historians who ignore these ideas do so at a cost to their analytical acuity.

## Summaries of chapters

This book expresses insights resulting from a two-year-long conversation on the embodiment and social construction of dis/abilities: first between the three editors and then among the invited contributors. In June 2021, the editors and contributors participated in a 1.5-day hybrid symposium. Prior to it, essayists produced full drafts for editorial and peer reviews. During the symposium, attendees spent the majority of the time identifying connections among the essays, positing insights that would weave through the book, and suggesting ways to deepen individual arguments and better align them with symposium themes. Working in "clusters" of participants from different disciplines and led by the editors, attendees reflected on their disciplinary approaches to interrogating dis/ability and the similarities and dissimilarities among them. At the symposium conclusion, each cluster summarized the questions and themes which emerged from its conversations. Next, Lauri Umansky, US social historian and co-editor of the pathbreaking volume *The New Disability History* (Longmore & Umansky 2001), teased out the significance of cluster discussions for the next stage of revisions. This rigorous intellectual exchange not only sharpened the interdisciplinarity of this volume but enhanced its cohesiveness. The result is an exciting four-part discussion of dis/abilities which focuses on both the tension between embodiment and social construction theories and the intersectionality of identities.

### *Foundations: experience and theories*

The first section collects two essays that examine the importance of looking at dis/abilities from the perspective of lived experience. In the first, "The art of regarding still life," Mullins, a practicing psychoanalyst, reflects on the consequences of her own diagnosis of multiple sclerosis and challenges the medical world's framing of her experience. She uses the concept "in betweenness" to grapple with what it means to be caught between different cultures—the able-bodied and dis/abled—and between two senses of self. The first is the subject that feels despair; the second is a self that can reflect on feeling despair. Using still life painting as a metaphor, Mullins describes the dialectics between being seen as a still object in a medical setting and as being an active subject who immerses herself in a life experience.

Crossley's chapter, "Embodiment's contributions to appreciating life with disability and to advancing justice," succinctly summarizes how medical ideas about blacks and people with dis/abilities (or both) have had detrimental effects on the medical treatment of bodies of difference. She then presents how the social constructionist model brought to light the construction of bodies of difference. Despite the broader acceptance of the social constructionist model, medical professionals still hold biologically deterministic ideas. She argues that while it is important to continue promoting a social constructionist version of race and dis/abilities, it alone will not bring justice to those who are harmed by racism and ableism. She believes an embodiment approach will allow for a higher appreciation of the lived experience of blacks and people with dis/abilities (or blacks with dis/abilities), hence bringing justice to those whose lives were made unequal and inequitable.

### *Rehabilitation, disablement, and the state*

In a modern world where war and industry disaggregate the human body and disassemble the identities of those so afflicted, the state and private organizations assume responsibility for rehabilitating the dis/abled. As Jennifer Way, Radu-Harald Dinu, Sebastian Schlund, and Eric Miller argue, rehabilitation has as its goals the reinscription of gender identities, the return of the incapacitated to productive labor, and the reinstatement of them in the body politic. As this suggests, rehabilitation is infused by and reinvigorates nationalism and the prevailing social, economic, and political relations of the historical moment. What becomes clear is the extent to which the concept of rehabilitation is shaped more by institutions and less by those who are their beneficiaries.

Art historian Way analyzes key early 20th-century texts and photographs to unearth the underlying premises of occupational therapy in the United States. Specifically, she asks how craft making refashioned white male patients deemed mentally and physically dis/abled by inculcating them with prevailing conceptions of normalcy and productive work.[7] Way also excavates the origins of making-craft-as-therapy and locates them in prevailing anxieties about dis/ability generally and dis/abled men in particular. She contends that this approach reveals the centrality of craft as a therapeutic modality that also constructed the patient as a subject in service to interrelated social interests and needs, a process intended to aid their reintegration into mainstream society. Way's argument deconstructs for us the process by which ideas about normalcy and masculinity interact with therapeutic practices and the materiality of work to reposition the patient across diverse fields and society.

Dinu situates his analysis of national constructions of dis/ability within the communist regimes of Eastern Europe. His purpose is to interrogate the construction and management of the dis/abled in a non-liberal-democratic government. Dinu examines "defectology"—the medical model and psychology of dis/ability that held sway in communist Eastern Europe during the 20th century and especially after 1945. As the name implies, defectology characterized dis/abilities of all types as deficits requiring medical intervention. Radu asserts that this model arose as a byproduct of the communist ideal of the virile, healthy, and muscular "New Man," a cultural icon popularized throughout the Soviet bloc.

When measured against the New Man, the dis/abled fell short. Accordingly, they were subjected to physical rehabilitation to achieve social rehabilitation as productive members of the communist workforce.

By contrast, Schlund attributes discrimination against the dis/abled in postwar West Germany to three factors: the origins of one's impairment, whether the impairment was physical or mental, and gender ideology. Schlund is especially interested in the hierarchies, privileges, and mechanisms of discrimination that constructed national understandings of dis/ability. These structures and ideas blocked access by the dis/abled to the nation's welfare programs, the labor market, the education industry, and leisure time activities. To make his case, Schlund distinguishes the self-perceptions and representations of dis/abled male veterans and workers from those of dis/abled women. He does so to underscore the intra-group hierarchies among the dis/abled that coexisted with inter-group power relations across the able-bodied and dis/abled. Germany's approach to men and women with dis/abilities turned on whether a person with dis/abilities had performed traditionally male service to national defense or industry. Thus, the national impetus to rehabilitate and integrate the dis/abled did not extend to women until the 1970s, and then but slowly.

Miller's chapter uses a disablement model to explain how dis/ability plays a double role in policing: police fear being dis/abled while fighting crime so they demand the power to dis/able as a means of doing their job. He suggests that the police regard themselves as super-abled and feel justified in using disabling force on others. Therefore, policing is essentially the production of dis/ability. Using a disabilities studies lens, Miller asks that we move away from seeing dis/ability as a static state to using various intersectional theories of embodiment to critique dis/ability in relation to race and gender. An embodiment approach would allow us to understand the different ways in which individuals become—or resist becoming—dis/abled. Miller explains that despite popular belief, the police are more frequently called on to resolve minor domestic disputes or traffic offenses rather than to fight prototypical crime. A replacement of the dis/ablement model of policing should take into consideration the dignity and interests of vulnerable populations.

Taken together, these essays demonstrate the variability of both the constructions and embodied experiences of dis/ability and their origins in wide-ranging social and historical milieu. By taking interdisciplinary and intersectional approaches to their analyses of the contingency of thinking about dis/ability, the authors reveal the interplay of ideologies, processes, and systems that have shaped the terrain on which people with dis/abilities have asserted their personhood and contested their disenfranchisement.

### *Representation, liminality, and resistance*

The third section collects essays about how the bodies of people with dis/abilities are represented in different media in different times and spaces. When mainstream media exclude and marginalize the bodies of people with dis/abilities, media producers and fans carve out space to represent these bodies.

However, those representations do not always provide an alternative representation or afford persons with dis/ability a full subjectivity. In fact, they often reinforce ideological assertions of the inferiority of an impaired body and of heteronormativity. Consequently, these representations are resisted by those who are represented. The essays in this section show that representations are not merely discursive but have impacts on policies and laws.

Anna Vittinghoff and Anne-Lise Mithout, scholars in Japanese Studies, interrogate the arguments made by Japanese dis/ability rights activists from the 1940s through 2019. They show how these political and media discourses challenge the representations and understanding of people with dis/abilities.

Vittinghoff notes that in 2019, two candidates with disabilities from the Reiwa Shinsengumi, a left-leaning party, won their elections for the Japanese House of Councillors, the first to do so in the postwar years. While Vittinghoff notes that their victory marked a shift in Japanese attitudes about dis/ability, she historicizes a central tenet of the Reiwa Shinsengumi, namely, that the value of human beings resides not in their productivity but in their existence. Vittinghoff credits this idea to *uman ribu*, the mid-1970s Japanese women's rights movement that criticized postwar Japanese social relations. Ribu recognized that women and dis/abled people were similarly devalued by Japan's masculinist valorization of capitalist productivity and thus sought to make common cause with dis/abled activists. Vittinghoff argues that the ensuing and sometimes fractious collaborations were complicated by stakeholders' assessments of the differing costs and benefits for women and the dis/abled of the institution of reproductive rights and particularly, the legalization of abortion. Vittinghoff makes her argument by examining the intersectional analysis posed by the dis/abled ribu activist, Yonezu Tomoko. Over time, her ideas gained currency among dis/ability rights activists, and as a result, Tomoko's argument echoed through to the 2019 election. Vittinghoff's argument reminds us that the lens of dis/ability makes possible an intersectional analysis of Japanese grassroots and electoral politics and enables us to identify cross-cutting currents of thought that would otherwise elude us.

Mithout examines the documentary film *Sayonara CP* (1972, dir: Hara Kazuo) in order to understand visual representations of the dis/abled intent on challenging the medicalization and social devaluing of their lives. The film follows the lives of individuals with cerebral palsy who were affiliated with Aoi shiba no kai, the organization that launched the Japanese dis/ability rights movement during the late 1940s. According to Mithout, the film was a collaboration by the director and Aoi shiba no kai, but as she argues, the director represented his subjects in questionable and ableist terms. Despite its limitations, the film provided a vehicle for the protagonists to fashion self-representations that repudiated Japanese ableism and illumined the inaccessibility of the built environment. Mithout also furthers intersectional analysis by looking at the film's representation of women.

Rouse examines the fan fictions about *Voltron: Legendary Defender*. That anime story has a protagonist named Shiro who has a prosthetic arm and post-traumatic stress disorder (PTSD). Since Shiro's dis/abilities do not drive the plot, fans take the matter into their own hands. Rouse analyzes the tactics used by fans to normalize his body and to reinforce heteronormativity. Some writers replicate common dis/ability tropes, others "heal" his dis/abilities through romance. Others disregard his dis/ability and trauma altogether by reimagining Shiro as an able-bodied character with no past trauma. These tactics undermine the expression of subjugated knowledge about dis/abilities, which can and should be a function of fan fictions.

Lee asks media studies scholars to look beyond representations of dis/abilities and media accessibility and to pay more attention to the relationship between the body and technologies. One way to do this is to examine how the materiality of technologies actively shapes the body, in particular how technical devices normalize non-normative bodies. She looks at two assistive technological devices, eyeglasses and Google Glass, and describes them as forms of media that enable users to experience the world beyond their immediate spatial and temporal limits. In this case, assistive technology does not simply remedy a bodily "defect," it actively shapes, molds, and trains the body. Technologies challenge bodily limits and call into question what bodily normalcy is. For Lee, both medical and social constructionist models subscribe to a linear time-space or unidimensional vector, but accretions of knowledge and attitudinal change advance the human race. Lee argues instead that an embodiment-focused approach that also acknowledges social construction shows technologies create different spaces and times for human experience.

### *The political embodiment of personhood*

In the last section, we asked how institutions—the state, the court, the media—exercise biopower over their governed populations. The four essays collected here ask, which bodies matter? If a body matters, then how does it constitute civic personhood that is worthy of legal protection and procreation? On the flip side of the coin, what do institutions do to the impaired person? How can laws, rules, and norms enact civic dis/ablement by excluding some bodies that are deemed less worthy?

Barclay argues that after the American Civil War, Southern white supremacists appropriated anti-slavery rhetoric to characterize freedpeople as incapable of self-support and self-rule. Before 1860, abolitionists had characterized enslaved people in affective terms designed to appeal to the sensibilities of white audiences. Accordingly, abolitionists described the enslaved as pitiful and lacking in bodily agency, defense, and autonomy. After emancipation and the war's end, abolitionists reversed their claims and asserted that freedpeople were wholly able to navigate the South's changed social and political landscapes. However, Barclay argues, post-war exigencies such as the lack of material support for freedpeople—both able-bodied and dis/abled—undercut this argument. Southern white supremacists seized on this fact to argue that freedpeople could not be trusted with the levers of government and that by virtue of their race, they were irrevocably dis/abled. Barclay develops her argument against the backdrop of arguments for and against federal pensions for dis/abled Civil War veterans. By so doing she reveals how ideas about manliness, race, and dis/ability intersected to construct the status of both white and African American veterans.

In "Bending the laws of nature," Tkotzyk and Hebben aim to critically examine the role of the mass media in the dissemination of the knowledge of DNA hacking by questioning the relationship between media practices, the dis/abled body, and its perception and meaning in society. They use the show *Unnatural Selection* (2019) to illustrate the media's preoccupation with producing the perfect human. This show illustrates that DNA alteration is no longer a monopoly among scientists; biohackers and amateurs who possess DNA literacy can experiment with changing bodies and lives. Even though some biohackers see the gene-editing technology CRISPR as a democratic means for all to access genetic information, Tkotzyk and Hebben believe that this technology has the potential to reinvigorate the discriminatory ideas and practice of eugenics movements. As such, those who are DNA literate may create or recreate a new imbalance of power that allows them to exploit those who hope to live a "normal" life. They thus believe media producers should clarify whether they aim to educate the public about new possibilities or to warn them about the danger.

In Lininger's chapter "Deconstructing rules for proof of cognitive impairments," he explores the rules that apply in legal proceedings to determine whether a person lacks mental capacity. He asserts that statutes, jurisprudence, and ethical rules in this area are inconsistent. Recent decisions by the US Supreme Court have further undermined the cohesiveness of the law. This inconsistency disadvantages neurodivergent people because the procedural rules for proving incapacity to stand trial are burdensome and unfair. He seeks to accomplish three things in this chapter: an examination of theoretical underpinnings of the rules for proving mental incapacity; a description of the operation of current rules to the detriment of neurodivergent litigants and witnesses, particularly in criminal cases; and an exploration of the potential for reform. Most fundamentally, he believes that the criminal system should divert mentally ill people from prison to alternative sites that best suited to providing humane, productive, and appropriate treatment.

In the last essay "So that playing to win is not playing to die," Madeleine M. Plascencia uses the concept of a "brown commons" to explore how athletes of color face a field of oppression as a result of intersectional systems of race, class, and dis/ability. She focuses on sickle cell trait (SCT) to make her case. College athletes whose ancestors came from certain parts of the world are more prone to this genetic disorder; hence, African Americans are more likely to die during vigorous practices. Even though coaches recommend testing, athletes might deny having SCT because they would not be able to compete. Plascencia suggests that in the absence of legal protections, the testing can be racialized and class driven. Therefore, she advocates that SCT be seen as a dis/ability that is subject to legal protection under the ADA and other civil rights statutes.

All told, the essays in this collection provide a panoramic view of dis/ability across time and place, and, by so doing, reveal the mutability, heterogeneity, and particularities of dis/ability. Equally important, the authors deploy the ideas and methods of critical Disability studies to challenge and deepen framings of dis/ability within their respective disciplines. They do so by taking to heart the argument by Burch and Davis that dis/ability is "irreducible" to the body or to "universalized or essentialized interpretations" of dis/ability (Burch & Rembis 2014, p. 1). Rather, and as the authors demonstrate, dis/ability is produced by interlocking and evolving phenomena from across time and space: cultural and medical definitions of normalcy, the social and political relations that uphold and sustain these ideas, and the laws and technology that not only buttress these ideas and relations but also institutionalize the resulting barriers. We also learn how and why people with dis/abilities have accommodated and/or resisted discursive and material barriers to individual and collective agency. With these discussions, the authors bring into sharp relief the preconditions to liberation of the dis/abled

## Notes

1 Americans with Disabilities Act of 1990. Pub. L. 101-336. 26 July 1990. 104 Stat. 328. We prefer the term dis/ability. Dis/ability recognizes that concepts of ability and disability exist "in tension" with one another and that this dynamic is both generative and should be interrogated. In other words, the term suggests "the theoretical, practical and political work that takes place either side of the binary ... denoted by the presence of '/' (the slash)." Annamma et al. (2018) make the related point that the concept of dis/abilities not only highlights what a person can do rather than cannot do, but it also takes into account human ability in context. In other words, dis/ability is not a fixed condition, but a process of being and becoming. In contrast, the term "disability" fractures ability from inability unlike dis/ability which encompasses embodiment theory and social constructivism and the bridges between them that we seek to construct. Others, including McGinley and Cooper (2020), have adopted this approach.

2 Having used the new wheelchair signs to show change in the ways dis/abilities are thought about, we acknowledge that there are problems in focusing on immobility. Those are "visible" dis/abilities, and many are "invisible." Mental differences, such as being on one end of the continuum in terms of distractibility (and diagnosed as ADD-HD), might be invisible in someone who takes medicine, yet the person may sometimes show signs of their cognitive differences on other occasions. People with dis/abilities are tremendously heterogenous.

3 UPIAS. Archive today. Retrieved from: https://archive.is/20080703223248/http://www.gmcdp.com/UPIAS.html

4 Before we review the literature on embodiment and social construction approaches to dis/abilities, we must disclaim that none of us was trained in CDS. We have only recently actively engaged in the community of CDS scholarship. We identify ourselves as politically progressive, interdisciplinary scholars grounded in poststructuralism, political economy, cultural history and theories, critical race theory, and gender studies. While one of us is explicitly a CDS scholar, our lowest common denominator is critical theory in general. All three editors have published on gender and race issues in media, law, and history. Therefore, we do not claim to be veterans, but we are also not curious tourists who look for the rare and the exotic. Instead, we have found that critical disabilities studies, which we stumbled upon through our research, have provided insights into our intellectual and personal journeys.

5 For example, a parking space reserved for someone with a dis/ability may only allow others to see that person as someone with a dis/ability. But how would we view this person differently if we also take into account, among other identities, gender, race, and social class? How do we understand people with dis/abilities who do not own a car, and so travel on public transportation in order to run daily errands?
6 https://www.disabilitymuseum.org/dhm/index.html
7 On the four phases of rehabilitative treatment, of which occupational therapy second, see Laws (2011).

## References

Alper, M., (2017). *Giving voice: mobile communication, disability, and inequality*. Cambridge, MA: MIT Press.

Annamma, S. A., Ferri, B. A. and Connor, D. J., (2018). Disability critical race theory: exploring the intersectional lineage, emergence, and potential futures of DisCrit in education. *Review of Research in Education*. **42**(1), 46–71.

Asch, A., (2001). Critical race theory, feminism, and disability: reflections on social justice and personal identity. *Ohio State Law Journal*. **62**(1), 391–423.

Baynton, D. C., (1996). *Forbidden signs: American culture and the campaign against sign language*. Chicago, IL: University of Chicago Press.

Baynton, D. C., (2001). Disability and the justification of inequality in American history. In: P. Longmore and L. Umansky, eds. *The new disability history: American perspectives*. New York: New York University Press. pp. 33–57.

Baynton, D. C., (2008). Disability in history. *Disability Studies Journal*. **28**(3). Available from: https://dsq-sds.org/article/view/108/108

Blanck, P., (2021). Thirty years of the Americans with Disabilities Act: law students and lawyers as plaintiffs and advocates. *N.Y.U. Review of Law and Social Change*. **45**. Available from: https://socialchangenyu.com/harbinger/thirty-years-of-the-americans-with-disabilities-act/

Boellstorff, T., (2019). The opportunity to contribute: disability and the digital entrepreneur. *Information Communication and Society*. **22**(4), 474–490.

Bogdan, R., (1988). *Freak show: presenting human oddities for amusement and profit*. Chicago, IL: University of Chicago Press.

Burch, S., (2005). Disability history: suggested readings—an annotated bibliography. *The Public Historian*. **27**(2), 63–74.

Burch, S. and Rembis, M., (2014). Remembering the past. In: S. Burch and M. Rembis, eds. *Disability histories*. Urbana, IL: University of Illinois Press. pp. 2–13.

Collins, P., (2019). *Intersectionality as critical social theory*. Durham, NC: Duke University Press.

Collins, P. H. l. and Bilge, S., (2016). *Intersectionality*. Malden, MA: Polity Press.

Cooper, F. R., (2009). Our first unisex President? Black masculinity and Obama's feminine side. *Denver University Law Review*. **86**, 633–661.

Crenshaw, K. W., (1989). Demarginalizing the intersection of race and sex: a black feminist critique of antidiscrimination doctrine, feminist theory and antiracist politics. *University of Chicago Legal Forum*. **1**(8), 139–167.

Crenshaw, K. W., Gotanda, N., Peller, G. and Thomas, K. (1995). Introduction. In: K. W. Crenshaw, N. Gotanda, G. Peller and K. Thomas, eds. *Critical race theory: the key writings that formed the movement*. New York: The New Press. pp. xiii–xxxii.

Davis, D. and Boellstorff, T., (2016). Compulsive creativity: virtual worlds, disability, and digital capital. *International Journal of Communication*. **10**, 2096–2118.

Ellis, K., (2019). *Disability and digital television cultures: representation, access, and reception*. New York: Routledge.

Ellis, K., Kent, M., Locke, K. and Clocherty, C., (2017). Access for everyone? Australia's "streaming wars" and consumers with disabilities. *Continuum: Journal of Media and Cultural Studies*. **31**(6), 881–891.

Erevelles, N. and Minear, A., (2001). Unspeakable offenses: untangling race and disability in discourses of intersectionality. In: L. Davis, ed. *The disability studies reader*. New York: Routledge. pp. 354–368.

Eyer, K., (2021). Claiming disability. *Boston University Law Review*. **101**, 547–618.

Frank, A., (2006). Health stories as connectors and subjectifiers. *Health: An International Journal for the Social Study of Health, Illness and Medicine*. **10**(4), 421–440.

Fuller, L. K., (2016). *Female Olympians: tracing a mediated socio-cultural/political-economic timeline*. New York: Palgrave Macmillan.

Galis, V., (2011). Enabling disability: how can science and technology studies inform disability studies? *Disability and Society*. **26**(7), 825–838.

Garland-Thomson, R., (1997). *Extraordinary bodies: physical disability in American culture and literature*. New York, NY: Columbia University Press.

Garland-Thomson, R., (2001). Seeing the disabled: visual rhetorics of disability in popular photography. In: P. K. Longmore and L. Umansky, eds. *The new disability history: American perspectives*. New York: New York University Press. pp. 335–374.

Garland-Thomson, R., (2002). The politics of staring: visual rhetorics of disability in popular photography. In: S. L. Snyder, B. J. Brueggemann and R. Garland-Thomson, eds. *Disability studies: enabling the humanities*. New York: Modern Language Association of America. pp. 56–75.

Garland-Thomson, R., (2005). Feminist disability studies. *Signs: Journal of Women in Culture and Society*. **30**(2), 1557–1587.

Garland-Thomson, R., (2013a). *Disability studies: a field emerged. American Quarterly*. **65**(4), 915–926. doi:10.1353/aq.2013.0052.

Garland-Thomson, R., (2013b). Integrating disability, transforming feminist theory. In: L. Davis, ed. *The disability studies reader*. New York: Routledge. pp. 333–353.

Garland-Thomson, R., (2017). *Extraordinary bodies: figuring physical disability in American culture and literature*. 20th-anniversary ed. New York: Columbia University Press.

Gerschick, T. J., (2000). Toward a theory of disability and gender. *Signs: Journal of Women in Culture and Society*. **25**(4), 1263–1268.

Goggin, G., Ellis, K. and Hawkins, W., (2019). Disability at the centre of digital inclusion: assessing a new moment in technology and rights. *Communication Research and Practice*. **5**(3), 290–303.

Goggin, G. and Newell, C., (2002). *Digital disability: the social construction of disability in new media*. Lanham, MD: Rowman and Littlefield.

Goodbye CP, (1972). *Directed by Kazuo Hara*. Tokyo: Shisso Production.

Goodley, D., Liddiard, K. and Runswick-Cole, K., (2019). Provocations for critical disability studies. *Disability and Society*. **34**(6), 972–997.

Haegele, J. A. and Hodge, S., (2016). Disability discourse: overview and critiques of the medical and social models. *Quest*. **68**(2), 193–206.

Hall, M. C., (2019). Critical disability theory. In: N. Zalta, ed. *The Stanford Encyclopedia of Philosophy*. Available from: https://plato.stanford.edu/entries/disability-critical/

Hall, S., ed., (1997). *Representation: cultural representations and signifying practices*. Milton Keynes, UK: Sage.

Haraway, D., (2016). *A cyborg manifesto: science, technology, and socialist-feminism in the late twentieth century*. Minneapolis, MN: University of Minnesota Press.

Holmes, O. W., (1880). Book notices. *American Law Review*. **14**, 233–234.

Hunt-Kennedy, S., (2020). *Between fitness and death: disability and slavery in the Caribbean*. Urbana, IL: University of Illinois Press.

Jackson, D., Hodges, C. E. M., Molesworth, M. and Scullion, R., (2015). *Reframing disability: media, (dis)empowerment and voice in the 2012 Paralympics*. New York: Routledge.

Jeffreys, M., (2002). The visible cripple (scars and other disfiguring displays included). In: S. L. Snyder, B. J. Brueggemann and R. Garland-Thomson, eds. *Disability studies: enabling the humanities*. New York: Modern Language Association of America. pp. 31–33.

Kudlick, C. J., (2003). Disability history: why we need another "other". *The American Historical Review*. **108**(3), 763–793. doi: 10.1086/ahr/108.3.763.

Kunzel, R., (2018). The rise of gay rights and the disavowal of disability in the United States. In: M. Rembis, C. Kudlick and K. E. Nielsen, eds. *The Oxford handbook of disability history*. Oxford: UK: Oxford University Press. pp. 459–475.

Laws, J., (2011). Crackpots and basket cases: a history of therapeutic work and occupation. *History of the Human Sciences*. **24**(2), 65–81.

Loeser, C., Crowley, V. and Pini B., (2017). Introductory essay. In: C. Loeser, V. Crowley and B. Pini, eds. *Disability and masculinities: corporeality, pedagogy and the critique of otherness*. London: Palgrave. pp. xxv–lxxiv.

Longmore, P. K. and Umansky, L. eds., (2001). *The new disability history: American perspectives*. New York: New York University Press.

Martínez-Pére, J. and Del Cura, M., (2016). Introduction: exploring disability in the past: on perspectives, methodology and themes in disability history. *Asclepio; Archivo Iberoamericano de Historia de la Medicina y Antropología Médica*. **68**(2). Available from: http://asclepio.revistas.csic.es/index.php/asclepio/article/download/700/1030?inline=1

McGinley, A. and Cooper, F. R., (2020). Intersectional cohorts, dis/ability, and class actions. *Fordham Urban Law Journal*. **47**(2), 293–341.

McGinley, A. C., (2001). Enough!: eliminating police abuse of individuals of color with disabilities. *NEV. L.J.* **21**(3), 1081–1116.

McRae, L., (2019). Disciplining disability: intersections between critical disability studies and cultural studies. In: K. Ellis, R. Garland-Thomson, M. Kent and R. Robertson, eds. *Manifestos for the future of critical disability studies: volume 1*. London: Routledge. pp. 217–229.

Mills, M. and Sterne, J., (2017). Afterword II: dismediation—three proposals, six tactics. In: E. Ellcessor and B. Kirkpatrick, eds. *Disability media studies*. New York: NYU Press. pp. 365–378.

Minich, J., (2016). Enabling whom? Critical disability studies now. *Lateral*. **5**(1). Available from: http://csalateral.org/wp/issue/5-1/forum-alt-humanities-critical-disabilitystudies-now-minich/

Moser, I., (2006). Sociotechnical practices and difference: on the interferences between disability, gender, and class. *Science Technology, and Human Value*. **31**(5), 537–564.

Nagel, T., (1986). *The view from nowhere*. Oxford: Oxford University Press.

Nielsen, K. E., (2001). *A disability history of the United States*. Boston, MA: Beacon Press.

O'Connor, C., (2016). Embodiment and the construction of social knowledge: towards an integration of embodiment and social representation theory. *Journal for the Theory of Social Behavior*. **47**(1), 2–24.

Pernick, M. S., (1999). *The black stork: eugenics and the death of "defective" babies in American medicine and motion pictures since 1915*. Oxford: Oxford University Press.

Rembis, M., Kudlick, C. and Nielsen, K. E. eds., (2018). *The Oxford handbook of disability history*. Oxford: Oxford University Press.

Scarry, E., (1985). *The body in pain: the making and unmaking of the world*. Oxford: Oxford University Press.

Siebers, T., (2001a). Disability in theory: from social constructionism to the new realism of the body. *American Literacy History*. **13**(4), 737–754.

Siebers, T., (2001b). Disability and the theory of complex embodiment for identity politics in a new register. In: L. Davis, ed. *The disability studies reader*. New York: Routledge. pp. 278–297.

Siebers, T., (2006). In theory: from social construction to the new realism of the body. In: L. Davis, ed. *The disabilities studies reader*. 2nd ed. New York: Routledge. pp. 172–183.

Silvers, A., (2019). Feminist perspectives on disability. In: E. N. Zalta, ed. *The Stanford Encyclopedia of Philosophy* [online]. Available from: https://plato.stanford.edu/archives/fall2019/entries/feminism-disability/

Smit, C. R. and Enns, A. W. eds., (2001). *Screening disability: essays on cinema and disability*. Lanham, MD: University Press of America.

Smith, W. W., (2016). "Blind Tom" abroad: race, disability, and transatlantic representations of Thomas Wiggins. *Journal of Transatlantic Studies*. **14**(2), 164–175. doi:10.1080/14794012.2016.1169873.

Snyder, S. L., Brueggemann, B. J. and Garland-Thomson, R., eds., (2002). *Disability studies: enabling the humanities*. New York: Modern Language Association of America.

Stiker, H., (1999). *A history of disability*. Ann Arbor, MI: University of Michigan Press.

Trent, J. W., (1995). *Inventing the feeble mind: a history of mental retardation in the United States*. Berkeley, CA: University of California Press.

Wajcman, J., (1991). *Feminism confronts technology*. University Park, PA: Pennsylvania State University Press.

Walters, K. L., Mohammed, S. A., Evans-Campbell, T., Beltrán, R. E., Chae, D. H. and Duran, B., (2011). Bodies don't just tell stories, they tell histories: embodiment of historical trauma among American Indians and Alaska Natives. *Du Bois Review: Social Science Research on Race*. **8**(1), 179–189. doi:10.1017/S1742058X1100018X.

Wilkerson, A., (2015). Embodiment. In: R. Adams, B. Reiss and D. Serlin, eds. *Keywords for Disability Studies*. New York: New York University Press. pp. 67–70.

William-Searle, J., (2001). Cold charity: manhood, brotherhood, and the transformation of disability, 1870-1900. In: P. K. Longmore and L. Umansky, eds. *The new disability history: American perspectives*. New York: New York University Press. pp. 157–186.

Wilson, D. J., (2018). Disability—a historiographical survey. In: J. Podair and D. Dochuk, eds. *The Routledge history of twentieth-century United States*. New York: Routledge. pp. 349–358.

Young, I., (1990). *Justice and the politics of difference*. Princeton: Princeton University Press.

Part I

# Foundations: Experience and Theories

# 2 The Art of Regarding Still Life

*Pamela Mullins*

Susan Sontag who wrote *Illness as Metaphor* (1989) beat breast cancer and uterine cancer before finally succumbing to a third cancer sever years later. In the end, she exhausted all means possible in a futile attempt to avoid her own death. Her family and friends thought she was absurd in torturing herself to continue her search for a cure when she was so obviously on the brink of death. When they pleaded with her to stop all medical interventions, she was quoted as saying, "Too abstract death. Too concrete me" (Sontag 1989, p. 41). Though this is probably not an end-of-life choice that I would make, I am struck by just how embedded she was in her own lived experience. A person viewing the struggles of an "Other" with a disease or dis/ability makes a valuation of capabilities and very quickly contrasts that calculation with ratings of the past and projects those ratings into the future. However, this is not the experience of one living *in* a condition. Rather, the challenge for the person living it becomes an immersive experience, where coping in the moment becomes everything, where all that is present is precisely what is present in the moment.

Let me take you back to December 31, 1999. It is New Year's Eve and we are on the verge of not just a new year, but a new century and a new millennium! The phrase on everybody's lips was "Y2K," and we feared the possibility that when the calendar flipped chaos would ensue because our technological world might not be programmed to shift from the 1990s to 2000. The big question was: if digital calendars could not shift, would the power grid go down? There was widespread speculation and debate about this fear leading up to the new year. Ever the pessimist, I was biding my time until catastrophe hit. That day I was dialed in on the early new year turnovers. On live TV they covered the firework displays starting with the iconic Sydney Opera House, later the Kremlin in Moscow and Big Ben in London, as each place counted down the beginning of 2000. Reporters were breathlessly standing watch to see if glitches would wreak havoc with our wired world. They did not. As city after city had their celebrations without incident, I was slightly disappointed, as I usually am when my pessimism is not borne out. That's the thing about being a pessimist. Either you are right about being skeptical or you are bummed about being wrong. Kind of a no-win situation—kind of perfect, for a pessimist.

DOI: 10.4324/9781003257196-3

Meanwhile, I was having some weird back pain and a tendency to drag my left foot that had led to a brain scan the week before. Some odd symptoms had been showing up over the past couple of years that had resulted in this second MRI after an earlier CAT scan. Weird to have so many unfounded scans for an otherwise healthy person, I thought. The week after our electrical grid had successfully switched from 1999 to 2000, I found out that the faulty circuitry actually resided in me. Pessimism validated after all. I got a diagnosis of multiple sclerosis, a progressive neurologic disease where plaques form on neurons thereby blocking electrical signals trying to reach the body from the brain. I went from seeing myself in 1999 as a fairly healthy aging jock, in the flip of a calendar, to someone with a progressive dis/ability whose level of severity would unfold over the years and be impossible to predict.

Virginia Woolf, in her essay "On being ill," eloquently calls attention to a fascinating Cartesian split in literature. She notes that, with few exceptions, literature concerns itself predominantly with the mind in talking about love, conflict, and jealousy; and ignores the body. She goes on to wonder why this is so, since physical suffering is all consuming, taking one to places never visited before getting sick. Just listen to how she describes the experience of illness:

> Considering how common illness is, how tremendous the spiritual change that it brings, how astonishing, when the lights of health go down, the undiscovered countries that are then disclosed, what wastes and deserts of the soul a slight attack of influenza brings to light, what precipices and lawns sprinkled with bright flowers a little rise of temperature reveals … (Woolf 1926, p. 32).

When we are sick, we all want to get better as soon as possible despite whatever enlightenment we may have found in fever or lying still in contemplation. Indeed, we use the word "recovery" to indicate getting better, but re-covering is exactly that, the act of covering over an experience that, as Woolf points out, opens a glimpse to some extraordinary places. Not only do we try hard to cover over such pain or suffering, we do our level best to deny that it could ever befall us in the first place. Sontag refers to

> Illness as the night side of life, a more onerous citizenship. Everyone who is born holds dual citizenship, in the kingdom of the well and in the kingdom of the sick. Although we all prefer to use only the good passport, sooner or later each of us is obliged, at least for a spell, to identify ourselves as citizens of that other place (Sontag 1989, p. 22).

I want to focus on the psychic journey of living with a dis/ability, both in how that experience is shaped by the socio-cultural experience of living in the world and in how that influence gets reflected back and internalized. In doing so I want to emphasize the process of looking, both in how others' eyes impinge on us and in how we see ourselves. What I am trying to underscore is how much societal ableism is an objectifying experience that becomes an intrapsychic metabolism of objectification as well. Furthermore, I'd like to reflect on the universality of the grief process and its importance in making meaning of our lives. As I muse on these influences, I will demonstrate my process of how I see what I am going through. Finally, I want to share some of my experience of grieving and loss and the possibilities that these processes hold for being with experience in a deeper way. This is, of course, not meant to describe a universal experience of living with disease. Rather, it is a personal account of how I have navigated these universal phenomena.

I am trying to come to grips with an internal struggle between one sense of myself with a passport in the kingdom of the well and another sense of myself with a passport in the kingdom of the sick. In order to entertain these ideas, I am going to play with the words "Still Life." I am going to illustrate a threefold process which includes naming and embracing, grieving, and awakening in how we regard illness, disease, and dis/ability but I also want to use the same three components to show how we can *be* with it.

We will start with the concept of still life as in the painting of inanimate objects. How else could we begin to understand without first forming a picture of a thing? I would like to show you both the prejudice and value of reification in relation to others and in relation to self. Then I want to move on to *still* life as still in stopping, paying attention, and looking at the importance of grief and allowing ourselves to grieve. Finally, I want to emphasize the phrase still *life* as we look at still life as continuing on. Still life, *still* life, and still *life*, a three-part process of naming, grieving, and being-with.

## Still life as object

Still life is an art form that depicts inanimate objects captured in a moment of time. They are painted in such a way as to evoke the imagination of what has happened or is about to happen in the scene, and it is left to the viewer's imagination to conjure up the taste of the next bite or wonder what is in the next room. In still life paintings, we are both observing the objects portrayed and assigning them meaning even as those objects are evoking a mood in us. In essence, we are playing with them and they are playing with us.

Let's begin by looking at how experiences of illness, disease, and dis/ability become reified into objects. The philosopher Michel Foucault, in true phenomenological fashion, gives us the notion that power and knowledge are not given entities but rather exist in relation to each other. In a reciprocal way, power informs knowledge and knowledge informs power. In other words, they arise and are defined by their interaction with each other as opposed to either one being a predetermined given. Foucault said, "Power—that is, its exercise—perpetually creates knowledge and knowledge constantly induces effects of power" (Tremain 2015, p. 15). With this idea of each defining and clarifying the other, he notes the emergence of biopower, which takes as its object of knowledge life itself. He establishes biopower as arising around the second half of the 18th century. At this time, we witnessed the advent of scientific measurement and quantifiable data when phenomena such as birth and death rates, rates of reproduction and fertility coupled with economic and political concerns became biopower's first objects of knowledge and thus targets for control. Subsequently, we saw the first efforts of public hygiene, charities, and insurance systems developed to allocate resources. Norms were developed that are themselves artifacts of the discipline that has been created. In turn, these practices engendered a host of classifications of social anomalies through which some people have been divided from others and objectified with an explanatory label. Thus, we see the advent of norms based on statistics and the beginnings of an objectifying definition of dis/ability.

What is dis/ability? Simply put it is a deviation from a biomedical norm. Obviously, the term encompasses a wide variation of physical, mental, and emotional conditions. However, in all cases, the person is medicalized by virtue of being an outlier on a bell curve. The implications then are enormous. In measuring generalities for a population, outliers are partitioned off in order to maximize conditions for the majority. The outcasts become objects categorized into systems meant to manage them. Furthermore, in this process of medicalization, bodies become even more subdivided into units as they are sorted into hospitals or institutions. For example, a person who has lost a leg is then referred to as an amputee, as if the only salient detail of that human being is the missing limb.

For people with dis/abilities, a long laundry list of measures and institutions has emerged to bracket social anomalies. These include asylums, quality of life assessments, special education programs, regimes of rehabilitation, prostheses, sheltered workshops, home care services, and telethons, to name a few. These systems are helpful in many ways to those who encounter them, and they can also be intractable and all-consuming as they may dictate so many facets of one's life. Finally, the individual who has become objectified in this system becomes an object of oneself, living in a world that has reduced their experience of being in the world to an experience that is solely dominated by their dis/ability. Foucault refers to these three modes: (1) practices of classification, (2) dividing practices, and (3) self-subjectification practices. As a means of social control, human beings are categorized and bracketed off in the name of power.

Let me give you a sense of how it is to experience this type of objectification. A while ago I was at my biannual visit to my neurologist who left the room to have a look at the imaging from my latest MRI. Getting an MRI entails lying on a stretcher, having a hockey mask snapped down over your face, getting slid into a casket-like tube, and being told not to move, including trying not to swallow, for the next hour and a half. Inside, the MRI machine operates with the constant banging of loud magnets in varying rhythms for the duration of the scan. Finally, you are dragged out feeling like you have just been rescued from a cave. After this ordeal, I am typically not privy to the results of my test. On this particular day, he has a resident with him. As he reenters, he addresses only the resident as if I have no interest in what he has seen. "The brain is unremarkable," he says, meaning that there is little MS activity in my brain. (It happens to be predominantly in my spinal cord.) Now, to a medical person, this is a normal observation that the brain is unremarkable; but that brain happens to be mine. The depersonalization of his comment feels astounding to me. He has said without looking at me "the brain is unremarkable." And I pipe up, "Well maybe to you!" because I want him to notice the fully alive human being before him. He stops in his tracks and chuckles slightly and makes a comment to the resident about the importance of communication in a clinical setting.

Being disabled, one becomes entrenched in a classification system, further subdivided according to one's own particular affliction, and then an object of one's own reflection while living in such an overwhelming world. It is this aspect of objectification that I would like to focus on, the objectification of self. The phenomenological philosophical tradition that might help our examination here ironically gives dis/ability short shrift. For starters, we all know that philosophical thinkers are overwhelmingly white men, which is problematic in and of itself. Shelley Tremain (2013), a feminist philosopher, states:

> Dis/ability (unlike gender or race) is generally not conceived as a relation of social power in which everyone is implicated, but rather, is still widely regarded as an unfortunate politically-neutral characteristic … that some individuals possess and embody and about which there is little … to analyze (para. 24).

Ableism is even more pronounced in philosophical thinking as seen in writings by phenomenologist Hegel, who rather than including dis/ability in his observations bracketed off such phenomena and cited "cripples as monstrous" (Dryden 2013).

Although the field is not inclined to consider the disabled condition as a way of being in the world, we can use existentialism and specifically Heidegger's concept of the call, to find valuable ways to use philosophy to appreciate this kind of challenge. Heidegger uses the example of a hammer to reflect on how we are called when something breaks. When we use a hammer, we mostly don't think about it. It is predominantly used in a non-conscious way as a nondescript thing. But if it breaks, we have to stop and suddenly consider what a hammer is and how we use it, its "being" emerges. The same could be said for illness. So, going back to my sense of self, I suddenly was forced to shed the identity that I had hung onto for a life time, and like a broken hammer, I had to reflect anew about who I was and how I experienced being in the world. I was called in that break to pay attention, and existentialism tells us to heed the call and embrace the authentic moment that it offers.

But how exactly do we pay attention to the self as an object? To explore this question, we must focus on how the self experiences the self. For this, we will turn to Christopher Bollas to elucidate the concept of self as object, and further, the concept of self-being deepened by self experience. Bollas is a psychoanalyst who has written extensively on how the self is shaped by its world and perceives and expresses itself. Bollas writes, "The relation to the self as an object is clearly an important feature of our lived life" (Bollas 1987, p. 4). In other words, just as we think about our relationships with other people and how those connections shape us, our way of relating to ourselves, our self relation, has a profound impact on our lives. In the face of marginalization and objectification when the dis/abled person finds themself in such an intense place of invisibility, the challenge is to make the invisible *visible*, at least to themself. In the merger of philosophy and psychology, we see the challenge of embracing the objectification that we are both subjected to by the outside world and that we also do to ourselves. It is only in the process of claiming this experience that we can begin to be with it more fully.

## *Still* life as in coming to a stand still

I am at yet another neurology appointment a few years ago, sitting in the waiting room before being called into my doctor's office. This area is a bit different than other medical waiting rooms. It is filled with artifacts of what my life could become; canes, walkers, and motorized chairs that propel an individual up when they don't have the strength to stand. I simultaneously feel comforted that I don't need any of those devices now and freaked out that those devices may be in my future. The uncertainty of MS is that one never really knows what direction the disease will take. It can be relatively benign or relatively brutal, and though my disease has been termed mild, there are no reliable predictors of what that means for the future. Therefore, I generally hate these appointments where the unsteady balance that I work so hard to achieve mentally gets disrupted by the intrusion of medical inferences, blood draws, and the constant push to get an MRI that I invariably resist.

As I sit there, I am struck by the appearance of a woman in her thirties who frantically enters the room and seems confused about where the receptionist is or how to check in. Ah, first time and scared, I think to myself. I have no idea what symptoms have brought her here and while everybody else who comes as a patient gives a sympathetic and knowing nod which I always return; she briskly lights next to me with no notice of me or any of her surroundings. She is radiating anxiety and it is easy for me to surmise that she has just received her diagnosis. I am now 15 years removed from that devastating news and I have this sudden urge to throw my arms around her and say, "Oh honey, just relax. You've got a lot of good years ahead of you." She is called into her appointment shortly thereafter and I am placed in a room in the same hall. At the MS center, the rooms in which they see patients are all off the same hall, which has a 20-foot length marked off, kind of like a gauntlet. At the beginning of each doctor's visit, you are asked to walk the gauntlet and then turn around and do it again. Your doctor stands there with a stopwatch timing you, essentially to measure how much slower you get over time, thus giving some indication of progression by noting the deterioration in your ability to walk. In my first visit, my doctor approached it with enthusiasm egging me on to go faster. Over time it got more somber, where he noted, in typical fashion to his resident, not to me, how I was compensating in my gait for my difficulty in lifting my left leg. Eventually, he stopped timing me all together.

On this day though, after an initial greeting, my doctor leaves the room, as is his wont, to look at my MRI. He leaves the door ajar and I am able to see the woman from the waiting room just whipping up and down the hall in her timed walk. All she is doing is setting herself up for further disappointment down the road. But I recognize that fervor.

When I was first diagnosed, I was determined to summon my physical strength to outdistance this disease. I had been an athlete, an all-star rugby player on a national championship team, and a tennis player and coach. I had ridden my bicycle from one coast to the other and was still running six miles a day. I thought with the same determination I could out train any challenge my brain was trying to put in the way. Four months later with that resolve, I unintentionally rode my bike into the path of an oncoming car. As with the disease, I thought I could outrun the car. Now 15 years later, I can see this woman trying to do the same and I want to share with her the hard-earned wisdom I have gained from my own devastation.

What I got back in 2000 was a profound object lesson that I needed to STOP. I had finally given into despair. When I see the woman in the other office practically running through the timed walk, I am reminded of how this awful surrender brought me to my knees. Louise Gluck (1994) reminds us that despair

> demands resistance at the outset; to treat impoverishment as a prerequisite to wealth, to turn it into a kind of fraternity hazing, is to deny the experience. It must be feared and resisted; it must exhaust all available resources, since its essence is defeat (p. 133).

My resistance was to train feverishly while the woman from the waiting room attacked her first test to prove to herself she was ok. Gluck (1994) goes on to say,

> despair in our culture tends to produce wild activity: change the job, change the partner, replace the faltering ambition instantly. We fear passivity and prize action, meaning the action we initiate. But the self cannot be willed back. And flight from despair forfeits whatever benefit may arise in the encounter with despair (p. 133).

Suddenly, with my bike accident in which I broke my kneecap and from which I could no longer flee, I had a profound and different vantage point regarding the everydayness of my life. Fully immobilized with a cast on my right leg that stretched from my hip to my ankle, I wrote in my journal:

> If I can't use my body, a major defining part of me, then who am I and what does really matter? The capacity to leave that space open will allow

> something to enter through me, the process of creativity, or so I've been told. My panic is that it will just feel awfully empty. This is becoming who I am. It's not really a glitch anymore as opposed to something that shapes me.

Let's look at the self experience of despair induced by the diagnosis of this disease using Bollas as our guide. Bollas writes about two versions of self. The first is the immersive self. The immersive self is subject to feeling despair. However, from that experience, another complex version of self emerges, the self that can reflect on feeling despair. But how do we get from being lost in or overwhelmed by an experience to being able to reflect on it? Indeed, that was the question I was wondering about with trepidation in my journal. Bollas (1992) writes,

> The concept of *self experiencing* is ironic, as its referential ambiguity (does it mean the self that experiences or the experiencing of ourself?) is strangely true to the complexity of being human. All self experiencing involves this split, which can be described as a division between ourself as simple selves (when we are immersed in desired or evoked experience) and ourself as complex selves (when we think about experience) (p. 27).

He goes on to explicate a four-stage process in the dialectics of self experience where we move from this simple self immersion in an experience to a complex reflecting self. The first step is to use the object. In my journal entry, I chose my perception of my body as the object on which to focus—"I can't use my body." The second stage is to be played by the object—"then who am I and what matters?" Prior to my bike accident, I had not taken in my body in this way. Much like Heidegger's hammer, the first step is simply to use it, and the second step allows oneself to notice that it is broken. The third step in shifting from an immersive state to a reflecting one is to be lost in self experiencing. In my journal, I write about being lost in despair. In this state, the distinction between the object and the self is, according to Bollas (1992), "destroyed in the experiential synthesis of mutual effect" (p. 31). In other words, an interplay begins between the object carrying meaning and the experiencing self trying to make sense out of that interaction—a back and forth. As I note in my journal, in going through this process, I am filled with panic and emptiness. Finally, in the fourth stage, I am able to offer reflection as I observe the *self* as an object—I see it as something that shapes me, and I begin to appreciate the importance of leaving that space open. At the time I did not come up with a terribly convincing affirmation but was willing to incorporate my confusion about who I was and was hopeful (albeit a bit skeptical) that something more could emerge: "this is becoming who I am. It's not really a glitch anymore as opposed to something that shapes me."

One thing that is useful to notice with this example is how I, as the subject, reflect on myself, turning myself into an object of thought, i.e., "who am I?" As such I am simultaneously an actor in my own drama and a director deciding what the next scene will be: "a creative opening, or so I've been told." Thus, we see how, according to Bollas (1992), "the simple experiencing self and the complex reflecting self enable the person to process life according to different yet interdependent modes of engagement: one immersive, the other reflective" (p. 15).

Bollas writes about the back and forth of everyday experiencing in how objects are chosen by us to induce a certain experience but also how they can appear by chance for us to incorporate, and then how we synthesize them into our own psychic space. Further, the introduction of this new thing by choice or by chance begins to impact how we think about ourselves in our own self relation. Let's reflect back on that woman flying up and down the hall. The concept of self with MS becomes a very threatening object that she internalizes in that moment. I notice in response to her, 15 years into my diagnosis, how far I have come when I want to tell her to stay present and enjoy the moment that she has before her. Therefore, the very same diagnosis can be internalized in many different ways, thus influencing how we think about ourselves. Bollas (1992) writes, "Thus we oscillate between thinking ourself out through the selection of objects that promote inner experience and being thought out so to speak, by the environment which plays upon itself" (p. 4).

Parsing out the layers of experiencing in this way calls attention to the process of internalization. As the disease presents itself in a myriad of different ways and I cycle through this process of using it, being played by it, being lost in it, I find a way to reflect from an ever-varying vantage point. Through the continual repetition of this process, I begin to realize just how important it is to pay attention. In the complex self of self-reflection, I recognize so many ways to be with disease. I am not only the medicalized victim of a neurological condition. Rather, this challenge of encountering, sifting through, and making meaning opens my world to so many different vantage points. If I were to race that woman in the 20-foot timed walk, she would beat the pants off me. But I could run circles around her in having gone through a profound grieving process that has made evident so many ways to be.

In my process of being stripped away, I begin to develop an intimacy with this other self that I have tried so hard to outrace. I am gaining an understanding of the importance of grief which is felt through the acknowledgment of my own limitations. MS is the perfectly challenging existential disease for embracing grief. It wipes away the typical mask of well-being that we tend to operate with in the world. Further, it is full of surprises with no predictable course. Symptoms come and go with no particular cause and effect, so the sadness one feels is constantly shifting from a stiff leg here, to blurry eyesight there, to ringing in the ears, etc.

With these body scans and the grief that I learn to sit with, I begin to really grasp the existential notion that one must choose every moment. There is a wisdom in paying attention to the self in the way that Bollas explicates. Mark Doty, in *Still Life with Lemons and Oysters* (2001), echoes what Bollas has told us when he says the "world is a dialog between degrees of transparency, degrees of reflectivity and we are instructed by the objects that come to speak with us" (p. 5). And so I have to look. What I see is a landscape stripped of what I used to grow there. Much like trees losing their leaves in winter I begin to see whole vistas that had been hidden by the foliage. Doty (2001) refers to this dedication to look as "love, a sense of tenderness toward experience, of being held within an intimacy with the things of the world" (p. 4) and I would add with an intimacy toward oneself.

## Still *life* as possibility

I am going to start this section by discussing a poem from Emily Dickinson.

> I dwell in Possibility -
> A fairer House than Prose -
> More numerous of Windows -
> Superior–for Doors -
> Of Chambers as the Cedars -
> Impregnable of eye -
> And for an everlasting Roof
> The Gambrels of the Sky -
> Of visitors–the fairest -
> For Occupation - This -
> The spreading wide my narrow Hands
> To gather Paradise -

I chose this poem because Dickinson, famously reclusive herself, contrasts poetry to prose and exalts poetry in its capacity to say so much more. Poetry in its use of language points to meaning rather than explicating meaning and in that way is "More numerous of Windows/ Superior—for Doors." I also love the contrast with the spreading wide of narrow hands which I think reinforces Bollas's observations of use of object and Doty's plea for appreciating art: that the more closely we look, the more we see and, in that dedication, regardless of our vantage point, the vista discloses more and more. And so, it is that desire to receive what that moment offers that calls us to move beyond grief. As Doty (2001) says, "Not that grief vanishes, far from it, but that it begins in time to coexist with pleasure, sorrow sits right beside the rediscovery of what is to be cherished in experience" (p. 47).

You would think as I wax poetic about my gradual emergence from grief—where I both embrace that process and really choose to pay attention—that I could end right here imparting you with a little bit of wisdom and a challenge to embrace your own world. But you'd be wrong. Ten years later, I was involved in yet another bike accident. This time the culprit was a dog and this time, I didn't break my knee. I dislocated and broke my shoulder. But all the same ingredients were there: the hubris that I could outdistance my diagnosis, the sense of loss, the nothingness, and the grief. This whole process really does tend to cycle (quite literally for me) over and over.

I dedicated myself to physical therapy to recover and, while rehabbing my shoulder, I worked out with an upper arm exerciser which is like bike peddling for your arms. I proudly brought my shoulder back stronger than ever, and that spring while watching the Boston Marathon, I saw people participating using hand cycles, and I thought, I could do that! So I invested in a hand cycle. It looks like a recumbent bike but instead of using your legs to pedals you use your arms. It comes complete with 27 gears just like a touring bike and I fondly refer to it as my rig.

In Maine where I spend a lot of time, there is a beautiful bike path that meanders along an abandoned railroad track in the woods. I love to ride there every chance I get. On this route, I have encountered a bear, a moose, and a protective mother deer with her baby. I also go past a goat farm/day care. (In rural Maine, most things are multipurpose.) At times the goats are somehow halfway up the trees and I muse as I pass about how exactly they got there. Occasionally, they even like to run alongside me even if I nervously caution them that I don't think they should go too far from home. It's not a heavily traveled route so passersby always say hello and sometimes even stop to chat. One day last summer I was riding by the goat farm/day care and a kid who looked to be about ten was standing out there with his parents. As I was going by he exclaimed haltingly "That must be really hard … everyday … sometimes." And that is exactly right. It is indeed really hard … everyday … sometimes.

## Summary

I have been on the journey of living with MS for over 20 years. Since it is a progressive disease, I engage in a continual process of noticing and grieving changes and shifts in my functioning. What has surprised and enthralled me is precisely the process of looking, the continual variability, the uncertainty of what each day brings. What I hope that I have reinforced is just how important it is to look. Doty (2001) says, "First the principle of attention, simply that—a faith that if we look and look we will be surprised and we will be rewarded. Then a faith in the capacity of the object to carry meaning--to serve as a vessel" (p. 48). Still life paintings endure over centuries. The grief of *still* life is always there, but I hope that I have succeeded in showing you that still *life* is anything but.

## References

Bollas, C., (1987). *The shadow of the object*. New York: Columbia University Press.
Bollas, C., (1992). *Being a character*. New York: Hill and Wang.
Doty, M., (2001). *Still life with lemons and oysters*. Boston: Beacon Press.

Dryden, J., (2013). Hegel, feminist philosophy, and disability. *Disability Studies Quarterly*. **33**(4). doi:10.18061/dsq.v33i4.3868.

Gluck, L., (1994). *Proofs and theories, essays on poetry*. Hopewell, NJ: The Ecco Press.

Sontag, S. (1989). *Illness as metaphor and AIDS and its metaphors*. New York: Picador.

Tremain, S., (2013). Introducing feminist philosophy of disability. *Disability Studies Quarterly*. **33**(4). doi:10.18061/dsq.v33i4.3877.

Tremain, S., (2015). Foucault, governmentality, and critical disability theory today. In: S. Tremain, ed. *Foucault and the government of disability*. Ann Arbor, MI: University of Michigan Press. pp. 9–23.

Woolf, V., (1926). On being ill. *The New Criterion*. **4**(1), 32–45.

# 3 Embodiment's Contributions to Appreciating Life with Dis/ability and to Advancing Justice

*Mary Crossley*

## Introduction: wondering about the body

The first conference for health law professors that I attended included an unusual offering: a theatrical production. The short drama was the creature of bioethicist George Annas's imagination. The play's details have grown dim in my memory, but *Shelley's Brain* was about a human who somehow had lost all parts of his physical body except for his brain, which resided in a beaker and was connected to a voice generator. The brain was capable of cognition and speech, but had no body to command. This homage to Mary Shelley's *Frankenstein* raised the question: was this thinking, speaking brain-in-a-jar a person? Did the gathered audience of health lawyers and bioethicists understand it to be endowed with moral status and rights that accompany personhood?

*Shelley's Brain* has lingered for decades in my memory for its fundamental and largely unanswerable questions about the moral meaning of the human body in relation to the human mind. If the body were practically dispensable (as was the case in *Shelley's Brain*), would it also be ethically dispensable? Is one's body a critical part of being human, aside from serving as a vessel for a functioning brain?

Three decades later, I am writing a book about dis/ability, race, and health injustice (Crossley 2002), and those indelible questions still animate my thinking. Parts of that book project inform this chapter's exploration of how paying attention to bodies and embodiment is a vital complement to social constructionist accounts of dis/ability and race. Specifically, if classifications of race and dis/ability are derived from social understandings and decisions rather than biological fact, do Black people's[1] and dis/abled people's experiences of embodiment have any relevance to achieving justice for those groups? (Why) should we care what the experience of living in a body is like? If disadvantage associated with being Black or dis/abled comes from external attitudes and structures, why pay attention to bodily experiences?

Others have described the parallel historical evolution from biology-based understandings of Blackness and dis/ability to social constructionist understandings. For Blackness, the progress is often described as being from scientific racism to race as a social construct. For dis/ability, the phrases "medical model of

DOI: 10.4324/9781003257196-4

disability" and "social model of disability" are commonly employed. Historically, biological inferiority or defectiveness ostensibly associated with both Blackness and dis/ability were put forth as explaining those groups' disadvantage and legitimating control and inequality (Shifrer & Frederick 2019). The medical profession played an important role in bolstering those understandings. Today, by contrast, social constructionist understandings predominate in shaping academic research, public discourse, and public policy making.

In this chapter, I first argue that the consensus on social constructionist approaches remains tenuous, particularly (though by no means exclusively) in medical practice and research. There, persistent conceptions of Blackness and dis/ability as biologically based threaten to undermine social constructionist insights and their importance to pursuing social remedies for exclusion and other inequities. Some health professionals persist in attaching weight to bodily differences (real or assumed) in dis/abled people and Black people; the next section provides a few examples. This persistence highlights the need to continue promoting social constructionist understandings within health care. I also argue, however, that social constructionist understandings cannot alone do the work of advancing justice. To that end, the section "Embodiment's contribution" highlights two reasons why attention to embodiment is important not only for a richer appreciation of the lived experience of dis/ability but also as a matter of justice for all people.

## Medicine's continued attachment to biological understandings

### *Racial profiling in medicine*

For some physicians and medical scientists, beliefs in biological race are remarkably durable. Beliefs in innate racial biological differences still show up in clinical decision making (my focus here) and in medical and pharmaceutical research (Kahn 2008; Roberts 2011).

Racial profiling in medicine is an offshoot of racialized science's belief that diseases manifested differently in people of different races. The phrase "racial profiling" refers to targeting members of certain racial groups based on beliefs about shared behaviors or traits, rather than individualized, non-racial information. The phrase and the practice are more commonly associated with law enforcement. For example, "Driving while Black" describes Black men being pulled over by police for no reason (aside from skin color) or pretextual reasons. It appears in medicine when physicians treat a patient's apparent (to the physician) race as clinically significant in making decisions about diagnosis, prognosis, or treatment. Prominent physicians reject the use of racial profiling in clinical decision making, but some individual doctors still espouse race's usefulness as an aid to reaching decisions about a patient (Satel 2002). Beyond its weak scientific basis, racial profiling by doctors also poses a danger of reinforcing false medical beliefs and racial prejudices, as I have written about elsewhere (Crossley 2003).

Medical racial profiling is not confined to individual physicians' judgments about patients. It also appears in formal algorithms (like clinical guidelines) developed to help doctors apply massive amounts of medical knowledge to a patient's symptoms. The flimsy evidence base for using race in medical algorithms is the subject of increasing scrutiny (Vyas 2020), particularly as the development of medical algorithms powered by artificial intelligence renders the inclusion of race less visible and, thus, less disputable. Medical AI builds on knowledge generated by medical research and real-world medical practice. As a result, it assimilates and replicates biases (conscious or unconscious) pervading those practices. Biased input leads to biased output, shaping treatment and augmenting disparities (Khullar 2019; Krieger 2020).

For example, in 2019, scientists detected "racial bias" in an AI application used by health systems to identify patients who would benefit from additional medical support. Health systems use that information as a basis for intervening to lower patients' chances of experiencing health setbacks or complications (Obermeyer et al. 2019). To project individual patients' cost of future health care, the algorithm relied on large data sets of care received by actual patients. Those data, however, embody a well-documented health care disparity: Black people use less health care than White people. Statistically, Black people must be sicker to incur as much medical spending as White people. Sociologist Ruha Benjamin explains Black people's lower utilization of health care: "Black patients do not 'cost less,' so much as they are valued less" (Benjamin 2019, p. 421). Sure enough, the scientists' review of the algorithm's operation revealed that Black patients pegged as needing additional care equally to White patients were in fact much sicker. The algorithm asserts no racist ideology, but it effectively reinforces a pre-existing disparity by preferring White patients over sicker Black patients to receive intensive support.

### *Medical commitment to "fixing" dis/ability*

In the early 21st century, a debate challenging the limits of the social model of dis/ability has developed within bioethics. It centers around the question of whether dis/ability should be understood as a "mere" difference or a "bad" difference. Is dis/ability inherently bad in the sense of making dis/abled people worse off, or does it have no more negative value than differences like eye color? (See Barnes (2016) for a summary of the debate.) Some medical professionals still view dis/ability as a "bad" difference, to be vanquished or eliminated when possible. For them, fixing or altering a person's body remains the preferred response, rather than addressing social barriers (including their own prejudices and preconceptions) or deploying aids to increase functioning. These attitudes show a continued attachment to the medical model of dis/ability. They also reflect ableist preferences for performing activities "normally," meaning in the way that non-dis/abled persons typically perform them.

Multiple studies have documented how physicians tend to assume that being dis/abled diminishes the enjoyment of or satisfaction with life, when, in fact, surveys of people with varying dis/abilities show them to be about as satisfied with their lives as non-dis/abled people (Albrecht & Devlieger 1999; Lulé et al. 2009). A national survey published in 2021 confirms the persistence of these negative perceptions, finding that 82.4% of physician respondents believed that people with significant dis/ability have a worse quality of life than non-dis/abled people (Iezzoni et al. 2021). Some physicians acknowledge the risk that unconscious bias could negatively affect their evaluation of dis/abled patients (Kripke 2017), but many do not. A few examples demonstrate how ableist assumptions about reduced quality of life with dis/ability and devaluation of alternative modes of functioning can sell short dis/abled patients' interests.

The treatment Lex Frieden received for a crushed hip bone illustrates how physicians may overestimate a dis/abled patient's projected functional deficits and underestimate the value patients attach to alternative modes of functioning. Doctors may undervalue treatment that meets a need but does not "fix" the patient's dis/ability. Frieden, a research scientist, became paraplegic in 1967 from a spinal cord injury during a car crash. Nearly 40 years later, another car crash sent Frieden to the emergency room with a crushed hip bone. His doctor elected not to perform surgery to repair the broken hip. Knowing that Frieden would never walk again anyway, the doctor apparently reasoned that incurring the resources and risk that surgery entails was unjustified. But failure to repair his broken hip has meant that Frieden is in pain when using his wheelchair, a result that limits his ability to get around (Shapiro 2020).

Ableist biases in favor of normalizing function by eliminating or fixing impairment are also evident in attempts to restore walking after a spinal cord injury. This elusive "holy grail" prompts cutting-edge treatments including the use of surgery, electronic brain stimulation, and robotic exoskeletons (Novella 2015). But establishing restoration of walking (through grueling, expensive, and often painful treatments and rehabilitation) as the presumptive goal for persons with paralysis reflects a medical model of dis/ability. The social model, by contrast, contends that greater benefit would come from ensuring wheelchair users can go wherever they want. To be sure, some dis/abled people advocate strongly for research into normalizing treatments. Many, though, value accessibility (and broader measures to counter systemic ableism) over the pursuit of a "cure" (Hahn & Belt 2004; Pulrang 2020). Discounting the premium their dis/abled patients place on assistive measures to enable functioning in an atypical manner can lead physicians to substitute their own conceptions of what's best for dis/abled patients in determining what care to provide (Satz 2020). Only by rejecting the premise that life with dis/ability is flawed can medical professionals serve as valuable partners in enhancing health and functioning for people with dis/abilities.

In sum, when medical professionals rely on unvalidated and inaccurate understandings of race and dis/ability as biological rather than social categories, they risk harming their patients. That reliance also reinforces prejudices contributing to the very social and political choices that structure disadvantage and poor health for dis/abled people and Black people. Lingering adherence to aspects of the medical model of dis/ability and racialized science continues to situate the disadvantages experienced by dis/abled people and Black people in deviant bodies, rather than discriminatory structures and attitudes. For that reason, ongoing educational efforts to promote understanding of the social construction of race and dis/ability and to eliminate structural racism and ableism from medical practice and research are essential.

## Embodiment's contribution

### *Embodiment, subjectivity, and equal humanity*

Despite the preceding discussion's cautionary tale about the necessity of promoting social constructionist understandings within the medical profession, I now turn to arguing that social constructionist accounts standing alone are dangerously incomplete. Embodiment is important not only for richer appreciation of the lived experience of dis/ability (and arguably Blackness) but also as a matter of racial and dis/ability justice. Appreciating embodiment is critical for at least two reasons.

First, social constructionism focuses on the environments (physical, social, political, economic, and attitudinal) that individuals inhabit. In that sense, its focus is primarily external. Embodiment, by contrast, considers and attaches meaning to individuals' subjective experiences of inhabiting their bodies[2] as they navigate their environments. Embodiment melds the internal and external. It honors dis/abled people's individual, particularized subjectivity, and doing so seems key to acknowledging their equal humanity.

Just as dis/ability is not simply reducible to a body's departure from some norm (as the generally rejected medical model would assert), neither is it reducible to socially constructed barriers (as a pure social constructionist would argue). This is true particularly, but not exclusively, in cases where dis/ability carries with it chronic pain (Huang & Wasserman 2020). Embodiment is a necessary complement to social constructionism; a hybrid approach asks how social and cultural contexts affect the experience of living in a particular body. I do not identify as dis/abled, but my body is a core part of my experience of life. Sometimes my body offers me thrilling experiences; sometimes it disappoints or pains me. I expect the same is true of people who do identify as dis/abled. In its legion forms, embodiment is an aspect of shared humanity. Recognizing dis/abled people's equal humanity requires rejecting essentialized understandings of dis/ability.

Moreover, the bodily distinctiveness to which society attaches a label of Blackness or dis/ability can be sources of personal pride and valuable cultural connections. In one chapter of her book *So You Want to Talk about Race*, Ijeoma Oluo (2018) writes about Black hair and how she both loves her hair *and* recognizes that White people's often simultaneous fascination with and disdain for Black hair operates oppressively. For Black women particularly, their relationship with their hair (sometime referred to as their "hair journey") co-evolves in relationship to Black cultural identity and community *and* in the context of anti-Black racial discrimination and devaluation (Williams n/a).

Bodily aspects of dis/ability may similarly serve as sources of cultural connection and meaning. The best-known example is Deaf culture. But social and cultural connections forged around shared bodily features exist around other dis/abilities as well. In *Far from the Tree: Parents, Children, and the Search for Identity*, Andrew Solomon (2012) writes of the significant role that gatherings of Little People of America play for a significant number of people with dwarfism. Attendees at these gatherings share the challenges of navigating a world not constructed to account for people of short stature, but they also share emotionally bonding experiences of temporarily escaping a sometimes-isolating existence within their families or home communities. In another example, dis/abled dancers create choreography that uses their bodies to transform understandings of dance, the body, and personhood. Their work foregrounds embodiment as a source of unique artistic expression and provides a connection with other dis/abled artists (Seibert 2020).

Finally, assigning value to dis/abled people's subjective experience of embodiment is a necessary antidote to external, objectifying assessments of their experience. Traditionally, the medical model validated dis/ability's existence through physicians' reliance on objective measurements. This grant of professional authority to identify dis/ability's existence gave rise to a core critique of the medical model. But strict social constructionist views can also become a form of external assessment. Scholars or activists who describe socially and physically constructed barriers purely objectively, without accounting for the unique bodies or the emotional or cultural contexts in which dis/abled persons encounter those barriers, risk substituting one form of expertise for another.

### *Embodiment, emergent disability, and justice*

Embracing embodiment as a complement to social construction accounts promotes moving toward justice for a second reason. Focusing on how individual bodies become dis/abled helps to capture an aspect of dis/ability-and-race intersectionality that has not received as much attention as it warrants.

The starting point is data indicating that dis/ability is generally more prevalent among Black Americans than White Americans. Drawing conclusions from available data is complicated by inconsistent methods of defining and measuring dis/ability, along with a general dearth of data collection regarding dis/ability (Yee et al. 2017). That said, a few broad points can be made. First, dis/ability is generally (but not always) more prevalent among African American populations than among White non-Hispanic, Hispanic/Latino, and Asian populations (Yee et al. 2017). For example, one national survey found a higher prevalence of physical dis/ability and vision problems among Black Americans than among White Americans, but the latter had a higher prevalence of hearing problems. Black people are significantly overrepresented among adults with intellectual dis/abilities, while a higher percentage of non-Hispanic White people have a mental illness (Yee et al. 2017). Researchers have found that Black Americans have the highest prevalence of "complex activity limitations," a phrase that describes an impairment's effect on a person's ability to fully carry out social roles like working, keeping house, socializing, and caring for oneself (Ward & Schiller 2011). Across racial and ethnic groups, women are more likely to experience dis/ability than men, and the prevalence of dis/ability increases with advancing age (Warner & Brown 2011).

Finding that dis/ability is more widespread among older people is not remarkable. Far more troubling is that Black Americans appear to age more quickly than Whites in terms of developing dis/ability. Research suggests that Black people face an increased risk of disablement over time, as compared to White people (De Leon et al. 1997). One study found that Black women, in particular, "experience a trajectory of accelerated disablement" (Warner & Brown 2011, p. 1236). Survey data indicate that, at least after the age of 50, "the prevalence of physical disability for African Americans/blacks in any given age group was similar to the prevalence for non-Hispanic whites who were 10 years older" (Yee et al. 2017, p. 16). In short, evidence indicates that experiences of being Black are associated with—and may cause—accelerated aging and disablement for some people.

### *Race as a determinant of dis/ability?*

Research findings about the greater prevalence and acceleration of disablement among Blacks beg for explanation. When we consider interacting social and environmental factors, discrimination, and unequal treatment in the health care system, higher rates and earlier occurrence of dis/ability among Black people can be expected. We might think of these causes as social determinants of dis/ability (Fiorati & Elui 2015; Goyat et al. 2016; Wolbring 2011). Social epidemiologist Nancy Krieger calls this "the cumulative embodiment of multiple types of discrimination, deprivation, and other harmful exposures" (2012, p. 936, 942). Living in poverty, lacking access to quality education, encountering stressful or dangerous workplace conditions, and residing in neighborhoods marred by toxic exposures or chronic violence: all these make becoming dis/abled more likely, especially as a person ages (Singh & Lin 2013). For some, incarceration has disabling impacts (Ware et al. 2014). Black Americans disproportionately experience all these influences (Brown & Thorpe 2016; Latham 2012; Seabury et al. 2017; Singh & Lin 2013; Siordia 2015; Thorpe et al. 2014; Warner & Brown 2011). Add a dose of "weathering" from systemic and interpersonal racism that pervades American society. Receiving delayed, biased, or lower quality medical care can also produce disabling outcomes (Ansell 2017).

Higher risks of disablement are not confined to adults. Researchers have found that dis/ability is more prevalent among Black children than their White counterparts (Yee et al. 2017). Black babies in America are more likely to be born too small and to mothers who received too little prenatal care. Black children are more likely to live in racially segregated and impoverished neighborhoods, locales where social determinants threaten their disablement. Flint, Michigan provides an example. The city's 2013 decision to switch its drinking water supply from Detroit's water supply to the Flint River exposed residents to dangerously high levels of lead. Families in Flint (which is 57% Black) were left to drink, cook with, and bathe in lead-contaminated water. The percentage of Flint's children with elevated blood-lead levels—known to interfere with brain development—nearly doubled after the switch in water supply. In some neighborhoods, it nearly tripled (Denchak 2018). Six years after high lead levels were found in Flint's drinking water, one in five children entering Flint's public schools had dis/abilities qualifying them for special education services, up from fewer than one in seven in 2012–2013 (Mitchell 2019). In sum, young Black children are more likely to face disablement during early development, just as Black youths and young adults suffer more potentially disabling urban gun violence, and middle-aged Black people are more likely to become dis/abled before they reach old age.

### *Emergent disability: implications for justice*

In 1995, Katherine Seelman and Sean Sweeney described an "expanding or new universe of disability," where violence, substance abuse, inadequate prenatal care and low birthweight, environmental exposure to toxins, and injuries all contributed to escalating dis/ability rates. Among all the factors contributing to dis/ability, they identified poverty as the "primary screening indicator" for a heightened risk (Seelman & Sweeney 2002). Their insight is that a growing share of dis/ability results from impairments that are created or imposed rather than "naturally" or truly "accidentally" occurring. Other scholars have dubbed the multiplying of dis/abilities in communities experiencing poverty and disadvantage as "emergent disability" (Ribet 2010). Emergent disability may arise quickly and dramatically, when a person forced by financial need to cut short their education and take a dangerous job suffers a disabling injury. Or it may materialize more gradually, as ongoing exposure to environmental toxins damages a person's body or brain.

Viewed through the conceptual lens of emergent disability, the higher prevalence of dis/ability (and at younger ages) among Black Americans is a problem that requires both more empirical research and more thorough theoretical exploration. I will offer two preliminary observations. First, employing critical perspectives lays responsibility for more prevalent dis/ability among Black Americans at the feet of the state and free-market economy, rather than biology. Second, understanding how the overrepresentation of Black people among dis/abled people reflects racial injustice rather than biology may help us appreciate the sometimes fraught relationship between racial justice and the dis/ability rights movements.

The connections of earlier and more prevalent dis/ability among Black Americans to injustice are readily discernible. The concept of emergent disability suggests that the social, economic, and environmental deprivations disproportionately associated with being non-White must be seen as risk factors for becoming dis/abled. This reasoning clarifies that Black people's heightened risk of disablement does not spring from biological or natural differences along racial lines. Dr. Camara Jones makes the point precisely, describing race (along with other axes of inequity) as a *risk marker*, or an identifier of "how opportunity is structured and value is assigned in our society" (Jones 2014, p. S71, S73).[3]

This framing aligns with critical scholars' recognition that uneven distributions of privation and opportunity are not coincidental. They are not "natural" occurrences. Instead, the assignment of unequal risks of disablement links to deeper questions of social justice for dis/abled people and people of color (Pokempner & Roberts 2001). Thinking about emergent disability highlights this dynamic by "add[ing] a more materialist dimension to the social model of disability … reveal[ing] how the inequitable structure of society produces concrete physical and mental impairments that affect an individual's life chances" (Pokempner & Roberts 2001, p. 427). In short, it pushes the social model to acknowledge that unjust structures not only create or accept barriers to participation for people who already have an impairment, those structures also generate impairments.

And in American society, race is inextricable from this dynamic. Beth Ribet (2010) puts it simply: "disability is not simply racially charged, but often racially generated" (p. 241). Long histories of structural racism and contemporary discrimination and segregation leave Black Americans more likely to live in poverty, to receive less quality education, and to enjoy fewer employment prospects. The result is increased risk of becoming dis/abled, a disablement that in turn stunts upward social mobility (Pokempner & Roberts 2001). Across the life course, Black Americans face an unjustly unequal risk of unnecessary dis/ability.

Appreciating how the interplay of poverty, race, and dis/ability produces dis/ability should also yield more critical examination of the role of the state and markets in that process.

> Recognizing that disabilities are often caused by inequitable allocations of wealth and power implicates the state in creating disability, not just reacting to impairments in ways that disable. … [It] critiques the workings of the market rather than reinforcing its principles as neutral and inherently just (Pokempner & Roberts 2001, p. 458).

Ascribing responsibility for emergent disability to the state and the market economy it supports aligns with critical race and feminist scholars' work diagnosing racial, gender, and class oppression as founded on state policies and capitalist structures (Ribet 2010, p. 211). If that diagnosis is accurate, growing social and economic inequality in the United States portends increasing levels of emergent disability, with an increasingly Black or Brown face.

Appreciating the connection between emergent disability and race should compel us to consider how the dominant dis/ability rights movement has failed to address racism's role in constructing dis/ability. It pushes against precepts of the dominant dis/ability rights movement, sometimes described as "coded white" (Frederick & Shifrer 2019). To combat the medical model's message that dis/ability is a negative status to be avoided, even eliminated, the "mainstream" dis/ability rights movement has worked to end the stigma and disadvantage associated with dis/ability. The goal is to replace dis/ability shame with dis/ability pride. Dis/abled activists of color, however, have faulted organized dis/ability pride events for being dominated by White dis/abled people who refuse to include perspectives of non-White dis/abled people (Mulderink 2020). More to my current point, promoting dis/ability pride may simply miss the mark in cases of emergent disability. When a person's impairment (how their mind or body varies from some norm) is induced by unjust social structures, pride seems an inapt response.

Emergent disability thus challenges aspects of the "mainstream" dis/ability rights movement. Recognizing that unjust social, environmental, and economic structures generate dis/ability in ways that especially burden poor people and Black people stands in tension with some aspects of traditional advocacy for dis/ability civil rights. Understanding inequitable social structures as *causes* of dis/ability clarifies that legal rights (like those created by the Americans with Disabilities Act or other antidiscrimination laws) are insufficient to accomplish full justice if they attach only *after dis/ability* exists (Ribet 2011). Those laws do nothing to prevent the unjust imposition of dis/ability. Dis/ability rights narratives that fail to address racial and economic justice concerns will not accomplish dis/ability justice. Promoting dis/ability as "mere difference" rather than "bad difference" risks obscuring that emergent disability comes from oppression that weighs most heavily on darker and poorer bodies. Embodiment reminds us that dis/ability is fluid; it can arrive in a body gradually or suddenly. A pure social model asserts that dis/ability could effectively disappear if society eliminated all barriers to inclusion. But emergent disability reminds us that the origins of many dis/abilities lie in socially produced conditions that damage and degrade bodies that are disproportionately Black.

## Conclusion

In conclusion, important parallels exist between the socially constructed natures of race and dis/ability. Despite a broad consensus regarding social construction's role, however, traces of the medical model and racialized science remain visible in current-day medical practice and research. These residual influences highlight the continued work needed to dispel understandings of race and dis/ability founded on bodily difference.

But repudiating spurious beliefs in innate biological difference and inferiority does not require rejecting the body's centrality. People's bodies matter to them; bodies are the site of people's existence in the world. They help shape daily experience—for dis/abled people and non-dis/abled people—sometimes as sources of pain or challenge, sometimes as sources of joy or pride. Beyond the subjective importance of embodiment, bodies are also a site of the operation of oppressive social structures and living and working conditions. These conditions unjustly damage and degrade bodies, and in doing so disproportionately burden poor people of color. According to social epidemiologist Nancy Krieger, experiencing the social, economic, and environmental manifestations of racism produces "embodied inequality." Krieger's reference to embodiment is literal, providing an added dimension to understanding race and dis/ability as socially constructed (Krieger 2020).[4]

## Notes

1 Many of this chapter's points would also be applicable to persons who identify with other minoritized racial or ethnic groups. In my book, I focus on Blackness, and I do so here as well.
2 Throughout this discussion, I use the term "body" to encompass a person's mind as well.
3 In "Blackness as disability," Paul-Emile (2019) makes the related but distinctive point that Blackness is disabling *not* in the sense of causing impairment, but in the sense of preventing full participation in society.
4 Note that Krieger's work is not confined to racism, but it also encompasses other isms associated with injustice. At this point, the evidence base for the impact of racism is more thoroughly developed.

## References

Albrecht, G. L. and Devlieger, P. J., (1999). The disability paradox: high quality of life against all odds. *Social Science & Medicine*. **48**(8), 977–988.

Ansell, D. A., (2017). *The death gap: how inequality kills*. Chicago: University of Chicago Press.

Barnes, E., (2016). *The minority body: a theory of disability*. Oxford: Oxford University Press.

Benjamin, R., (2019). Assessing risk, automating racism. *Science*. **366**, 421–422.

Brown, T. and Thorpe, R., (2016). Race/ethnicity, stress, mobility limitations and disability among older men. *Gerontologist*. **56**(Suppl 3), 591.

Crossley, M., (2002). *Embodied injustice: race, disability, and health*. Cambridge: Cambridge University Press.

Crossley, M., (2003). Infected judgment: legal responses to physician bias. *Villanova Law Review*. **48**(1), 195–303.

De Leon, M. C. F. et al., (1997). Black-white differences in risk of becoming disabled and recovering from disability in old age: a longitudinal analysis of two EPESE populations. *American Journal of Epidemiology*. **145**(6), 488–497. doi:10.1093/oxfordjournals.aje.a009136

Denchak, M., (2018). Flint water crisis: everything you need to know. *NRDC* [online]. 8 November. Available from: https://www.nrdc.org/stories/flint-water-crisis-everything-you-need-know

Fiorati, R. C. and Elui, V. M., (2015). Social determinants of health, inequality and social inclusion among people with disabilities. *Revista Latino-Americana de Enfermagem*. **23**(2), 329–336. doi:10.1590/0104-1169.0187.2559

Frederick, A. and Shifrer, D., (2019). Race and disability: from analogy to intersectionality. *Sociology of Race and Ethnicity*. **5**(2), 200–214. doi:10.1177/2332649218783480

Goyat, R., Vyas, A. and Sambamoorthi, U., (2016). Racial/ethnic disparities in disability prevalence. *Journal of Racial and Ethnic Health Disparities*. **3**(4), 635–645. doi:10.1007/s40615-015-0182-z

Hahn, H. D. and Belt, T. L., (2004). Disability identity and attitudes toward cure in a sample of disabled activists. *Journal of Health and Social Behavior*. **45**(4), 453–464. doi:10.1177/002214650404500407

Huang, C. J. and Wasserman, D., (2020). Chronic pain as a challenge for disability theory and policy. In: I. G. Cohen et al., eds. *Disability, health, law and bioethics*. Cambridge: Cambridge University Press, pp. 129–140.

Iezzoni, L. I. et al., (2021). Physicians' perceptions of people with disability and their health care. *Health Affairs (Project Hope)*. **40**(2), 297–306. doi:10.1377/hlthaff.2020.01452

Jones, C. P., (2014). Systems of power, axes of inequity. *Medical Care*. **52**, S71–S75.

Kahn, J., (2008). Exploiting race in drug development: BiDil's interim model of pharmacogenomics. *Social Studies of Science*. **38**(5), 737–758. doi:10.1177/0306312708091928

Khullar, D., (2019). A.I. could worsen health disparities. *The New York Times* [online]. 31 January. Available from: https://www.nytimes.com/2019/01/31/opinion/ai-bias-healthcare.html

Krieger, N., (2012). Methods for the scientific study of discrimination and health: an ecosocial approach. *American Journal of Public Health*. **102**(5), 936–944. doi:10.2105/AJPH.2011.300544

Krieger, N., (2020). Measures of racism, sexism, heterosexism, and gender binarism for health equity research: from structural injustice to embodied harm – an ecosocial analysis. *Annual Review of Public Health*. **41**(1), 37–62.

Kripke C., (2017). Patients with disabilities: avoiding unconscious bias when discussing goals of care. *American Family Physician*. **96**(3), 192–195.

Latham K., (2012). Progressive and accelerated disability onset by race/ethnicity and education among late midlife and older adults. *Journal of Aging and Health*. **24**(8), 1320–1345. doi:10.1177/0898264312459345

Lulé, D. et al., (2009). Life can be worth living in locked-in syndrome. *Progress in Brain Research*. **177**, 339–351. doi:10.1016/S0079-6123(09)17723-3

Mitchell, C., (2019). In Flint, schools overwhelmed by special education needs in aftermath of lead crisis. *Education Week* [online]. 28 August. Available from: https://www.edweek.org/ew/articles/2019/08/28/special-ed-concerns-loom-large-after-flint.html?cmp=soc-edit-tw

Mulderink, C. E., (2020). The emergence, importance of #DisabilityTooWhite hashtag. *Disability Studies*. **40**(2). doi:10.18061/dsq.v40i2.6484

Novella, S., (2015). Helping the paralyzed walk. *Science Based Medicine* [online]. 2 September. Available from: https://sciencebasedmedicine.org/helping-the-paralyzed-walk/

Obermeyer, Z. et al., (2019). Dissecting racial bias in an algorithm used to manage the health of populations. *Science*. **366**(6464), 447–453. doi:10.1126/science.aax2342

Oluo, I., (2018). *So you want to talk about race*. New York: Seal Press.

Paul-Emile, K., (2019). Blackness as disability? *The Georgetown Law Journal*. **106**, 293–364.

Pokempner, J. and Roberts, D. E., (2001). Poverty, welfare reform, and the meaning of disability. *Ohio State Law Journal.* **62**, 425–463.

Pulrang, A., (2020). Disabled people's feelings about cures are more complex that you may think. *Forbes* [online]. 7 September. Available from: https://www.forbes.com/sites/andrewpulrang/2020/09/07/disabled-peoples-feelings-about-cures-are-more-complex-than-you-may-think/?sh=4d53d72a36c6

Ribet, B., (2010). Surfacing disability through a critical race theoretical paradigm. *Georgetown Journal of Law and Modern Critical Race Perspectives.* **2**, 209–252.

Ribet, B., (2011). Emergent disability and the limits of equality: a critical reading of the UN Convention on the Rights of Persons with Disabilities. *Yale Human Rights and Development Law Journal.* **14**, 155–204.

Roberts, D., (2011). *Fatal invention: how science, politics, and big business re-create race in the twenty-first century.* New York: New Press.

Satel, S., (2002). I am a racially profiling doctor. *The New York Times* [online]. 5 May. Available from: https://www.nytimes.com/2002/05/05/magazine/i-am-a-racially-profiling-doctor.html

Satz, A. B., (2020). Healthcare as eugenics. In: I. G. Cohen et al., eds. *Disability, health, law and bioethics.* Cambridge: Cambridge University Press. pp. 20–32.

Seabury, S. A., Terp, S. and Boden, L. I., (2017). Racial and ethnic differences in the frequency of workplace injuries and prevalence of work-related disability. *Health affairs (Project Hope).* **36**(2), 266–273. doi:10.1377/hlthaff.2016.1185

Seelman, K. D. and Sweeney, S., (2002). The changing universe of disability. *American Rehabilitation.* **21**(3), 2–13.

Seibert, B., (2020). To see and be seen: these dancers make disability visible. *The New York Times [online].* 1 December. Available from: https://www.nytimes.com/2020/12/01/arts/dance/heidi-latsky-kinetic-light-disability-dance.html

Shapiro, J., (2020). People with disabilities fear pandemic will worsen medical biases. *National Public Radio* [online]. 15 April. Available from: https://www.npr.org/2020/04/15/828906002/people-with-disabilities-fear-pandemic-will-worsen-medical-biases

Shifrer, D. and Frederick, A., (2019). Disability at the intersections. *Sociology Compass.* **13**(10). doi:10.1111/soc4.12733

Singh, G. K. and Lin, S. C., (2013). Marked ethnic, nativity, and socioeconomic disparities in disability and health insurance among US children and adults: the 2008-2010 American community survey. *BioMed Research International.* **2013**, 627412. doi:10.1155/2013/627412

Siordia C., (2015). Disability prevalence according to a Class, Race, and Sex (CSR) hypothesis. *Journal of Racial and Ethnic Health Disparities.* **2**(3), 303–310. doi:10.1007/s40615-014-0073-8

Solomon, A., (2012). *Far from the tree: parents, children, and the search for identity.* New York: Scribner.

Thorpe, R. J. et al., (2014). Racial disparities in disability among older adults: finding from the exploring health disparities in integrated communities study. *Journal of Aging and Health.* **26**(8), 1261–1279. doi:10.1177/0898264314534892

Vyas, D. A., (2020). Hidden in plain sight: reconsidering the use of race correction in clinical algorithms. *New England Journal of Medicine.* **383**, 874–882. doi:10.1056/NEJMms2004740

Ward, B. W. and Schiller, J. S., (2011). Prevalence of complex activity limitations among racial/ethnic groups and Hispanic subgroups of adults: United States, 2003-2009. *NCHS Data Brief*. **73**, 1–8. Available from: https://pubmed.ncbi.nlm.nih.gov/22617095/

Ware, S. et al., (2014). It can't be fixed because it's not broken: racism and disability in the prison industrial complex. In: L. Ben-Moshe, C. Chapman and A. Carey, eds. *Disability incarcerated: imprisonment and disability in the United States and Canada*. New York: Palgrave Macmillan. pp. 163–184.

Warner, D. F. and Brown, T. H., (2011). Understanding how race/ethnicity and gender define age-trajectories of disability: an intersectionality approach. *Social Science & Medicine*. **72**(8), 1236–1248. doi:10.1016/j.socscimed.2011.02.034

Williams, A., (n/a). The connection between hair and identity in black culture. C+R Research. Available from: https://www.crresearch.com/blog/connection-between-hair-and-identity-black-culture

Wolbring, G., (2011). People with disabilities and social determinants of health discourses. *Canadian Journal of Public Health*. **102**(4), 317–319. doi:10.1007/BF03404058

Yee, S. et al., (2017). *Compounded disparities: health equity at the intersection of disability, race, and ethnicity*. Berkeley, CA: Disability Rights Education and Defense Fund. Available from: https://dredf.org/wp-content/uploads/2018/01/Compounded-Disparities-Intersection-of-Disabilities-Race-and-Ethnicity.pdf

# Part II

# Rehabilitation, Disablement, and the State

# 4 Subjects of Industry: Craft Therapy, Its Photography, and Healing American Soldiers of World War I

*Jennifer Way*

## Introduction

In *The New Disability History* (2001), Rosemarie Garland-Thomas identified key tropes that shape popular photographs of disabled subjects. Building especially on her analysis of Sander Gilman's research concerning the ways, as Garland-Thomas (2001) notes, that "photographs of disabled people recapitulate cultural ideas about disability at the same time they perpetuate those beliefs" (p. 336), this chapter explores how, during the World War I era, craft therapy and its photography accommodated convalescing American soldiers to changing ideas about their disabilities, which were shifting from primarily injuries of the mind and body to include deficits of attitude and behavior. Interestingly, while the photographs that Garland-Thomas (2001) studied "sequester[ed] disability within the discourses of science and medicine" (p. 337), the examples considered here serve two purposes. First, they indicate that photographs associated with the military, government, and key non-governmental organizations recorded injured troops practicing craft fabrication as a new medicalized, object-based therapy intended to heal them. Second, these photographs helped to constitute and narrate craft's potential to rehabilitate these men to live a life far beyond sequestration—enabled, thanks to craft fabrication, to participate as useful members of mainstream American society, as then defined.

As with previous wars involving Americans, injured soldiers and veterans of WW1 might be cared for by family and community or in domiciliary institutions with government pensions helping to support their needs over the long term. However, the number of soldiers who sustained injuries and lived could deplete these resources. As one consequence, the United States, like other Western industrial states, deployed new technologies and procedures to heal injured troops and rehabilitate them for independence in the worlds of civilian work and life (Bell 2018; Cohen 2006; Gerber 2000; Linker 2011; Perry 2014; Rose 2008; Rostker 2013).

Yet, put to this purpose, craft fabrication brought a history associated with the care of people having mental illnesses and physical injuries whom society marginalized if not shut away, for example, in asylums (Rose 2008). Likewise, as craft therapy entered military base hospitals abroad and military and civilian

DOI: 10.4324/9781003257196-6

hospitals along with the Red Cross Institute for Crippled and Disabled Men in the United States, it iterated elements of the concurrent Arts and Crafts Movement. In the United States, some Arts and Crafts practitioners held that industrial society and work crippled everyone, and craft should be instrumentalized as a tool for reforming the nature of work (Boris 1998).

## Craft as therapy

Based on his study of how the British mitigated the war's "excessive incidence of mental diseases" (Salmon 1917, p. 33) through re-education, Dr. Thomas William Salmon's *The Care and Treatment of Mental Diseases and War Neurosis in the British Army*, 1917, helped to shape American approaches to treating mental injuries from war, including shell shock (Salmon 1917). Shell shock comprised "neuropsychiatric" injuries characterized by mental and emotional ailments borne by the "invisibly wounded" (Stagner 2014, p. 166). In *Reconstruction Therapy*, 1919 medical doctor and psychiatrist William Rush Dunton observed that these wounded men suffered not simply from their injuries but also from dwelling on them intensively and repeatedly. As recourse, he recommended "anything that diverts the patient from unhealthy thought is to be classed as occupation" (Dunton 1919, p. 43). The US Federal Board for Vocational Training restated Salmon's and Dunton's observations in noting that WW1 soldiers were "particularly susceptible" to mental injury due to "the strain of trench warfare, the idle hours of waiting, the submission to discipline, and lack of individual initiative" (US Federal Board for Vocational Education 1918, p. 44). Their susceptibility followed these men into places of healing and rehabilitation, where they needed to avoid "self-pity and a brooding condition of mind" (p. 12).

Insofar as Salmon, Dunton, and other psychiatrists drew upon European contexts for treating mental illness (Stagner 2014), it is unsurprising that they recommended craft as a therapeutic modality. Its history with socially marginalized populations indicated that craft fabrication could be deployed institutionally. Also, craft practices such as weaving, knitting, and basket making (Hall & Buck 1915) among other crafts were becoming more widely practiced in Europe and the United States, avocationally and vocationally, and American doctors were experimenting with ways that handicraft could remedy mental illness caused by social experiences and situations, including war (Hall & Buck 1915). Photographs of war-related neuropsychiatric patients abroad and in the United States sometimes showed them making craft objects outdoors or on porches (Figure 4.1). At the US Armed Expeditionary Forces Base Hospital 117 in LaFauche, France, which served war neurosis cases from the front lines with the intention to rehabilitate patients and return them to combat (Schwab 1919), emphasis on working outdoors with natural materials reiterated a lineage of work therapy in Europe for treating the insane with agricultural work (Schwab 1919). In Europe and the United States, this aspect of craft intersected with the growing popularity of the Mental Hygiene Movement that advocated a

**A patient weaving**

*Figure 4.1* The experiment in occupational therapy at Base Hospital 117, A.E.F.

back to nature approach to achieve a wholesome life offsetting the crowding, pollution, and disease associated with urban spaces and the working-class people who lived there.

As with "mental re-education," the "functional restoration" about which Douglas McMurtrie of the Red Cross Institute for Healing Crippled and Disabled Men wrote, had roots in Europe, too. Especially influential were the work of the Society for Assistance to the Maimed, Crippled, and Injured in Denmark, and France's training of its war wounded in Lyons, where injured soldiers made paper boxes, bound books, beaded and worked in fur and wood (McMurtrie 1919) as well as chair caning, cabinet making, and weaving (Kinder 2007). While functional restoration returned the patient to utility through the purpose-oriented making of objects, other reasons recommended craft as a strand in all stages of what Dunton called occupational therapy. For example, its materials and tools tended to be simple, cheap, and available, or readily and inventively sourced on the spot; and the processes and techniques of craft fabrication could accommodate a wide range of skills and abilities (US Federal Board for Vocational Education 1918).

Although men practiced many types of crafts therapeutically, they favored weaving in fibers and reeds. Artisan and therapist Louis James Haas, who worked in craft occupations, began publishing on the topic before the war and during the 1920s while he served as Director of Men's Occupations at the Bloomingdale Hospital in White Plains, New York. Haas held that patients in bed require an occupation "with the briefest possible explanations and demonstrations, simple in technic, appealing to the eye, with results that can be measured at the end of each short period of work" (Haas 1925, p. 135). Many photographs from the period also feature small groups of men weaving baskets of all sizes with reeds (Figure 4.2). Haas specified how weaving fibers into containers such as baskets fostered healing owing to "the oft times tedious repetition of motions required to produce the weaves used in making baskets that are really interesting" (Haas 1922, p. 381). Moreover, these repeated motions held a "confused man's thoughts" to "something real and tangible, pushing his fears ever so slightly into the background" (p. 382). Once weaving fibers connects the mind with the body and both with the process, the caregiver intensifies this "point of tangency" "by gradually raising the level of the work just as rapidly as

*Figure 4.2* Convalescing WW1 soldiers weaving baskets and engraving a wooden box.

the clearing of the confused mind permits it to grasp and accomplish more" (p. 381). The expectation was that thinking leads to doing by interacting with materials. Presumably, in a feedback loop, the doing shapes or re-shapes the mind and leads to mental healing, while interacting with materials facilitates physical rehabilitation. As this occurs, Dunton advised, physicians should chart the progress of their patients by having the craft teacher keep records about the patient's attention, concentration, and ability in doing the work, along with their initiative (Dunton 1919). These behaviors provided a means for physicians to monitor and assess his healing.

The 1918 Vocational Rehabilitation Act divided physical and vocational reconstruction, with the military overseeing the former and the Federal Board of Education supervising the latter. Still, in practice, the two often merged (Kickel 2001; Kinder 2015). During the same year, the US Federal Board for Vocational Education suggested that beyond healing and diversion, occupation offered "a definite effect on the mind and spirit, and consequently it generated a favorable reaction on the physical condition, too" (US Federal Board for Vocational Education 1918, p. 35). The Board echoed the widely held notion that healing the mind led to improvements for the body that led to "functional restoration" (US Surgeon-General's Office 1927) or an enabling of the patient to live independently and contribute to society. By representing patients fabricating craft objects, photographs were confirming their progress toward this state, even for soldiers who had lost limbs (Figures 4.3–4.5).

*Figure 4.3* Soldier weaving in bed, 1918, National World War I Museum and Memorial.

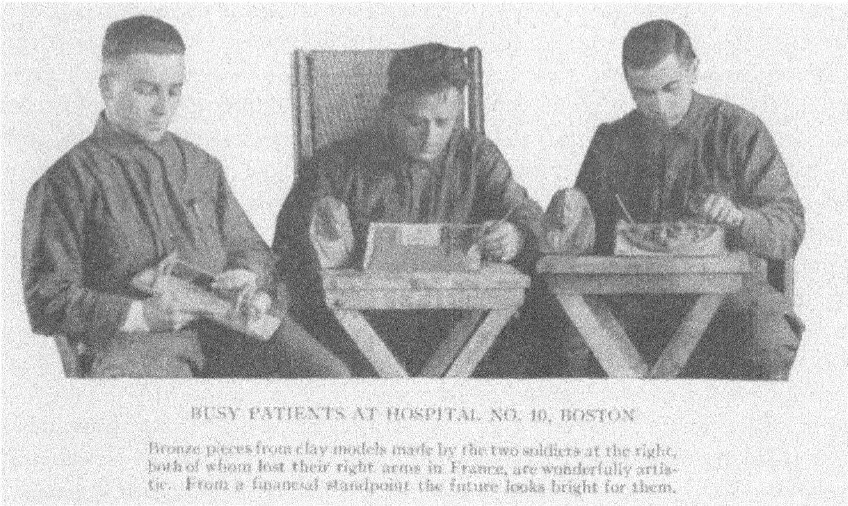


*Figure 4.4* To the returning soldier, 1919.

## Revising dis/ability? Craft and the "new industrialism"[1]

Although its roots reached back to England during the mid-19th century, the Arts and Crafts Movement remained active during WW1 and had potential to impact notions of function and work for convalescing soldiers on the grounds of dis/ability. Implicit in Arts and Crafts was the notion that industrial work and society were harmful and needed reform. Although some of the focus here was on the plight of the factory worker, this notion also expanded the population of the disabled to include everyone subjected to capitalist industrialism and its subsuming of the human factor to the profit motive. A solution was needed that thwarted dis/ability by reforming work and life to benefit human-based integration of the mind, body, and spirit.

In the United States, practitioners of the Arts and Crafts Movement leveraged making craft objects as a means of reforming contemporary work and society (Clark & Kaplan 1987) by repairing elements of industrialization and urbanization they considered deleterious (Boris 1998). These included poorly made objects consisting of cheap materials; hierarchical divisions of labor that alienated workers from themselves, their activities and products, one another, and the users of things they made; and pollution, overcrowding, and unsanitary and unsafe conditions for workers and consumers, often associated with urban living (Boris 1998). As Arts and Crafts scholar Eileen Boris notes, from their critiques of the ills of contemporary capitalist society, Arts and Crafts "sought to fashion a 'new industrialism'" (Boris 1998, p. 208, 212). Their reform comprised a "craftsman ideal-skilled workmanship, organic unity of thought and labor, [and] individuality of expression" (Boris 1998, p. 220) as well as agency in

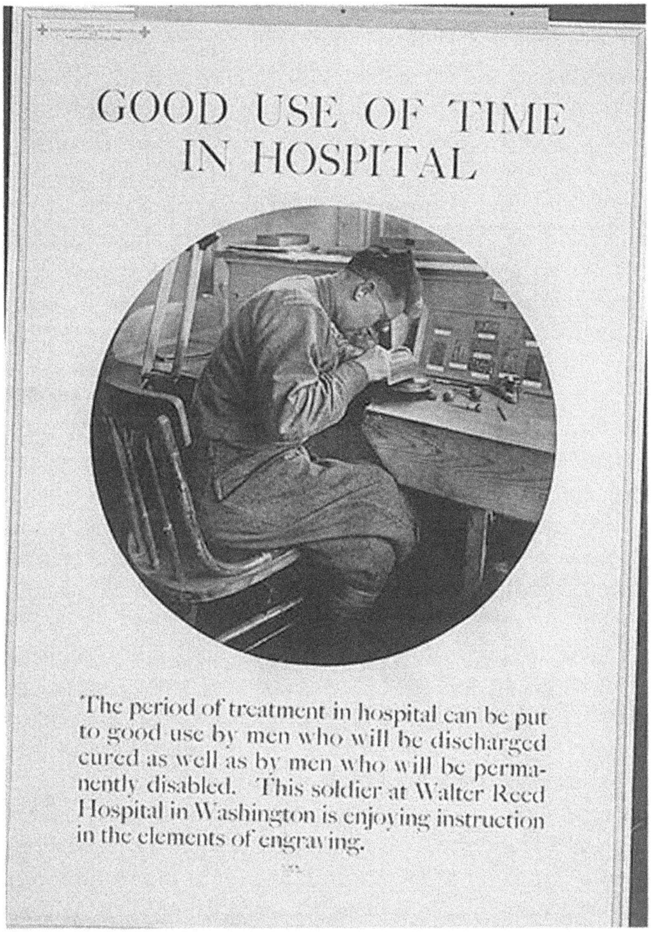


*Figure 4.5* Good use of time in hospital, 1919.

making beautiful and useful objects perceived as wholesome and supportive of the body, mind, and spirit of the maker and consumer. These objects would be fabricated in a "more satisfying labor and a holistic environment closer to nature" (Boris 1998, p. 210) that diminished social binary divisions between work and art, and life and art and fostered not class divisions but community through fellowship (Boris 1998). Consequently, subjects impaired by capitalist industrialism and urbanization were prescribed craft fabrication as a mode of healing work (Boris 1998). In contrast to workers experiencing a separation of their agency from their body to advance capitalist profit, the Arts and Craft Movement asserted that craft fabrication could re-integrate all facets of the self.

Some organizations and individuals associated with Arts and Crafts helped to pave the way for deploying craft fabrication as a therapy for convalescing soldiers.

For example, sanitoria and workshops already were becoming known for the Arts and Crafts ideas and practices that informed their uses of craft as a therapeutic modality (Work for Nerves 1905). Dr. Herbert James Hall, who first worked with middle-class women neurasthenics and eventually with disabled veterans (Jenkins 2009), recommended that using the hands to make small direct actions invited the mind to follow "in a simpler, more methodical way" (Hall 1910, pp. 12–13) and this in turn promoted "accuracy and precision of movement" (Hall 1905, pp. 30–31). The results were the remedying and normalizing of "disability as a nervous exhaustion" (Hall & Buck 1915, p. xi). Women predominated among those Arts and Crafts practitioners who served as Reconstruction Aides—civilian women who taught convalescing troops to make craft objects using "knitting, beadwork, basketry, mat-weaving, printing, wood carving, painting and pottery, bronze casting, jewelry and metalsmithing" (Gavin 1994, p. 40; see also Andersen & Reed 2017; Frank 1992; Low 1992; US Surgeon-General's Office 1927). Some straddled mental health care and occupational work, such as Jessie Luther who, during WW1, directed occupational therapy for soldiers at the Walter Reed Hospital (Rompkey 2001). Before that, Luther collaborated with Hall at his sanitorium in Marblehead, Massachusetts (Hall 1905).

Whether through an awareness of the revitalization of craft in the Arts and Crafts Movement or fostered by the pathways laid by the recommendations and practices of specific medical and craft authorities, some tenets of craft as a model for reforming work resonate in photographs of convalescing WW1 soldiers. Further, we might consider these images as evidence that the very troops harmed by technologies that industrialized nations brought to bear on them in intending to cause harm, especially benefitted from the recuperative and life-sustaining craftsman ideals as they fabricated craft objects.

For example, photographs depict men working harmoniously in the company of one another (Figures 4.2–4.4 and 4.6), in wards (Figure 4.3) and workshops (Figures 4.2 and 4.4–4.6). Although the men do not appear to interact directly with one another, their demeanors imply a pleasant, collegial environment in which no man stands out as a manager supervising or controlling others, and female Rehabilitation Aides appear to play a quiet role in tending to the men's projects (Figure 4.2). Photographs show projects at all stages (Figures 4.1–4.4 and 4.6) indicating, especially in the presence of multiple men, that different rates of fabrication were permitted (Figures 4.2 and 4.4). This suggests some degree of agency as well as diversity in matters of productivity. Groups in which individuals work in different craft media (Figures 4.2 and 4.4) contrast expectations that manufacturing comprises workers endlessly repeating the same few gestures to operate one machine or part of a machine. Photographs of men working indoors include spaces filled with natural light from windows (Figures 4.2 and 4.6) or they are shown working outside (Figure 4.1). Both scenarios imply a beneficial connection with nature augmented by the natural materials with which the men work. As they integrate natural materials together

*Figure 4.6* War Neuroses, 1919.

and strengthen and secure their connections—thread to thread, reed to reed, thus tending to emerging shapes, even as they lie prone (Figure 4.3), their fabrication is healing rather than harmful. Furthermore, the Arts and Crafts Movement's "socialist faith in the machine as a precondition for greater abundance for all" (Boris 1998, p. 213) could support diversity in minds and bodies having varying needs for the types of tools and equipment needed to make in concert with the broad reformist aims of the Arts and Crafts Movement (Edwards 1987).

## Crafting ability through occupation

However, craft therapy did not follow the impulse of the Arts and Crafts Movement in privileging craft fabrication as a means to reform work. Rather, as crafting facilitated healing for injured troops, photographs and their associated captions and articles less represented the activity as a broad reform of work than they promulgated "culturally fabricated narrative[s] of the body" (Garland-Thomas 2001, p. 347). These reflected existing ableist American ideas and practices (Millett-Gallant & Howie 2016) about usefulness and productivity.

For one thing, in contrast to the Arts and Crafts Movement's attention to experiencing pleasure in making craft, and Hall's claim that "aesthetic quality and therapeutic reward … [are] not mutually exclusive" (Morton 2011), photographs did not describe the emotions or feelings of craft therapy patients. Though the young man weaving outside his base hospital in France may appear to smile (Figure 4.1), his base hospital issued a report insisting that healing mental illness neither engaged with artistic quality nor generated pleasure. The assertion cleaved an important element of the Arts and Crafts reform of work from the convalescing war subject's experience (Schwab 1919).

To be sure, at his sanitorium Hall considered craft workshops as "a group of industries" comprising "hand weaving, wood carving and metal work" (Hall 1908, p. 31) undertaken to fulfill commissions (Work for Nerves 1905, p. 7). He even presented his artisan-run Marblehead Pottery as a model for a new iteration of work linking "the factory and the individual craftsman … where it should be possible to meet expenses without cheapening the product" and retain "the craftsman spirit" (Hall 1908, p. 30) including "the human interest and personal touch which can hardly be attained in a large pottery" (Hall 1908, p. 30). Still, representations of craft therapy lacked references to the patient's spirit or individual touch. Furthermore, craft therapy might justify a "segmentation of labor" (Boris 1998, p. 217). Following their rehabilitation, businesses might hire veterans for some jobs and not afford them opportunity to apply to others. As John Culbert Faries, Director of the Institute for Crippled and Disabled Men, observed, "The effort is not made to give trade training, but rather to fit a man for a special process suitable to his particular disability" (Faries 1919, p. 10).

Photographically, this agenda resulted in images that pictorially diminish attention to patient's mental and physical injuries and highlight their mastery of fabrication skills. Moreover, while Faries acknowledged the "long process from the time the man enters the hospital until he is placed in industry" (New York Academy on Medicine 1921), the photographs do not explore the duration or experience of the process. Nor do they reveal men as weak, experiencing pain, or overtaken by a condition of the mind or body, states traditionally associated with the feminine. Consequently, while the medicalizing of their care constituted a radical departure from relying on pensions and women at home (Linker 2011), and as craft, so laden with domestic associations with the feminine, entered into the rehabilitative therapy for injured soldiers, photographs confirm the continuation of heteronormative gender roles in which women support and encourage the work of men.[2]

Photographs feature men practicing skills independently, even in bed and as amputees (Figure 4.3). Out of bed, they show that many men dispensed with pajamas and robe to wear the same tailored shirt and trousers as their peers. In a group setting, the clothing conjures a uniform of sorts, which hints at the institutional if not professional as opposed to recreational purpose of their therapy (Figures 4.2 and 4.4–4.6).

Photographs narrated the men's ability by describing their behavior, too. Above all, the men appear serious and focused. They do not look at one another or talk. Instead, they concentrate on their own work visually, which suggests their ability to control their minds and bodies in a group setting (Figures 4.2, 4.4, and 4.6) and as they work alone (Figures 4.1, 4.3, and 4.5). Captions further characterized their activity as a wise use of time, which implies that the men were aware of its value as a resource on which they could and should capitalize (Figures 4.4–4.6). "From a financial standpoint the future looks bright for them," declares the caption for a photograph of three solider-patients at a Boston hospital published in *Carry On, Magazine on the Reconstruction of Disabled Soldiers and Sailors*, published jointly by the US Public Health Service, the Army, and the Red Cross Institute for Crippled and Disabled Men (Leatherbee 1919). One works on a belt and two who each lost an arm model clay busts of an Egyptian person that will be cast in bronze.

It could be bright for those healing from mental injury, too. In *The Journal of the American Medical Association*, Dr. Theodore H. Weisenburg of the Philadelphia General Hospital averred that war neurosis cases were difficult, including those treated in New York at Plattsburg Barracks, US Army General Hospital No. 30, which specialized in neuropsychiatric cases, and those the hospital received could not be cured abroad (Weisenburg 1919). Yet, *Carry On* reproduced from the same hospital a photograph of two soldiers operating a large loom, and the caption noted the hospital's success with the "mental education" of occupational work for war neuroses (Figure 4.6). Although their mental injuries remained invisible, the photograph and caption confirm the men's ability to run a complex machine for weaving without medical or craft specialists overseeing their work.

Coupling healing with achieving ability for civilian jobs came from the government, medical experts, and non-governmental organizations worrying about and engaging with troop's preparation for existing types of work, not work as imagined by the Arts and Crafts Movement. The US Federal Board for Vocational Education worried that the idle time of receiving medical treatment would render patients as "incurable loafers" who would "degenerate after a long convalescence into that chronic invalidism which is mental rather than physical" (US Federal Board for Vocational Education 1918). Echoing Salmon's framing of craft occupation as re-education and his warning against non-productive occupations, and Hall and Buck urging attention to managing the patient's mind to heal from illness and war injury (Hall & Buck 1915), for

Dunton, men "learn[ing] motion unconsciously and naturally" (Dunton 1919, p. 117) should be purposed for healing and "vocational re-education" (p. 118). Essentially, these experts were redefining dis/ability by shifting it away from injuries as deficits to abilities as attitudes and skills that pointed towards employment. To prevent troops from sinking into degeneracy, the Division of Special Hospitals and Physical Reconstruction created within the Office of the Surgeon General undertook to "secur[e] employment for them [upon being] discharged" (US Surgeon-General's Office 1927, p. 4).

Outside of official governmental channels, organizations like the Institute for Crippled and Disabled Men, which worked with the Surgeon General's Office and, from its establishment in 1917–1920, with the American Red Cross (Byrom 2001), echoed the social imperative to integrate healing with training men to achieve economic independence. "We have learned to conserve things, we must now learn to conserve men," Faries (1919, p. 4, 5) observed. Conserving men meant harnessing their post-war minds, bodies and attitudes to reject the dis/ability of idleness and moral deterioration that generated "parasitic, social units" (Faries 1919, p. 3) and resulted in a diseased society (Faries 1919, p. 5).

Faries echoed medical experts and the government in explaining that rehabilitation aimed "to render [the patient] fit to resume his standing as a productive unit in society after something has happened to render him for the time being unfit" (Faries 1919, p. 5). This agenda did not require returning the soldier's mind or body to its pre-war state. In *Reconstructing the Disabled Soldier*, McMurtrie (1918) published a photograph of a one-armed man filing metal, explaining that "some men prefer to work with their stump and abandon an artificial appliance" (p. 21). In contrast to the Arts and Crafts Movement's account of dis/ability as deficiencies in one's self and life caused by industrial work and society, with reforming society and work as the solution, these discourses of the injured soldier eschewed his living as a "cripple" and instead refused to treat dis/ability as a limitation to getting a job and living independently in society as it already existed (Albrecht 1992).

Overarchingly, the message resonated the theme of overcoming injury by achieving an ability to work (DeVolder 2017), and it echoed throughout 15 black and white photograph panels with descriptive text that the Red Cross Institute for Crippled and Disabled Men exhibited in 1919. The panels feature men practicing occupations as they convalesce or enter civilian life, mostly in the United States but with some representation of activity in France, Italy, and India, too. The series begins with "First steps to usefulness," a title that frames the meaning of the photographs as a narrative that shifts the injured man from inadequacy and worthlessness to having social worth through work. The image that depicts a man in bed, designing on a bed easel. Subsequent photographs indicate that the Institute supported modes of fabrication ranging from craft to skilled mechanical work.

One features a seated man who leans into his engraving work (Figure 4.5). The man's missing right leg is indicated by a baggy, empty trouser leg extending from his waist over his left knee, disappearing underneath the workbench.[3] The photograph's internal framing evokes the circular lens of the camera homing in on the man, a visual strategy that highlights the deportment of his body as he balances with his leg on the edge of the chair to lean over a workbench. He wears a loupe on his right eye all the better to see his material and use an assortment of nearby graver handles as he steadies his work in progress on an engraver's sandbag (Figure 4.5). Interestingly, although the caption for the photograph references using one's time in a hospital (Figure 4.5), the image provides no hint of a hospital setting. Although rehabilitation took place in institutional settings, photographs indicate that the burden for healing was placed on the individual to triumph over his impairments and achieve productivity on a pathway to economic self-support, and the images emphasized his activity, not the hospital setting or its staff.

Instead, in an age when photography denoted truths about the working class and the nature of work in industrial society, for the records of government-supported occupational therapy programs, the Institute of Crippled and Disabled Men, and periodicals for military and medical readers such as *Carry On* and *Mental Hygiene*, photographs of men practicing craft therapy confirmed their worth for post-war American society through work. "America may have some physical cripples returned from the front, but she must have no social or economic cripples resulting from her participation in this war for justice and humanity" (McMurtie 1918, p. 49). McMurtrie warned Americans concerned with the welfare of these men and the economic health of the nation. The same idea could be understood as a warning that failing to strengthen men whom the war weakened could lead to enduring mental weakness as an index of the weakening of American economy and society if not also Western civilization (Stagner 2014).

## Conclusion

Instead of reforming industrial society and work toward health and pleasure, craft therapy and its photography helped to repurpose men injured by war for civilian employment. For these men, photographs of craft therapy contributed to defining dis/ability not as a condition of their minds and bodies but as a lack of effort they might fail to make toward achieving usefulness. Extrapolating from this situation, craft therapy and its photography messaged strong support for the United States mainstreaming ableism.

According to the social model of dis/ability, ableist societies dis-enable people by making it difficult or impossible for them to access and experience inclusion concerning places, other people, resources, activities, and experiences. Ableist societies establish normative expectations about bodies and minds, and they seek to hold their members accountable to them. These expectations include that selves do not change through deterioration or impairment, nor do they seem to vary by place or time. Rather, changes that are socially valued improve the body and mind toward manifesting society's highest standards. Ableist societies may expect everyone to aspire to achieve them, no matter if these comprise race, age, beauty, or other characteristics. More fundamentally, ableist societies determine what counts as human by "setting the measure of body and mind that gives or denies human status to individual persons" (Siebers 2008, p. 8). By way of omission, erasure, hiding, and silencing, they devalue people who do not aspire to achieve normative standards of wellness and beauty or who cannot (Bauman & Mazzeo 2012). It follows that ableist societies devalue mental and physical impairments by associating them with weakness and abnormality. A consequent lack of access and inclusion renders people who are impaired as disabled, and they may be shunned and pathologized "to signify inferior human status" (Siebers 2008, p. 6) and considered not seen fit to belong in public spaces and life (Baynton 2001).

The government- and non-government-based medical care of disabled American soldiers helped to instrumentalize craft fabrication to enable the men to belong to the mainstream of American life. By downplaying if not avoiding depicting their impairments, and stressing their skills, productivity, behavior, and demeanor as the men worked in ostensibly natural settings of fabrication, photography contributed to the maintenance of ableist norms for men. In these photographic constructions of the men as successful workers, their identity as workers could mitigate against their experience of deleterious "social meanings, symbols, and stigmas attached to dis/ability identity" (Siebers 2008; see also Shakespeare 2018; Wendell 1996) and normalize them while benefitting the economy by adding workers instead of paying for their long-term care.

## Notes

1 Attributed to Boris (1998).
2 On needing to persuade men to appreciate rehabilitation as opposed to expecting a military pension that precluded them from working, see Linker (2011, pp. 122–123).
3 Other scenes in the photograph series show men farming, carpentry, auto mechanics, typing, running motion picture equipment, and mechanical drafting.

## References

Albrecht, G., (1992). *The disability business, rehabilitation in America*. Newbury Park, CA: Sage Press.

Andersen, L. T. and Reed, K., eds., (2017). *The history of occupational therapy: the first century*. Thorofare, NJ: SLACK.

Bauman, Z. and Mazzeo, R., (2012). *On education: conversations with Riccardo Mazzeo*. Cambridge, UK: Polity.

Baynton, D., (2001). Disability and the justification of inequality in American history. In: P. K. Longmore and L. Umansky, eds. *The new disability history: American perspectives*. New York: New York University Press. pp. 33–57.

Bell, L., (2018). Medical developments in World War One. *British Library Newsletter*. 7 November. Available from: https://www.bl.uk/world-war-one/articles/medical-developments-in-world-war-one

Boris, E., (1998). Dreams of brotherhood and beauty. In: W. Kaplan, ed. *The art that is life: the arts & crafts movement in America, 1875–1920*. Boston: Bullfinch Press.

Byrom, B., (2001). A pupil and a patient, hospital-schools in progressive America. In: P. K. Longmore and L. Umansky, eds. *The new disability history: American perspectives*. New York: New York University Press. pp. 133–156.

Clark, R. J. and Kaplan, W., (1987). Arts and crafts: matters of style. In: W. Kaplan, ed. *'The art that is life': the arts & crafts movement in America, 1875–1920*. Boston: Museum of Fine Arts with Little, Brown and Company.

Cohen, D., (2006). Disabled veterans. In: G. L. Albrecht, ed. *Encyclopedia of disability*. New York: Sage Publications.

"Convalescing WW1 soldiers weaving baskets and engraving a wooden box, July 1, 1922, Walter Reed Hospital." (Reeve 041863). Silver Spring, MD: Otis Historical Archives, National Museum of Health and Medicine.

DeVolder, E., (2017). *Overcoming the overcoming story: critical disability informed genealogies of compulsory heroism*. Ph.D. dissertation, University of British Columbia.

Dunton, W. R., (1919). *Reconstruction therapy*. Philadelphia, PA: W.B. Saunders.

Edwards, R., (1987). The art of work. In: W. Kaplan, ed. *'The art that is life': the arts & crafts movement in America, 1875–1920*. Boston: Museum of Fine Arts with Little, Brown and Company.

Faries, J. C., (1919). Re-educating the disabled man. *American Journal of Care for Cripples*. **8**(1), 10.

Frank, G., (1992). Opening feminist histories of occupational therapy. *The American Journal of Occupational Therapy*. **46**(11), 989–999.

Garland-Thomas, R., (2001). Seeing the disabled, visual rhetorics of disability in popular photography. In: P. K. Longmore and L. Umansky, eds. *The new disability history: American perspectives*. New York: New York University Press. pp. 335–374.

Gavin, L., (1994). Reconstruction aides in World War I: a brand new profession. *MINERVA: Quarterly Report on Women and Military*. **12**(4), 65–74.

Gerber, D. A., ed., (2000). *Disabled veterans in history*. Ann Arbor, MI: University of Michigan Press.

Gilman, S., (1996). *Seeing the insane*. Lincoln, NE: University of Nebraska Press.

Good Use of Time in Hospital, (1919). Red Cross Institute for Crippled and Disabled Men. Retrieved from the Library of Congress, LC-USZC4-7384 DLC.

Haas, L. J., (1922). How needs have controlled the selection of crafts. *Archives of Occupational Therapy*. **1**(5), 381.

Haas, L. J., (1925). Weaving frame for bedside occupation. *Occupational Therapy and Rehabilitation*. **4**(2), 135.

Hall, H. J., (1905). The systematic use of work as a remedy in neurasthenia and allied conditions. *Boston Medical and Surgical Journal*. **112**(2), 30–31.

Hall, H. J., (1908). Marblehead pottery. *Keramic Studio*. **10**, 31.

Hall, H. J., (1910). Work-cure. *Journal of the American Medical Association*. **1**(54), 12–13.

Hall, H. J. and Buck, M. M. C., (1915). *The work of our hands, a study of occupations for invalids*. New York: Moffat Yard & Company.

Hickel, K. W., (2001). Medicine, bureaucracy, and social welfare: the politics of disability compensation for American veterans of World War 1. In: P. K. Longmore and L. Umansky, eds. *The new disability history: American perspectives*. New York: New York University Press. pp. 236–257.

Jenkins, S. G., (2009). *The national society of craftsmen, New York, New York (1906–1920) & the New York Society of Craftsmen (1920–1957): a craft continuum from the arts and crafts movement*. Washington, DC: History of Decorative Arts, Smithsonian Associates and Corcoran College of Art and Design.

Kickel, K. W., (2001). Medicine, bureaucracy, and social welfare: the politics of disability compensation for American Veterans of World War 1. P. K. Longmore and L. Umansky, eds. *The new disability history, American perspectives*. New York and London: New York University Press. pp. 236–257.

Kinder, J. M., (2007). *Encountering injury: modern war and the problem of the wounded soldier*. Ph.D. dissertation, University of Minnesota.

Kinder, J. M., (2015). *Paying with their bodies: American war and the problem of the disabled veteran*. Chicago: University of Chicago Press.

Leatherbee, R. W., (1919). To the returning soldier. *Carry on Magazine on the Reconstruction of Disabled Soldiers and Sailors*. **1**(8), 14–15.

Linker, B., (2011). *War's waste: rehabilitation in World War 1 America*. Chicago: University of Chicago Press.

Low, J. F., (1992). The reconstruction aides. *American Journal of Occupational Therapy*. **46**(1), 38.

McMurtrie, D. C., (1918). *Reconstructing the disabled soldier*. New York: Red Cross Institute for Crippledand Disabled Men.

McMurtrie, D. C., (1919). *The disabled soldier*. New York: Macmillan.

Millett-Gallant, A. and Howie, E., (2016). Introduction. In: A. Millett-Gallant and E. Howie, eds., *Disability and art history*. London: Routledge. pp. 1–11.

Morton, E., (2011). The object of therapy: Mary E. Black and the progressive possibilities of weaving. *Utopian Studies*. **22**(2), 331.

New York Academy of Medicine, (1921). Meeting on occupational therapy. The Committee on Public Health of the NY Academy of Medicine: Correspondence, Reports, Documents, 1921–5, draft report. 18 February. Retrieved from: UNT Public Health Archives.

Perry, H., (2014). *Recycling the disabled: army, medicine, and modernity in WW1*. Manchester, UK: Manchester University Press.

Rompkey, R., (2001). *Jessie Luther at the Grenfell Mission*. Montreal: McGill-Queen's University Press.

Rose, S. F., (2008). *No right to be idle: the invention of disability, 1850–1930*. Ph.D. dissertation, Illinois: University of Chicago.

Rostker, B., (2013). *Providing for casualties of war: the American experience through World War II*. Santa Monica, CA: Rand Corporation.

Salmon, T. W., (1917). *The care and treatment of mental diseases and war neuroses ('Shell Shock') in the British Army*. Bethesda, MD: Uniformed Services University of the Health Sciences. Available from: https://digitalcollections.lrc.usuhs.edu/digital/collection/p16005coll4/id/22358/

Schwab, S. J., (1919). The experiment in occupational therapy at Base Hospital 117, A.E.F. *Mental Hygiene*. **3**, 581.

Shakespeare, T., (2018). *Disability: the basics*. New York: Routledge.

Siebers, B., (2008). *Disability theory*. Ann Arbor, MI: University of Michigan Press.

Stagner, A. C., (2014). *Defining the soldier's wounds: US shell shock in international perspective*. Ph.D. dissertation, University of California Irvine.

US Federal Board for Vocational Education, (1918). *Letter, training of teachers for occupational therapy for the rehabilitation of disabled soldiers and sailors.* 30 January. Washington, DC: Government Printing Office.

US Surgeon-General's Office, (1927). *The Medical Department of the United States Army in the World War,* volume XIII. Washington, DC: Government Printing Office.

War Neuroses, (1919). *Carry on magazine on the reconstruction of disabled soldiers and sailors.* **1**(5), 2.

Weisenburg, T. H., (1919). Traumatic neuroses in war and peace. *Journal of American Medical Association.* **73**(7), 596–599.

Wendell, S., (1996). *The rejected body: feminist philosophical reflections on disability.* New York: Routledge.

Work for Nerves, Handicraft Sanatorium for Rundown Patients, (1905), *The Adair County News.* 30 August. 7.

# 5 Medical Discourses on Dis/ability in State Socialist Romania: A Critical Genealogy

*Radu-Harald Dinu*

## Introduction

Today few would object to the assertion that scientific categories are determined by collective norms and social practices. Ever since Ludwik Fleck's publication of *Genesis and Development of a Scientific Fact* (Fleck 1935), we have acknowledged that the scientific endeavor is anything but a disinterested observation and classification of biological entities "out there" and is, rather, determined by what Fleck called "thought styles" and "thought collectives." However, during the 1930s, Fleck's outlook on science was still on the fringes. Medicine was largely regarded as an autonomous realm where scientists could not only decipher and explain but also perform dispassionate interventions into the human body. Being one of the most esteemed academic disciplines, the medical field was imbued with a triumphalist narrative of scientific advancement which can be traced back to the 19th century (Canguilhem 1989; Hacking 1990). In state socialist contexts, the faith in the promises of modern science was equally an offspring of modernity and marked by the optimistic view "that scientific and industrial progress ... removed all restrictions on the possible application of planning, education, and social reform" and the belief "that social problems can be finally solved" (Bauman 1991, p. 29). Being widely recognized as the epitome of scientific progress, medicine inscribed itself into this modernist narrative that lasted until the fall of state socialism in Eastern Europe.

Against this background, this chapter sets out to explore medical discourses on dis/ability in state socialist contexts, with particular focus on Romania. It delineates the nexus between medical and political visions of dis/ability and of various scientific disciplines' commitment to categorize and cure human conditions that questioned socialist ideals of normality. The study focuses on a sample of Romanian medical and educational literature published between the late 1940s and early 1970s. The ways in which these texts classified and framed dis/ability revolve around two broader themes that are explored in this chapter: *defectology*, an interdisciplinary field of disability research which originated in the Soviet Union, and *labor productivity* that emerged as a guiding principle during state socialism to integrate the dis/abled into socialist society.

DOI: 10.4324/9781003257196-7

Extracts from the Romanian sources are woven into an analytic narrative and contextualized in relation to existing literature on medicine, science, and dis/ability.

## Social constructivism, embodiment theory, and the dis/abled body

Ever since the 1960s, Western scholars have followed a constructivist path when investigating the expansion of medical authority, criticizing the extent of medical control over human behavior and the related transformation of physical or intellectual differences into pathologies (Conrad 2007; Wright & Treacher 1982). Disability studies have in many ways reflected these epistemological contentions and applied them to their own field of inquiry. Some of these constructivist stances have come under attack by disability scholars who have offered alternative understandings of the impaired body as simultaneously biological *and* social. In pointing out the limits of social construction, Tobin Siebers has advocated for a "renewed acceptance of bodily reality" and "a sense of realism" in dis/ability theory (Siebers 2008, p. 66). A similar approach has recently been proposed by Elizabeth Barnes, who contended that we may not be able to provide accounts of dis/ability centered around objective similarities shared by human bodies. With their embrace of embodiment theory, Siebers and Barnes demonstrate that disablement is not exclusively determined by societal norms or discourses; rather, dis/ability is attributable to the (physical) body because bodies matter to us (Barnes 2016). This chapter falls in line with these assertions and argues that the body under state socialism mattered on a very concrete, corporeal level, not least because it became the main arena where disputes on hereditary and environmental causes of dis/ability were settled by medical experts. At the same time, the body, over which physicians have traditionally been given the preferential right of interpretation, had connotations far beyond questions of well-being or disease. This applies all the more to socialist societies where medical concepts of health and illness, normality and abnormality had strong political ramifications (Starks 2008).

## Soviet thought styles

The gradual Sovietization of Eastern Europe after 1945 was not only a matter of high politics; this process also entailed a sustained transfer of scientific thought and a rich regional exchange of expertise (Marks & Savelli 2015). In Romania, the socialist regime's formative years after 1947 were equally marked by the adaptation of Soviet blueprints in science, a process orchestrated by various state-controlled institutions such as the Academy of the Romanian People's Republic (Milcu 1962). *Lysenkoism* and *Pavlovism* emerged as major paradigms and informed most scientific disciplines during this period (Doboş 2015; Oghina-Pavie 2017; Turda 2020). Named after the Soviet biologist Trofim Lysenko, Lysenkoism rejected the most fundamental tenets of modern genetics, overemphasized environmental factors, and promoted concepts such as the "inheritance of acquired characteristics" and a belief in the transformative power of man over nature (Krementsov & deJong-Lambert 2017, p. x). Similarly, Ivan Pavlov's classical conditioning principles were reframed as a social engineering technique designed to enhance the socialist New Man, or, as the Soviet psychologist Sergei Rubinstein phrased it, "to efficiently shape and educate the mental traits of the constructive man in communist society" (Brătescu 1999, p. 389). The Bucharest-based Institute of Neurology was renamed after Ivan Pavlov, and the head of this institution, neurologist Arthur Kreindler, advocated for an adoption of Pavlov's models (Kreindler et al., 1949). Pavlov's theory was also applied to the public health sector and the health care system with the aim of ameliorating workers' "nervous systems" and creating favorable conditions for their reintegration into labor (Marcu 1953; Velt 1953).

## The defective body

The medicalization of disability in state socialist countries was primarily concentrated in the interdisciplinary field of defectology. Though some have attributed the beginnings of this Soviet type of disability research to Lev Vygotsky's studies during the 1920s, defectology can be traced back to Vsevolod Kashchenko, a child psychologist who coined the term in pre-revolutionary Russia (McCagg 1989; Stepanova 2018). Defectology combined various educational, psychological, and medical traditions into a deficit-oriented approach to treating disability (Byford 2018) and was eventually divided into four subdisciplines: *surdopedagogy* for the deaf, *typhlopedagogy* for the visually impaired, *oligophrenopedagogy* for the intellectually dis/abled and *logopedics* for those with speech "defects" (Lubovsky 1974). Although defectologists focused on sensory, physical, and cognitive impairments in children, the discipline had much wider, biopolitical ramifications. Many defectologists were driven by the prospect of ultimately "eradicating" physical and mental "defects" (D'iachkov 1967, p. 47). As Anatoly Lunacharsky, the head of the People's Commissariat for Education, put it in 1920, "defectiveness depends not so much on bad inheritance as on the milieu. Change conditions, and there will not remain a trace of defectiveness in these children" (D'iachkov 1967, p. 46). Kaschenko, whose research received comprehensive state funding during the 1920s, similarly made sure to demonstrate not only the medical but also the economic and social benefits of his discipline. Comparing impairments to the missing parts of a machine, the utopian "war against defectiveness" ultimately aimed to transform dis/abled children into "functioning" Soviet citizens (Galmarini-Kabala 2016). The ideological underpinnings of Soviet defectology were thus informed by modernist driving forces, following overarching trends of scientific progress. These core aspects fell in line with the Soviet state's objective to limit deviations from social and political norms by means of integrating individuals into mainstream production (Byford 2018).

Stalinism brought about an abrupt break in defectological research in the Soviet Union and in July 1936 the Central Committee condemned the field as "antiscientific." Since leading defectologists used psychological measurement methods that were closely associated with western psychology, the party denounced these tendencies as "bourgeois perversions" (Bogoiavlenski & Mecinskaia 1963, p. 502). Only during the Khruschev Thaw was defectology given back "some of its old social mission" (McCagg 1989, p. 57). Vygotsky's works became cited again, but some of his comparatively progressive approaches from the 1920s fell into oblivion after Stalin's death. His opposition to segregating dis/abled from "normal" children—as this, in his words, would have created "a new breed of human being"—thus never gained ground in defectology or in the Soviet educational system (Vygotsky et al. 1993, p. 36).

## Romanian trajectories

The implementation of Soviet defectology in Romania was facilitated by the Institute of Pedagogical Sciences in Bucharest and its affiliate at the University of Cluj, where the first defectological research units were established in 1956 (Mare et al. 1968, p. 250). The Cluj branch was eventually transformed into an independent center, and Alexandru Roşca was appointed as the first chair for defectology in 1960 where he and his colleagues founded *Problems of Defectology and Psychopathology*, the first Romanian journal within this field. Roşca already had made his mark as a prolific psychologist during the interwar years, debuting with a PhD thesis on "mental debilities" in children and a study on juvenile delinquency (Roşca 1931, 1932). However, his career first gained momentum during the postwar years when he openly embraced Soviet models in disability research (Marea Adunare Naţională 1969). The influence of Soviet defectology is also reflected by the fact that Roşca maintained a wide network of a number of Soviet psychologists and defectologists such as Alexander Luria, Boris Lomov, and Maria I. Zemtsova, whose works were frequently invoked by Romanian defectologists (Roşan 2015).

A concise appraisal of this eminent academic field can be found in a handbook on medical psychology and pedagogy from 1962, edited by Paul Popescu-Neveanu, another main proponent of the Sovietization of Romanian science. The chapter on defectology outlined the discipline's emphasis on compensating models for both bodily and neuropsychological disfunctions. The notion of "deficiency" was defined as "a pathological state of functionality," affecting "individuals' working capacity and leading to disorders in their adaption to the physical and social environment." All temporary or "light" forms of deficiencies "which do not reduce individuals' capability to comply with the necessities of labor" were excluded from the definition (Bara & Pop 1962, pp. 449–450).

While seemingly scientific in form, Romanian defectology was political in motivation. Based on Pavlov's theory, the authors contrasted socialist defectology with contemporary "bourgeois defectology," denouncing the latter for promoting "reactionary and pseudo-scientific" ideas. In capitalist societies, "the role of heredity for the development of deficiencies is overstated," the authors claimed, and the "potential of rectifying deficiencies through education is brushed aside." In contrast, "Marx and Engels' dialectical and historical materialism" and Pavlov's physiology were believed to constitute a new base of defectology and inform special education programs "in the spirit of communist principles" (Bara & Pop 1962, pp. 455–458). These assumptions had wide-ranging implications for the evaluation of deafness: the diagnostic category of cortical deafness (deafness resulting from lesions in the temporal lobes of the brain), for example, was repudiated as "anti-scientific" since it was not in line with Pavlov's model of higher nervous activity (Bara & Pop 1962, p. 489). Since ideological allegiance was a prerequisite for career advancement, medical surveys and periodicals frequently made obligatory and ritualized references to the Pavlovian thought collective. Summarizing the evolution of their discipline after 1944, Valeriu Mare emphasized that the "ideological fundaments" of socialist defectology had radically departed from "outdated" Western scientific approaches. In socialism, "disorders" were no longer considered "irreversible," and individuals no longer deemed "irrecuperable." On the contrary, due to the "exceptional plasticity" and "enormous potential" of individuals' "higher nervous activity," compensatory measures would reestablish an equilibrium "between the human organism and the social environment" (Mare et al. 1968, p. 250).

Research in juvenile delinquency was also subjected to the Pavlovian framework. The pediatrician Mihai Peteanu delineated the state of the art in an article from 1961, acknowledging that "neurotic states" in children occur and disappear "according to the laws of conditioned responses" and are solely triggered by environmental factors, among which the author identified "educational failures" as the most frequent. Further, he reasoned, "Bourgeois influences on education ... [combined with] miserable material conditions and permanent unemployment" explained the perseverance of neuroses in capitalist societies. By controlling these environmental factors, Peteanu believed that "neuropsychiatric disorders" would eventually disappear. By "securing the mental health of its citizens," or so Peteanu reasoned, the socialist order "provides a higher neuropsychiatric tonus by eliminating conflictual situations." Children would consequently be transformed into "valuable citizens, well integrated into society and their labor collective." Quoting his colleague Arthur Kreindler, Peteanu reassured readers that "neuroses will cease to exist in the communist society. People will talk about them in the same manner as we talk about medieval plague outbreaks today" (Peteanu 1961, pp. 121–125). In other works, the study of juvenile delinquency was frequently associated with "oligophrenia" or congenital dementia. Bara and Pop stated that "imbeciles" need to be subjected to a "special system of education and surveillance" as these individuals would otherwise enter upon "antisocial careers, marked by theft, begging, prostitution, vagrancy or delinquency, etc." (1962, p. 501). These various claims reveal how medical discourses on disability were infused with socialism's civilizing mission.

The main field of defectological research, however, focused upon sensory impairments such as vision or hearing loss, although there were no sharp dividing lines from other areas of specialization. A cursory survey of the discipline's main scientific journal, *Problems of Defectology*, and a research synthesis from 1968 confirm this picture: three-quarters of the total scientific output before 1967 focused on what was then called "typhlology," the study of blindness, and "surdology," the study of hearing impairments (Mare et al. 1968, p. 251). Even in the case of visual impairment and deafness, politically informed notions of normality and abnormality shaped many of the medical judgments. Experts stated that individuals who lose their vision would allegedly "become inert, passive, indifferent, insecure, nervous, irritable, etc.," while the use of guide dogs or the white cane was deplored as an erroneous, "bourgeois" trend since it would transform the blind into "passive elements" and hamper their mental activities (Bara & Pop 1962, p. 466; Damaschin 1968b, p. 38). Sensory impairments were largely regarded as "curable," and in the case of deafness, experts strictly advocated oralist approaches which would eventually bring about a "demutization" (*demutizare*) of the deaf (Pufan 1966). Sign language was, in contrast, considered detrimental to communication since it would not comply with the requirements of "logical and advanced way of thinking which is specific for humans" (Bara & Pop 1962, p. 493).

## Deflating the Soviet appeal

The epistemological adherence to the Soviet paradigm as described earlier lasted only two decades since Romania's communist leadership started to gradually emancipate itself from the Soviet Union. Initiated by Romania's first communist leader Gheorghe Gherorghiu-Dej during the late 1950s, and further intensified by his successor Nicolae Ceauşescu after 1965, this paradigm shift was not only palpable within the political and cultural sphere but also had considerable repercussions on science. While prewar scientists, formerly stigmatized as "bourgeois," were increasingly vindicated, Soviet models lost ground. Thus, in the course of the 1970s, Lysenko's "inheritance of acquired characteristics" and Pavlov's neurophysiology were rejected, the former being labeled as "incompatible" with modern biology (Săhleanu 1976a, p. 112) and the latter as "highly questionable" (Săhleanu 1976b). An essay collection on the history of special education in Romania from 1968 is revelatory in this respect. Instead of shedding light on Soviet mentors, the volume exclusively paid homage to various Romanian scientists and educators from the prewar period, formerly branded as "reactionary." Dimitrie Rusticeanu, for example, a prewar special needs educator who had acted as head of the Royal Institute for the Blind and Deaf-Mutes in Cernăuţi (Chernivtsi) before 1940, was lauded for promoting "pure oralism" and the "eradication" of sign language in deaf education (Sorescu 1968, p. 173). While Romanian defectologists started to acknowledge their intellectual debts to domestic traditions, Soviet concepts were not completely abandoned. Romanian works from the prewar period proved to be compatible with the Soviet state of the art as both advocated for oralist approaches. Experts could still condemn psychometrics as a "Western" aberration (Mare et al., 1968, p. 253), but the 1970s brought about a significant shift in Romanian disability research. Scholars began to embrace Western genetic models, such as Lewis Terman's IQ studies and Mendelian inheritance, and gradually incorporated these formerly stigmatized paradigms into their research agendas (Bologa 1972, p. 469; Păunescu 1973). Dorin Damaschin, chair of psychology at the University of Bucharest and a specialist in defectology, went the farthest in incorporating these impulses albeit along eugenicist lines. In a programmatic paper presented in August 1969 at the University of Bucharest, Damsachin demanded a radical repositioning of his field that accorded with his belief that "[g]enetically gifted" individuals contribute to "positive genetic feedback" by handing down their hereditary characteristics to the next generations, according to natural selection principles. Individuals with "unmistakable genetic deficiencies," in contrast, create a "negative genetic feedback." Due to modern medical science, these individuals have "a higher chance of survival" and thereby pass on their "genetical defects" to future generations. In concluding his digression on eugenics, Damaschin asserted that the transmission of chromosomal and other strongly hereditary illnesses is a reality that allows for new hypotheses and new certitudes in the diagnosis and education of oligophrenics, of juvenile delinquents, of logopathy and deafness. New perspectives for studying human cytogenetics were opening up and confirmed the necessity to explore the problems of eugenics (Damaschin 1970). These stances were indeed a novelty in socialist Romania.

At the same time, Damaschin safeguarded himself against potential accusations of promoting "reactionary" theories and demarcated his own eugenicist vision from "dehumanizing" concepts. The "problems of human eugenics in our country," he concluded, "are conceived on moral grounds, and on the grounds of socialist humanism," which stood in sharp contrast to the abuses of scientific racism (Damaschin 1970, p. 95). These core arguments were further expounded in a monography on defectology published a few years later, in which Damaschin urged fellow scientists to carry out research on "the problems of heredity and marriage" and to "apply resolute measures" in order to remedy various "deficiencies" (Damaschin 1973, pp. 23–24). However, the author remained vague in this respect and did not explicitly state what kind of "resolute measures" he envisioned. In another article, Damaschin was more blatant and recommended introducing "obligatory measures" in order to curtail marriages and "hereditary deficiencies" among the dis/abled (Damaschin 1968a, p. 36). These statements clearly challenged Romanian law at the time, which prohibited marriage with the "mentally insane" (*alienatul mintal*) and "mentally weak" (*debilul mintal*) but did not target other forms of disability (Marea Adunare Națională 1954). Even though Damaschin did not further elucidate if "obligatory measures" involved negative eugenics, his claims evidently reawakened the prewar eugenicist discourse by regarding marriage among the dis/abled as a potential threat to the hereditary composition of the population.

Damaschin's progressivist aim to "eradicate" all sorts of deficiencies must be read against this background. Eugenicist measures to diminish congenital dis/abilities and rehabilitation programs were two sides of the same coin, both aimed at "normalizing" the dis/abled: "In our age, new and unimagined perspectives for the compensation and recovery of all deficiencies are evolving. [They will] cause a revolution in rehabilitation and bring the deficient man closer and closer to the capabilities of the normal man" (Damaschin 1973, p. 69).

## Dis/ability through the lens of labor productivity

Labor productivity was a core component of socialist ideology and was grounded in the belief that it would "beat capitalism at its own game" (Siegelbaum 1988). Romanian economic policy mirrored these ideas in various respects. During the early postwar period, labor regimes were informed by Taylorist organization principles, scientific management, and state control (Anonymous 1953; Păcuraru 1966; Petrovici & Faje 2019). Both Romanian technocrats and Soviet representatives were "enthralled by the promises of socialist productivity," as Adrian Grama highlighted, and the term "quickly became the rallying cry of the socialist party" (Grama 2019, p. 13).

Since socialist regimes habitually attributed social categories to work capacity, dis/ability needs to be interpreted through the lens of productivity. Even though socialist regimes generally used their welfare systems as a showcase for "socialist humanism," welfare programs for the dis/abled were not egalitarian but rather were stratified (Fieseler 2014). In the Soviet Union, authorities began to measure disability by the loss of work capacity and, consequently, individuals were not to be classified as dis/abled because of their impairment but rather because of their incapacity to work (Bernstein 2019).

## Dis/ability and work capacity in the Romanian state

The onset of industrialization brought about an increase in industrial injuries and resulted in the creation of new medical domains. Social hygiene and occupational medicine emerged as new disciplines that were devoted to improving worker health and preventing industrial injuries (Mihăilă 1971). Mihail Maurer, who was chair for the medical evaluation of work capacity at the University of Bucharest, stated that a physician's task is not only to "ensure a worker's optimal physical and mental state" but also to "contribute to the growth of productivity by utilizing man and his best performance" (Maurer 1967, p. 67).

The most common narrative in specialist literature on occupational medicine was frequently imbued with socialism's success story: in an article from 1957, the authors stated that due to "new methods, developed by medical-traumatological science in the Soviet Union," severe industrial accidents causing impairments were "hardly ever happening" (Voinea & Balenty 1957, p. 68). The intersection between medicine and labor productivity became another locus where scientists negotiated designations of dis/ability, often modeled in line with the ideal of the socialist "New Man."

Originating in Soviet Stalinist culture, the idealized figure of the able-bodied, socialist worker as male infused both political campaigns to maximize labor productivity and visual and literary works that portrayed the New Man as virile, determined, clean-cut, and square-jawed. Against this background, femininity and disability became obverse categories, denoting social inferiority (Kaganovsky 2008). The myth of the socialist New Man was thus not only haunted by the figure of the emasculated, mutilated body that questioned the very ideal of the enhanced, virile worker, but also by a purported feminization (Bernstein 2014). In this context, rehabilitation programs were conceived as a means to re-establish traditional gender roles. Even though Romanian medical literature was silent on that matter, experts implicitly reinforced labor productivity as a masculine domain. Not only were (male) war veterans and civilians with dis/abilities tacitly lumped together with the aim to uniformly incorporate these groups into production (Averbah et al. 1953); additionally, accessible professions for the dis/abled were categorized along traditional gender lines, such as carpentry for men and household chores for women (Fromm 1969).

The most critical institutional settings in which these cultural scripts were enforced were the so-called medical expert commissions for evaluating individuals' work capacity. In Romania, a central institute for the medical evaluation of work capacity and local expert commissions were founded in 1951 and fashioned after the Soviet model (Ilea et al. 1963). These bodies had the task of evaluating the degree of an individual's impairment and were staffed with experts from various medical professions (Frolova 1979). The evaluation targeted both dis/abled civilians and war veterans and fulfilled the function of justifying state-sponsored rehabilitation and compensation programs. With their medical gaze, these commissions undoubtedly had the greatest impact on the lives of the dis/abled under socialism (Bernstein 2019). Medical expert commissions were generally instructed to apply rigid criteria for classifying people with dis/abilities, which stood in sharp contrast to the official rhetoric on socialist humanism. Only those whose conditions had acquired "a permanent and constant character" were to be categorized as "invalids," "and only after the inefficiency of different treatments [had] been proven." Individuals with "temporary disabilities" and those "whose work capacity can be restored" were to be disqualified from "a premature allowance of invalid pensions" (Averbah et al., 1953, p. 9). Mihail Maurer similarly underlined that a "deficiency as such does not constitute a sufficient condition for assessing the degree of labor incapacity" (Maurer 1967, p. 63). As in the Soviet Union, the classification system for dis/abilities comprised three categories based on the criterion of how much work capacity individuals had retained (Marea Adunare Națională 1959, 1966). Category I included those who had completely lost their work capacity and needed full-time care; Category II encompassed those who were not in need of state-subsidized care; and Category III included persons whose conditions allowed a transfer to less demanding, intermittent, or reduced work. An amputation of fingers or of parts of the lower limbs, for example, was not regarded as sufficient to classify workers as "invalid" (Averbah et al. 1953, p. 22). The handbook also advised physicians on various methods to "objectively" assess whether patients were feigning their impairment. In cases where physicians doubted their patients' alleged paralysis, for example, they were instructed to position the patient in a supine position, lift his hand, and ask him to drop it slowly. If this descending movement was performed too slowly, there were no grounds to diagnose any serious paralysis (Averbah et al. 1953, p. 590).

## Work as therapy

State concerns for work capacity engendered the promotion of labor as an effective therapeutic tool. As a means of individual emancipation, it was also in line with the official rhetoric of constructing a socialist society. While rejecting charity as an erroneous, capitalist trend that allegedly prevented the dis/abled from flourishing, Soviet officials "promoted labor as the only medicine that cured the social pain of individualism in adults as well as in children" (Galmarini-Kabala 2019, p. 194). Studies published during the postwar period echoed these stances when discussing the reintegration of persons with neuropsychiatric disorders into mainstream industry. Dmitry Melekhov, a Soviet psychiatrist, wrote that "work is one of the premises of mental health. … Hence, putting the afflicted back into work after they have overcome the most acute phases of illness is of utmost importance" (Averbah et al. 1953, p. 711). With reference to congenital mental deficiencies, medical expert commissions were advised to prescribe "oligophrenics at least simple working tasks in order to enhance their work capacity and to make them socially admissible," as they otherwise would "inevitably degenerate and take a path of antisocial behavior" (Averbah et al. 1953, p. 724). Victor Săhleanu, Romania's leading medical anthropologist at the time, similarly endorsed the therapeutic benefits of work: "Education through work is essential to any pedagogical process" and "better than any medicine," he wrote in 1971. Endowing labor with a social Darwinist aura, Săhleanu defined the adjustment to working life in terms of natural selection principles: those who "do not manage to adjust [to working life] can be helped by medicine." An "eliminatory selection process" would "sort out employees through accidents, diseases, retirement, etc. and rearrange the current human tableau of professions" (Săhleanu 1971, pp. 248–250).

## Conclusion

Valeriu Mare, one of the leading defectologists in Romania, wrote in 1968 that "everything which has been done for the deficients is an act of incomparable ethical beauty and a living expression of socialist humanism" (Mare et al. 1968, p. 254). This statement reflects the utopian underpinnings of disability research in state socialism. By analyzing medical discourses, this chapter demonstrated how concepts of dis/ability were defined by scientists and how socialist understandings of labor productivity were incorporated into disability research. This is not to claim that medical science was informed by a simple determinism, as a field exclusively driven by external, ideological imperatives. Even if medicine was strongly informed by and contributed to officially sanctioned policies, it did so as medicine. Scientific discourses thus enforced distinct notions of ab/normality and helped to shape the utopian belief that disabilities can be corrected and even eradicated. Alternative denominations such as "special psychopedagogy" were brought into the discussion in the 1970s, but the field of defectology survived well into the post-socialist transition period in both Romania and other post-socialist countries. To be sure, many of the methods discussed by defectologists, such as oralism in deaf education, were not so much determined by socialist imperatives but rather part of a global trend. Attempts to "make the deaf-mutes talk" have been made since the 1800s in Romania (Baican & Ionescu 1884). Virdi (2020) and Schmidt (2020) have similarly shown how the obsession to "cure" deafness through various oralist approaches dominated Anglo-American scientific cultures during the 20th century. However, in contrast to Western, liberal societies, in socialist countries, the power and organization of the medical profession did not come under attack. While the deinstitutionalization and the disability rights movements in the West demanded community care, independent living, and accessibility since the 1960s, these claims were widely silenced in state socialist countries.

## References


Anastasiu, G., (1968). *Contribuţii la istoria învaţământului special din România: Culegere de studii*. Bucharest: Editura Didactică şi Pedagogică.

Anonymous, (1953). Să sprijinim muncitorii în lupta pentru ridicarea productivităţii muncii. *Munca*. 27 September. 1.

Averbah, A. I., et al., (1953). *Expertiza medicală a capacităţii de muncă. Studii*. Bucharest: Editura de Stat.

Baican, E. and Ionescu, N., (1884). *Noţiuni de articulaţie sau instrucţiuni pentru a face să vorbească surdo-muţii*. Bucharest: Unknown.

Bara, S. and Pop, Ş., (1962). Elemente de defectologie. In: P. Popescu-Neveanu et al., eds. *Psihologie şi pedagogie medicală, defectologie: manual pentru şcolile tehnice sanitare*. Bucharest: Editura Medicală. pp. 445–552.

Barnes, E., (2016). *The minority body: a theory of disability*. New York: Oxford University Press.

Bauman, Z., (1991). *Modernity and ambivalence*. Cambridge, UK: Polity Press.

Bernstein, F., (2014). Prosthetic promise and Potemkin limbs in late-Stalinist Russia. In: M. Rasell and E. Iarskaia-Smirnova, eds. *Disability in Eastern Europe and the former Soviet Union: history, policy and everyday life*. London: Routledge. pp. 42–66.

Bernstein, F., (2019). The history of disability during Stalinism. In: K. Boterbloem, eds. *Life in Stalin's Soviet Union*. London: Bloomsbury Academic. pp. 115–137.

Bogoiavlenski, D. N. and Mecinskaia, N. A., (1963). Psihologia învaţării. In: A. N. Leontiev et al., eds. *Psihologia în U.R.S.S.* Bucharest: Editura Ştiinţifică. pp. 495–548.

Bologa, V. L., (1972). *Istoria medicinei româneşti*. Bucharest: Editura Medicală.

Brătescu, G., (1999). *Catre sanatatea perfecta: O istorie a utopismului medical.* Bucharest: Humanitas.

Byford, A., (2018). Lechebnaia pedagogika: the concept and practice of therapy in Russian defectology, 1880–1936. *Medical History.* **62**(1), 67–90.

Canguilhem, G., (1989). *The normal and the pathological.* New York: Zone Books.

Conrad, P., (2007). *The medicalization of society: on the transformation of human conditions into treatable disorders.* Baltimore, MD: Johns Hopkins University Press.

Damaschin, D., (1968a). Defectologie: criterii orientative de cercetare şi învăţămînt. *Revista învăţământului superior.* **3**, 35–41.

Damaschin, D., (1968b). Beiträge zum Problem der Kompensation der Erblindung und zur elektronischen Modellierung des Auges. *Zeitschrift für angewandte Psychologie.* **175**(1/2), 29–53.

Damaschin, D., (1970). Orientări şi perspective în învăţămîntul special şi în cercetarea ştinţifică şi în defectologie. *Revista de pedagogie.* **1**, 94–99.

Damaschin, D., (1973). *Defectologie, teoria si practica compensatiei: Nevăzători, ambliopi, orbi-surdomuti.* Bucharest: Editura Didactica si Pedagogica.

D'iachkov, A. I., (1967). The development of Soviet defectology. *Soviet Education.* **10**(5), 44–55.

Doboş, C., (2015). Psychiatry and ideology: the emergence of "asthenic neurosis" in communist Romania. In: S. Marks and M. Savelli, eds. *Psychiatry in Communist Europe.* New York: Palgrave Macmillan. pp. 93–116.

Fieseler, B., (2014). Soviet-style welfare: the disabled soldiers of the "Great Patriotic War." In: M. Rasell and E. Iarskaia-Smirnova, eds. *Disability in Eastern Europe and the former Soviet Union: history, policy and everyday life.* London: Routledge. pp. 18–41.

Fleck, L., (1935). *Entstehung und Entwicklung einer wissenschaftlichen Tatsache. Einführung in die Lehre vom Denkstil und Denkkollektiv.* Basel: Schwabe.

Frolova, O. G., (1979). Medical labor commission of experts. In: *Great Soviet encyclopedia (1970–1979).* New York: Macmillan. Available from: https://encyclopedia2.thefreedictionary.com/Medical+Labor+Commission+of+Experts

Fromm, W., (1969). Das Blinden- und Sehschwachenbildungswesen in der Sozialistischen Republik Rumänien. *Die Gegenwart.* **23**(12), 279–281.

Galmarini-Kabala, M. C., (2016). *The right to be helped: deviance, entitlement, and the Soviet moral order.* Ithaca, NY: Cornell University Press.

Galmarini-Kabala, M. C., (2019). Between defectological narratives and institutional realities: the "mentally retarded" child in the Soviet Union of the 1930s. *Bulletin of the History of Medicine.* **93**(2), 180–206.

Grama, A., (2019). *Laboring along: industrial workers and the making of postwar Romania.* Berlin: De Gruyter Oldenbourg.

Hacking, I., (1990). *The taming of chance.* Cambridge, UK: Cambridge University Press.

Ilea, T. et al., (1963). *Invăţămîntul medical şi farmaceutic din Bucureşti.* Bucharest: Institutul de Medicină şi Farmacie.

Kaganovsky, L., (2008). *How the Soviet man was unmade: cultural fantasy and male subjectivity under Stalin.* Pittsburgh, PA: University of Pittsburgh Press.

Kreindler, A. et al., (1949). *Comemorarea savantului I.P. Pavlov.* Bucharest: Academia Republicii Populare Române.

Krementsov, N. and deJong-Lambert, W., (2017). "Lysenkoism" redux: introduction. In: W. deJong-Lambert and N. Krementsov, eds. *The Lysenko controversy as a global phenomenon, volume 1.* New York: Palgrave Macmillan. pp. 1–34.

Lubovsky, V. I., (1974). Defectology: the science of handicapped children. *International Review of Education*. **20**(3), 298–305.

Marcu, I., (1953). Aplicând metoda spitalelor raționale fruntașe din Macarovo si Vinogradov. *Munca*. 2 July. 2.

Mare, V., Popescu, G. and Sorescu, V., (1968). Unele aspecte ale dezvoltării învațămîntului special şi a defectologiei din ultimii ani. In: G. Anastasiu, ed. *Contribuţii la istoria învaţământului special din România: Culegere de studii*. Bucharest: Editura Didactică şi Pedagogică. pp. 245–254.

Marea Adunare Națională, (1954). *Legea 4/1953*. Buletinul Oficial 1. 4 January.

Marea Adunare Națională, (1959). *Decretul 292/1959*. Buletinul Oficial 20. 10 August.

Marea Adunare Națională, (1966). *Legea 27/1966*. Monitorul Oficial. 1 January.

Marea Adunare Națională, (1969). *Decretul 493/1969*. Buletinul Oficial 77. 14 July.

Marks, S. and Savelli, M., eds., (2015). *Psychiatry in Communist Europe*. New York: Palgrave Macmillan.

Maurer, M., (1967). *Expertiza medicală și recuperarea capacității de muncă*. Bucharest: Editura Medicală.

McCagg, W., (1989). The origins of defectology. In: W. O. McCagg and L. Siegelbaum, eds. *The disabled in the Soviet Union*. Pittsburgh, PA: University of Pittsburgh Press. pp. 39–62.

Mihăilă, I., (1971). Dezvoltarea cercetărilor de fiziologia muncii în institutul de igienă și sănătate publică din Bucureşti. In: G. Brătescu, ed. *Din trecutul medicinii muncii în România: Comunicări și note*. Bucharest: Editura medicală. pp. 241–246.

Milcu, Ş. M., (1962). Îndrumarea ştiinţei în Republica Populară Romînă de către Partidul Muncitoresc Romîn. In: V. Bologa et al., eds. *Din istoria medicinii romîneşti şi universale*. Bucharest: Editura Academiei. pp. 505–513.

Oghina-Pavie, C., (2017). The national pattern of Lysenkoism in Romania. In: W. deJong-Lambert and N. Krementsov, eds. *The Lysenko controversy as a global phenomenon, volume 2*. New York: Palgrave Macmillan. pp. 73–102.

Păcuraru, I., (1966). Cu privire la munca productivă şi neproductivă în socialism. *Lupta de Clasă*. **5**(12), 57–69.

Păunescu, C., (1973). *Limbaj şi intellect*. Bucharest: Editura Ştiinţifică.

Peteanu, M., (1961). Manifestări nevrotice la copii legate de greşeli de educaţie. *Probleme de Defectologie și Psihopatologie*. **2**, 121–165.

Petrovici, N. and Faje, F., (2019). Sociological approaches to work in Romania since 1945. In: P. Stewart et al., eds. *The Palgrave handbook of the sociology of work in Europe*. New York: Palgrave Macmillan. pp. 347–383.

Popescu-Neveanu, P. et al., (1962). *Psihologie şi pedagogie medicală, defectologie: Manual pentru şcolile tehnice sanitare*. Bucharest: Editura Medicală.

Pufan, C., (1966). Aspecte ale operaţiilor de analiză şi sinteză logică la surdomutul în curs de Demutizare. *Probleme de defectologie*. **5**, 197–124.

Roşan, A., (2015). *Psihopedagogie specială: Modele de evaluare şi intervenţie*. Bucharest: Polirom.

Roşca, A., (1931). *Debilitatea mintala: aspectul psihologic, pedagogic și social al problemei copiilor debili mintali*. Bucharest: Editura Instit. de Psihologie al Universitatii.

Roșca, A., (1932). *Delincventul minor*. Bucharest: Editura Instit. de Psihologie al Universitatii.

Săhleanu, V., (1971). Medicina Muncii ca medicină antropologică. In: G. Brătescu, ed. *Din trecutul medicinii muncii în România: comunicări și note*. Bucharest: Editura medicală. pp. 247–250.

Săhleanu, V., (1976a). *Mică enciclopedie de biologie şi medicină: concepte, concepţii, controverse*. Bucharest: Editura ştiinţifică şi enciclopedică.

Săhleanu, V., (1976b). *Concepţii despre om în medicina contemporană*. Bucharest: Dacia.

Schmidt, M. A., (2020). *Eradicating deafness? Genetics, pathology, and diversity in twentieth-century America*. Manchester, UK: Manchester University Press.

Siebers, T., (2008). *Disability theory*. Ann Arbor, MI: University of Michigan Press.

Siegelbaum, L. H., (1988). *Stakhanovism and the politics of productivity in the USSR, 1935–1941*. Cambridge, UK: Cambridge University Press.

Sorescu, V., (1968). Dimitrie Rusticeanu, înaintaş de frunte al defectologiei Româneşti. In: G. Anastasiu et al., eds. *Contribuţii la istoria învaţământului special din România: Culegere de Studii*. Bucharest: Editura Didactică şi Pedagogică. pp. 165–195.

Starks, T., (2008). *The body Soviet: propaganda, hygiene, and the revolutionary state*. Madison, WI: University of Wisconsin Press.

Stepanova, M. A., (2018). Pedagogika iskljuchitel'nogo detstva V.P. Kashhenko: k 110-letiju Sanatorija-shkoly dlja defektivnyh detej v zavedyvanii doktora V.P. Kashhenko. *Klinicheskaja i special'naja psihologija*. **7**(3), 1–23.

Turda, M., (2020). Subversive affinities: embracing Soviet science in late 1940s Romania. *Studies in History and Philosophy of Science: Part C, Studies in History and Philosophy of Biological and Biomedical Sciences*. **83**, 1–8.

Velt, R., (1953). *Învăţătura lui I. P. Pavlov în medicina teoretică şi practică*. Bucharest: Editura de Stat pentru Literatură Ştiinţifică.

Virdi, J., (2020). *Hearing happiness: deafness cures in history*. Chicago: University of Chicago Press.

Voinea, A. and Balenty, P. V., (1957). Prevenirea şi tratamentul de urgenţă al traumatismelor în indistria grea. *Viaţa Medicală*. **2**(6), 68–78.

Vygotsky, L. et al., (1993). *The collected works of L.S. Vygotsky: the fundamentals of defectology (abnormal psychology and learning disabilities, Vol. 2)*. New York: Plenum.

Wright, P. and Treacher, A., eds., (1982). *The problem of medical knowledge: examining the social construction of medicine*. Edinburgh: Edinburgh University Press.

# 6 Embodied Inequalities: Intersections of Dis/abilities and Gender in West Germany (1950–1990)

*Sebastian Schlund*

During the four decades of the Bonn Republic, i.e., the Federal Republic of West Germany before reunification, the everyday life and social integration of dis/abled people undoubtedly improved in many aspects. Discrimination against dis/abled people at the legal and political level, in professional life, and in the areas of education and leisure activities decreased. Architectural barriers were dismantled, and the accommodation of most mentally handicapped people in separate institutions, which was often characterized by structural and physical violence, was reduced. At the time of German reunification, people with dis/abilities had more chances to participate in all fields of social life as opposed to the immediate postwar period. All these observations are truisms, they cannot surprise anyone who has even briefly studied the history of dis/ability in Germany. All these observations are at the same time undifferentiated and inherently normative: they also hint at the specificity of dis/ability history as a discipline committed to both activism and knowledge production. Yet, it is not the task of academic dis/ability history to write a biased success story that glosses over fractures, contradictions, and the simultaneity of change and continuity (Lingelbach 2019).

Therefore, this chapter will focus on disparities, frictions, and unequal treatment, on internal hierarchies among people with dis/abilities, and also on the transformations that shaped the history of dis/abled people in the Federal Republic.

Using an intersectional approach, I argue that both the privileges of certain groups of dis/abled people, the lasting discrimination of others, and the rhythm of incremental juridical and societal transformations can be more precisely understood if the interrelation of dis/ability with other identity markers such as gender is integrated into the analysis. By applying an intersectional lens to the contemporary history of dis/ability in West Germany, the factors triggering and driving, as well as hindering change, can be identified and explained. However, an all-encompassing intersectional analysis of all groups of dis/abled persons in all periods will not be carried out. Rather, in order to accentuate the analytical benefit of an intersectional lens, it is applied where it best explains hierarchies,

DOI: 10.4324/9781003257196-8

continuities, and change, i.e., where interdependencies of the various categories are particularly significant. Intersectional analysis is appropriate where debates on the social status of certain groups of dis/abled persons were debates on gender hierarchies or on notions of virility or gendered bodily aesthetics.

This chapter—based mainly on historical research and following a roughly chronological order—first focuses on war-dis/abled men, who assumed their relatively privileged status owing to their gender and the cause of their impairment. They formed the most influential group of dis/abled persons during the period under review. Next, the chapter critically reviews later emotionally charged public debate in the context of the thalidomide scandal as well as processes of societal transformation in the 1960s and 70s, which brought about new ways of assessing the living conditions of formerly neglected groups of dis/abled persons, namely physically dis/abled children and women. Analyzing contemporary discourses on both groups highlights the importance of accounting for the specific interdependence of dis/ability and youth, as well as of dis/ability and prevalent notions of gender (roles). The last part of the chapter revolves around explaining why people with intellectual dis/abilities lacked a powerful lobby, focusing on the specific impact of the diagnosis of mental impairment as a type of dis/ability. I conclude by showing how an intersectional approach can explain most, but not all contemporary hierarchies, structures of social prejudice, and amplitudes of public awareness of the complex phenomena of dis/ability.

## Intersectionality, intracategorial and intercategorial complexity

Intersectional analysis aims at investigating the simultaneous interaction of forms of discrimination such as racism, sexism, or—with reference to the category of dis/ability—ableism. After intersectional perspectives were initially taken up in the study and teaching of law in North America (Crenshaw 1989), it has not only crossed geographical but also disciplinary borders. In Germany, Sociology and the emerging field of Gender Studies were among the first disciplines to integrate intersectionality into their analytical tool kit. As a result, and in contrast to the Anglophone academic sphere, German intersectionality research is characterized by a focus on gender rather than on race. This also applies to the recent adaption of intersectionality in German historiography (Bähr & Kühnel 2018; Schnicke 2014). A steadily growing number of publications on questions of which and how many categories should be included in historical case studies (Winker & Degener 2009) and the interconnectedness of micro- and macro-level foci ultimately spawned a trend toward applying intersectional methodology to primary source material.

As a sub-discipline heavily influenced by sociologically inspired Disability Studies, German Disability History was at the forefront of this recent methodological change of perspective. Several publications in Disability History have already committed to an intersectional approach (Jacob et al. 2010; Raab 2007; Schlund 2017). Through these and other studies, it has become clear that intersectional analyses of dis/ability in both current and historical contexts must first address the variances and differentiations that are obscured by the catch-all term dis/ability. Second, it is important to relate dis/ability to further categories of inequality in order to paint a more detailed picture of mechanisms of both discrimination and privilege. To put it in terms of intersectional theory formation, *Intra- and inter*categorial complexities shape the sometimes highly different experiences of dis/ability depending on the social and temporal context.

According to Leslie McCall, intracategorial complexity refers to the distinctions and internal differentiations within a group of people who share the same category of inequality (McCall 2005). Transferred to the field of contemporary Disability History, an intracategorial lens offers the possibility of interrogating the supposed collective of "dis/abled people" in a much more precise and nuanced way.

This study will demonstrate that two intracategorial factors greatly shaped the self-image of dis/abled Germans as well as their opportunities of social participation and eligibility for welfare state benefits: the cause of impairment and the type of impairment. As far as the cause of the impairment is concerned, a distinction can be made between war-dis/abled and—in contemporary terms—"dis/abled civilians." Civil dis/abilities include several phenomena such as physical, mental, or psychological impairment since birth or resulting from an accident or an illness. However, the dichotomy of war injury and civil dis/ability was the main cause for the unequal treatment of persons with dis/abilities in the legal sphere and for identity-related self-perceptions that continued well into the 1970s. In terms of the type of impairment, there was a sharp dividing line between physically and mentally impaired persons who had differing opportunities of social integration and participation. People with mental impairment had and still have a much harder time being included on an equal footing at school, in the labor market, or in autonomous organization of leisure time activities.

These specific hierarchies shaped through intracategorial complexity can be understood more precisely by taking into account the *inter*categorial relation of the categories gender and dis/ability. Both constructions of masculinity and of femininity were renegotiated through their interplay with ableism. Those negotiations played out through discourses strongly related to the body of dis/abled people and aimed at aesthetics associated with predominant concepts of gender roles. Contemporarily, a group of female authors pointed out this interdependence through the apt title "Gender: Disabled, Special Characteristic: Woman" (Boll et al. 1985). Together, three factors—the cause of impairment, type of impairment, and gender—created complex, only slowly changing structures of privilege and discrimination that shaped the lived experiences of people with dis/abilities, as will be shown in the following sub-chapters focused on the design of labor market policy, the welfare state, and leisure time activities.

## Honorary Germans? War-dis/abled men in postwar Germany

In relation to all three of these areas, war-dis/abled men were very privileged in the first two decades after the war. We may well ask what explains this hegemony given that dis/abled veterans were a symbol for the "lost" war of a regime that no longer existed.

The most obvious reason for this phenomenon is the size of the group of war-dis/abled men, whose 1.5 million members represented more than two-thirds of all dis/abled persons in a 1950 census (Rudloff 2005). Because of their numbers alone, no government could afford to disregard the wishes of this considerable group of voters. Second, war-dis/abled men were almost exclusively of working age. Owing to their age and their privileged access to rehabilitation programs, they were comparatively quickly available for the labor market and hence for economic reconstruction—in contrast to dis/abled children or dis/abled women, for example. Finally, women at that time—regardless of whether they were dis/abled or not—were much less likely to be employed than they are today. And integration into the labor force was regarded as the primary goal of social policy governing people with dis/abilities: those who returned to work were characterized as useful members of society and not as a burden on the state's welfare and pensions system (Lingelbach 2020). Thus, the slogan "work instead of pension" was linked to a utilitarian cost-benefit calculation. Moreover, in the first postwar decades, the assumption was widespread that social integration of dis/abled persons was best achieved through labor.

Another factor was the so-called "Aufopferungstatbestand" or personal sacrifice. State policy toward dis/abled persons was characterized by the principle that war-dis/abled men were entitled to preferential treatment because they had made an all too personal sacrifice for their country, albeit one that had embraced fascism. As a result, there was a consensus among the state bureaucracy and all major parties that war injuries should be accorded a higher "moral value" than civil dis/abilities (Rudloff 2003). Remarkably, however, the act of sacrifice alone was not enough to classify the war-dis/abled as "honorary citizens of the nation," (*Ehrenbürger der Nation*) as a contemporary term put it (Löffelbein 2013). This required an extraordinary kind of determination: only those dis/abled veterans who—in the understanding of the time—compensated for their "deficiencies" through increased effort and did not make themselves comfortable at the expense of the state were deserving not only of financial aid but also moral recognition by society (Rudloff 2003).

In his dissertation on interest organizations of dis/abled people in the Federal Republic, Jan Stoll dealt extensively with identity formation among highly influential associations of war victims (*Kriegsopferverbände*). In the 1950s, they continually advocated that privileged entry to the labor market through quotas should only be granted to war-dis/abled people (Stoll 2017). Additionally, they were not only active as lobby groups, but they offered war-dis/abled men a feeling of community, comradeship, and mutual assistance as they struggled with the psychological consequences of war and with the contradiction of being both a physical symbol of the traumatic war and, potentially, a "honorary citizen of the nation." In addition, they saw themselves as men who did not conform to the prevailing physical standards of masculinity. Their group identity was fed first by their experiences of wartime and its aftermath with which they had to cope together, but second by their dissociation from people with civil dis/abilities. Thus, one association exclusively composed of war victims stated in 1952: "what created and holds our community together, the common experience of wartime deployment and military comradeship" could not be shared with "pathetic" dis/abled civilians (Stoll 2017, p. 56).

The discrimination against civilian dis/abled people by war-dis/abled men was particularly manifest in leisure activities. Numerous clubs for dis/abled sports founded after the war were almost exclusively communities of dis/abled veterans. In a doubly homosocial sphere, they not only cultivated their camaraderie but also made themselves physically fit for work. They also confirmed their persisting masculinity and unbroken virility through athleticism. As a result, many war-dis/abled men associated a specific image of masculinity with their equally specific form of impairment in order to compensate for their dis/ability. One result of this connection was their self-identification as a kind of elite among the dis/abled. As the chairman of the Essen dis/abled athletes, Ernst Dieckhöfer, expressed in 1962 (Dieckhöfer 1962): "We athletes have to be the elite among the dis/abled, in stark contrast to the miserable, dubious cripples who display their injured limbs and are to be found as beggars on the streets or as antisocial people at night at the train station" (p. 172). Dieckhöfer was alluding to typical prejudices against dis/abled people, who as "beggars" burdened society. This quote also makes particularly clear the interrelation between contemporary ideas of dis/ability as a personal deficit that is to be compensated for by performance and will, and the preferential treatment by the state that one has to earn through the strength of character.

Between the 1960s and the founding of the Federal Republic of Germany in 1990, a combination of the cause of impairment and concepts of gender—in this case, an ideal of masculinity—defined the internal hierarchy of the entire group of dis/abled people. War-dis/abled men's privileges, hence, resulted from both an intracategorial distinction and a patriarchy focused on maintaining traditional gender roles. The fact that up to this point my narrative has focused but little on civilian dis/abled persons in general and dis/abled women and children or mentally dis/abled people in particular relates to the circumstances of the time: their concerns hardly ever appeared in the debates about the rights and needs of dis/abled people.

## The thalidomide transformation

When and why were the fault lines that split the group of dis/abled people into privileged or marginalized subgroups abolished or at least diminished (Lingelbach & Waldschmidt 2016)? There is broad agreement among German Disability Historians that this phase is to be located between the late 1960s and the mid-1970s. This period includes, for example, the harmonization of state benefits for the rehabilitation of war-dis/abled and civilian dis/abled persons regarding welfare and care policy. It was no longer the cause of the impairment that was decisive for the granting of support, but the individual goal of rehabilitation (Bösl 2016). Second, the state intensified efforts to improve the education of dis/abled children and teenagers to improve their position in the job market: an expansion of special schools was followed by the establishment of a nationwide system of special training centers for (nearly) all groups of dis/abled people (Rudloff 2006). Third, the representation of the interests of dis/abled people began to transform significantly. Demographic changes shifted the quantitative weight of the overall group of dis/abled people away from the war-dis/abled to younger, civilian dis/abled people. The latter also felt that they were not adequately represented by the traditional war victims' associations. They established their own clubs and focused on a more vigorous form of criticism, targeting various forms of social discrimination in everyday life, such as architectural barriers. This marked the beginning of a protest movement of dis/abled people in the mold of New Social Movements that became increasingly visible to the public over the next two decades (Stoll 2017). Further, accelerating change affected recreational activities. In educational institutions for (mostly young) dis/abled people, they demanded more self-determination and scope for shaping their leisure time (Lingelbach & Stoll 2013).

This remarkable accumulation of processes of change in different spheres of society, all of which were aimed at reducing intracategorial inequality and the social integration of dis/abled people, had several causes. A general climate of social change and of protesting traditional hierarchies was prevalent in the Federal Republic, as in many other "Western" countries. This general climate also affected debates on improving the everyday life of all people with dis/abilities in Germany. From 1969 onward, this atmosphere of social transformation met with a government that for the first time was not led by the Christian-conservative CDU, but by a coalition of Social Democrats and Liberals. This coalition government was open to the dismantling of rigid hierarchies and generally oriented its social policy to the needs of formerly marginalized groups of people. These included those people with dis/abilities who had been disadvantaged in the previous 20 years because of the cause and type of their impairment and their gender.

The third and probably most powerful reason for the extraordinary culmination of transformational developments was the thalidomide scandal which for many years had already affected political decision-makers, the media, and the attitudes of the non-dis/abled majority society toward dis/ability for several years. The sleeping pill Contergan containing the ingredient thalidomide had been distributed by the pharmaceutical company Grünenthal from 1957 onward, and caused—when taken by pregnant mothers—"malformations" of limbs and internal organs in their children. In Germany, prenatal exposure to the drug affected between 4,000 and 5,000 children, of whom no more than 3,000 survived the first months of life (Crumbach 2018).

The thalidomide scandal became public in 1962 and had a profound impact on both the living conditions of dis/abled people and on public awareness of dis/abled persons in general. The latter can be illustrated by the creation of *Aktion Sorgenkind*. It was founded in 1964 by the state-run television station ZDF as a mixture of state lottery and charity organization. Extremely popular quiz and entertainment shows on ZDF were devoted entirely to advertising the *Aktion Sorgenkind* campaign, thus bringing its work into the living rooms of a population that had previously hardly been concerned by the topic of dis/ability. The work of *Aktion Sorgenkind* became a wake-up call that alerted people to the neglect of dis/abled people themselves and their parents or families. Accompanying brochures pointed out the lack of infrastructure for dis/abled people from nurseries and attendance at special schools to support in vocational training and finally in taking up a job (Lingelbach 2010). Despite the announcement that the primary aim of the campaign was to generate empathy rather than pity, *Aktion Sorgenkind* certainly relied on the emotional, sympathetic approach of the population. The very name of the organization indicates that already *Sorgenkind* roughly translates as "child that causes worries and requires special care." Thus, the impact of the thalidomide scandal on public consciousness was so severe because the category of dis/ability was linked to the category of age—in this case, youth. There can be no doubt that the age and vulnerability of children impaired by thalidomide triggered an emotional response from large parts of the population.

While the 1960s was a period in which public attention was generated by the scandal criticism of it did not yield change for dis/abled youth until the turn of the 1970s. The "thalidomide children" were now at an age where they would be expected to go to school, join a sports club, and in the foreseeable future they would be trained for a profession. Consequently, it was at this moment that the thalidomide issue combined with social and political climate change to produce changing perception of what it meant to be dis/abled. Dis/ability was no longer associated just with men or with wartime injuries. Dis/ability was now understood as the pitiful fate of children, caused not by war, but by a sleeping pill. This change in meaning, which can hardly be overestimated in its effect, contributed significantly to increasing recognition of the diversity of dis/abled people. Likewise, their needs and those of other people with dis/abilities would no longer be interpreted solely on the basis of the cause of their impairment.

## Dis/abled housewives: impairment, gender, and the body

Historical change rarely occurs simultaneously and uniformly for all groups of people. An intersectional lens, especially a combined intra- *and* intercategorial one, enables us to adequately grasp and explain the complexity of social inequality. In Federal Germany, the marginalized social position of dis/abled women was determined not only by the category of dis/ability but also by the category of gender. Therefore, a detailed analysis of how change came about for dis/abled women can only be achieved by an intercategorial analysis of the transformation of gender ideology and the changes in the perception of dis/ability.

The first two postwar decades of Federal German gender history have been described as a phase of conflict-laden, gradual change in gender roles that affected only certain areas of life. The rising absolute number of employed women should not hide the fact that the growth rates were primarily in poorly paid positions in the service sector. This imbalance was also cemented by the establishment of part-time jobs for women and sprang from the image of the housewife and child-raiser that prevailed during this period, although it was eroding. Although part-time work was considered a possible, progressive solution to the problems for women of balancing family and career, the model of the male breadwinner as provider remained in place.

The structural disadvantaging of women and the discrimination of dis/abled people—i.e., sexism and ableism—were particularly strongly linked in those areas where the prevailing distinction of gender roles was questioned. For example, all measures of vocational integration during this period were not only aimed at the war-dis/abled but also directed exclusively at men (Bösl 2009). The seeds of transformation which afforded non-dis/abled women more autonomy, self-determination and equality, did not yet affect dis/abled women.

Whereas dis/abled men in the 1950s and 1960s were expected to fill the role of being the sole breadwinner, dis/abled women's roles (like those of able-bodied women) were generally associated with staying at home and looking after the household. Consequently, the physical impairment of dis/abled women was identified as particularly crucial. An article from 1954 described the connection between "typical" gender roles and the "problem" that dis/abled women represented in a striking way. Published in *Der Versehrtensportler*, the monthly journal of the Sports Association for the Disabled, the author raised several evocative questions (Inhauser 1954): "How should this woman and with her all the other dis/abled women do their housework? Can one afford domestic help with these income levels? Should those men who have a handicapped wife bear these additional social burdens alone?" (p. 2). Viewed in this gendered fashion, the physical impairment of women is represented as rendering her incapable of fulfilling her housewifely duties, but also as an additional (financial) burden on the husband. It is also noteworthy that the chapter was explicitly intended as an advertisement, encouraging dis/abled women to take up sports. In contrast to dis/abled men, women were not supposed to get in shape for their job, but for their function as housewives, which was obviously considered a natural role.

The two categories of dis/ability and gender do not merely reinforce each other, they intersect, resulting in a specific form of discrimination. This becomes particularly clear when body images, ideals of beauty, and aesthetic concepts are included in the analysis. The outward appearance of dis/abled women whose bodies do not conform to a supposed norm is central to understanding the interrelation between dis/ability and gender. Dis/abled women were assumed to be less attractive than non-dis/abled women. Therefore, they were expected to have difficulties finding a husband, let alone a non-dis/abled one (Die versehrte Frau 1951). Accordingly, a dis/abled woman was considered less of a woman than their able-bodied counterparts. Authors from the decidedly feminist branch of the German dis/ability movement alluded to this fact as early as the 1970s by contending that dis/abled girls were confronted with a "non-recognition of their femininity." They learned "they will not be 'real women,' that they are not beautiful and desirable, and that the classic female role as partner and mother is, for them, out of the question" (Köbsell 2007, p. 33).

The fact that the body of dis/abled women was under special scrutiny throughout the entire period under study indicates that the change in stereotypes for this specific group of dis/abled persons took on a rhythm of its own and was characterized by the interdependence of ideas of dis/ability and femininity. As early as 1951, one (female) author "drew attention to the importance of aesthetic body preservation" and stated that "innate female vanity" should not tolerate "letting body and soul degenerate" (Die versehrte Frau 1951, p. 3). When dis/abled women became more numerous and visible in dis/abled sports in the early 1970s, inspired by social trends of liberalization and emancipation, many men reacted with mockery, arguing, the "deficient" bodies of dis/abled women should not be displayed in public. If dis/abled women were to participate in sports events at all, they should do so in "typical" women's sports such as dancing or gymnastics. Moreover, observers were surprised that dis/abled women took part in swimming competitions even though this destroyed their carefully arranged hairstyles (Schlund 2017). Ableist and sexist stereotypes therefore converged in the assessment of the dis/abled female body, resulting in a particularly persistent formula of intersectional discrimination.

## Those who had no lobby: persons with mental impairment

The intercategorial interaction of dis/ability and gender had even more serious consequences for mentally impaired females. Britta-Marie Schenk's research on genetic counseling in Germany shows that people with intellectual dis/abilities were deprived of reproductive self-determination in the Bonn Republic. This fundamental right was denied to them by medical experts and their own parents because of their cognitive impairment. Often the parents of mentally dis/abled girls and women decided to sterilize their daughters without their knowledge or consent (Schenk 2016).

From an intersectional point of view and in this historical context, the relationship between physical and mental impairment and between the women's movement and the movement for the dis/abled is particularly compelling. For while the women's movement celebrated the legal milestone of winning the right to abortion up to the 12th week as a triumph of women's self-determination (1976), large parts of the dis/ability rights movement, which was dominated by physically dis/abled persons, protested. Rather than acknowledging abortion as a step toward the equality of women, they saw the danger of women aborting a dis/abled child after receiving a prenatal diagnosis. Particularly radical-thinking members among the advocates of dis/ability rights, who provocatively called themselves the "cripple movement," even interpreted the right to abortion as a memento of National Socialist eugenics. As they viewed it, more than 30 years after the war, a fatal distinction could again be made between worthy and unworthy lives (Schenk 2019).

In these debates, the people least represented were those whom it primarily concerned: people with mental impairment. Here, as in previous decades, it became clear that, compared to physically dis/abled people, they had much less power to shape their own lives, less right to self-determination and less of an opportunity to form a political interest group. Both medical experts and the state degraded people with mental impairment to second-class citizens, owing to their perceived lack of intellectual capability. All transformations and improvements in the living conditions of dis/abled people in the Federal Republic benefited people with intellectual dis/abilities after a considerable delay or not at all. While the school system was opened and expanded for physically dis/abled children, mentally dis/abled children remained in separate institutions. While the general labor market was made more accessible for physically dis/abled young adults, their mentally dis/abled peers had to remain in isolated facilities. While more and more physically handicapped people in sports clubs practiced the sports they enjoyed most, there was an ongoing debate about whether mentally handicapped people understood the basics of competitive sports at all (Schlund 2017). The fact that the Special Olympics, founded in the United States as early as 1968, did not come to reunited Germany until the early 1990s reveals the existence of an isolated parallel world in which this most disadvantaged group of dis/abled people lived—and in some respect is still living.

Since 1958, the *Lebenshilfe für das geistig behinderte Kind* (literally *Life Aid for the Mentally Impaired Child*) has been working to combat the social isolation of mentally handicapped people in all spheres of public life. The association was founded by affected parents as a self-help organization that fought against the persistent prejudices that both non-dis/abled and physically impaired people continued to cultivate toward mentally dis/abled people. The Lebenshilfe still exists today and has contributed a great deal to the reduction of prejudices against mentally dis/abled people over the past decades (Stoll 2017). However, against the backdrop of the continuing discrimination and separation of this group of people most affected by negative attitudes, and notwithstanding the undisputed achievements of the association, the history of ambivalence toward mentally dis/abled people in the Federal Republic persisted (Schenk 2019).

## Conclusion

The example of mentally dis/abled persons shows that a singular success story of the integration of dis/abled people in the Federal Republic of Germany cannot be narrated (Lingelbach 2020). Moreover, this case is a reminder that *dis/ability* is less the medical diagnosis of physical or mental impairment than the dis/ability of self-determination, of successfully voicing protest and forming an interest group, of working toward the removal of structural and mental barriers, of eventually improving one's recognition and position in society. An intersectional analysis of these capacities for change making reveals they are contingent on the interacting factors of the cause of the impairment, the type of impairment, and gender. Privileges for certain groups of dis/abled persons, and the ongoing discrimination against others, in the Bonn Republic were very much based on the social construction of both gender and the specific evaluations of war-dis/ability, civil dis/ability, and mental dis/ability. Further, the bodies of the persons affected by these hierarchizations not only carried symbolic meaning but also were visible markers of status: the bodies of dis/abled veterans were reminders of the war, and at the same time functioned as symbols of reconstruction in the context of utilitarian rehabilitation programs. Demonstrations of unbroken physical ability through sports pertained to both notions of "overcoming" dis/ability as well as prevalent images of masculinity. Bodies of physically impaired women were assessed along the lines of contemporary beauty ideals, while the bodies of mentally impaired women became objects of discussions on reproductive control. All these intricate linkages point at the strong interdependency of social construction and embodiment—one does not work without the other.

With regards to the methodology applied in this chapter, it is only through the intracategorial distinction between the war-dis/abled and the civilian dis/abled and through the link to hegemonic notions of masculinity that the privilege of war-dis/abled men in the first two postwar decades could be deciphered. And it is only through the inclusion of body-related images of femininity that the special form of the long-lasting discrimination of physically dis/abled women can be explained. In both cases, it was persistent and only slowly changing gender roles that contributed to the internal hierarchy within the overall group of dis/abled people. Both cases also demonstrate that the interplay of dis/ability and gender can contribute to the constitution of privileges and the formation of a specific form of discrimination. Therefore, it should not be forgotten that the analysis of social inequality does not only include the explanation of discrimination but also the explanation of privilege. These layers of intricate hierarchies could only be revealed through combining intracategorial distinctions of type and cause of impairment with prevalent gender images. Therefore, intersections of dis/abilities and gender had to be put into relation with other aspects of identity.

Moreover, historical analyses have to take into account the coincidence (in both meanings of the word) of different, initially unrelated phenomena ultimately contributing to change, as was the case with the thalidomide scandal, the changing demographics of dis/abled persons, and the political tidal change of the late 1960s and early 1970s. The previously rigid internal hierarchies of the group of dis/abled people would therefore not have been destabilized at this rate without external impulses. For formerly marginalized people with dis/abilities in the Federal Republic, change occurred only through interaction with coalition partners from outside their own peer group—however significant the contribution of the dis/ability movement may have been.

Such findings, sometimes pointing at the contradictions inherent in the self-empowering activism of feminist movements and dis/ability rights groups, as seen by debates on abortion and prenatal diagnostics, remain to be discussed in further research projects. Whereas in the early days of German Disability History, conclusions on embodied inequalities at the intersection of dis/ability, gender, and age were a mere by-product of pioneering empirical research, an intersectional methodology has now become a systematic approach, a vantage point from which a more nuanced understanding of contemporary dis/ability history can be achieved.

## References


Anonymous, (1951). Die versehrte Frau. *Der Versehrtensportler*. **1**, 3.

Bähr, M. and Kühnel, F., eds., (2018). *Verschränkte Ungleichheit: Praktiken der Intersektionalität in der Frühen Neuzeit*. Berlin: Duncker & Hublot.

Boll, S. et al., (1985). *Geschlecht: behindert, besonderes Merkmal: Frau: Ein Buch von behinderten Frauen*. Munich: AG-SPAK-Publ.

Bösl, E., (2009). *Politiken der Normalisierung. Zur Geschichte der Behindertenpolitik in der Bundesrepublik Deutschland*. Bielefeld, Germany: Transcript.

Bösl, E., (2016). Die Geschichte der Behindertenpolitik in der Bundesrepublik aus Sicht der Disability History. *Aus Politik und* Zeitgeschichte. **23**(2010), 6–12.

Crenshaw, K. W., (1989). Demarginalizing the intersection of race and sex: a black feminist critique of antidiscrimination doctrine, feminist theory and antiracist politics. *Chicago University Legal Forum*. **40**(1), 139–167.

Crumbach, A. H., (2018). *Sprechen über Contergan. Zum diskursiven Umgang von Medizin. Presse und Politik mit Contergan in den 1960er Jahren*. Bielefeld, Germany: Transcript.

Dieckhöfer, E., (1962). Hier spricht der VSG-Vorsitzende als einer für viele! *Der Versehrtensportler*. **11**, 172–173.

Inhauser, L., (1954). " … und da warf er eine Handgranate": Erste Sportkur für versehrte Frauen in Isny. *Der Versehrtensportler*. **6**, 2.

Jacob, J., Köbsell, S. and Wollrad, E., eds., (2010). *Gendering Disability: Aspekte von Behinderung und Geschlecht*. Bielefeld, Germany: Transcript.

Köbsell, S., (2007). Behinderung und Geschlecht. Versuch einer vorläufigen Bilanz aus Sicht der deutschen Behindertenbewegung. In: J. Jutta and E. Wollrad, eds. *Behinderung und Geschlecht. Perspektiven in Theorie und Praxis Dokumentation einer Tagung*. Oldenburg, Germany: BIS-Verlag. pp. 31–49.

Lingelbach, G., (2010). Konstruktionen von 'Behinderung' in der Öffentlichkeitsarbeit und Spendenwerbung der Aktion Sorgenkind seit 1964. In: E. Bösl, A. Klein and A. Waldschmidt, eds. *Disability History. Konstruktionen von Behinderung in der Geschichte. Eine Einführung*. Bielefeld, Germany: Transcript. pp. 127–150.

Lingelbach, G., (2019). Der Stand der Forschung zur Geschichte von Menschen mit Behinderungen in Deutschland. *Geschichte in Wissenschaft und Unterricht*. **70**(H. 1/2), 5–21.

Lingelbach, G., (2020). Die Entwicklung der bundesrepublikanischen Gesundheitsfürsorge für Menschen mit Behinderungen in intersektionaler Perspektive. *Medizin, Gesellschaft und Geschichte*. **38**, 105–126.

Lingelbach, G. and Stoll, J., (2013). Die 1970er Jahre als Umbruchsphase der bundesrepublikanischen disability history? Eine Mikrostudie zu Selbstadvokation und Anstaltskritik Jugendlicher mit Behinderung. *Moving the Social*. **50**, 25–52.

Lingelbach, G. and Waldschmidt, A., (2016). Einleitung. In: G. Lingelbach and A. Waldschmidt, eds. *Kontinuitäten, Zäsuren, Brüche? Lebenslagen von Menschen mit Behinderungen in der deutschen Zeitgeschichte*. Frankfurt am Main: Campus. pp. 7–27.

Löffelbein, N., (2013). *Ehrenbürger der Nation. Die Kriegsbeschädigten des Ersten Weltkriegs in Politik und Propaganda des Nationalsozialismus*. Essen, Germany: Klartext.

McCall, L., (2005). The complexity of intersectionality. *Signs*. 30(3), 1771–1800.

Raab, H., (2007). Intersektionalität in den Disability studies. Zur Interdependenz von Behinderung, Heteronormativität und Geschlecht. In: A. Waldschmidt and W. Schneider, eds. *Disability studies, Kultursoziologie und Soziologie der Behinderung. Erkundungen in einem neuen Forschungsfeld*. Bielefeld, Germany: Transcript. pp. 127–148.

Rudloff, W., (2003). Überlegungen zur Geschichte der bundesdeutschen Behindertenpolitik. *Zeitschrift für Sozialreform*. **6**, 863–886.

Rudloff, W., (2005). Rehabilitation und Hilfen für Behinderte. In: G. Schulz, ed. *Bundesrepublik Deutschland 1949–1957. Bewältigung der Kriegsfolgen, Rückkehr zur sozialpolitischen Normalität*. Baden-Baden, Germany: Nomos. pp. 515–557.

Rudloff, W., (2006). Rehabilitation und Hilfen für Behinderte. In: H. G. Hockerts, ed. *Bundesrepublik Deutschland 1966–1974. Eine Zeit vielfältigen Aufbruchs*. Baden-Baden, Germany: Nomos. pp. 559–590.

Schenk, B.-M., (2016). *Behinderung verhindern. Humangenetische Beratungspraxis in der Bundesrepublik Deutschland (1960er bis 1990er Jahre)*. Frankfurt am Main: Campus.

Schenk, B.-M., (2019). Selbstbestimmte Fortpflanzung? Behinderung und Geschlecht in der Bundesrepublik. *Geschichte in Wissenschaft und Unterricht*. **70**(1/2), 71–87.

Schlund, S., (2017). *Behinderung' überwinden. Organisierter Behindertensport in der Bundesrepublik Deutschland (1950–1990)*. Frankfurt am Main: Campus.

Schnicke, F., (2014). Terminologie, Erkenntnisinteresse, Methode und Kategorien – Grundfragen intersektionaler Forschung. In: F. Schnicke and C. Klein, eds. *Intersektionalität und Narratologie. Methoden-Konzepte – Analysen*. Trier, Germany: WVT Wissenschaftlicher Verlag Trier. pp. 1–32.

Stoll, J., (2017). Jan Stoll: Behinderte Anerkennung? *Interessenorganisationen von Menschen mit Behinderung in Westdeutschland seit 1945*. Frankfurt am Main: Campus.

Winker, G. and Degener, N., (2009). *Intersektionalität. Zur Analyse sozialer Ungleichheiten*. Bielefeld, Germany: Transcript.

# 7 Policing Dis/ability

*Eric J. Miller*[1]

## Introduction

It is no exaggeration to say that in the contemporary United States, there is a dis/ability issue on either end of a nightstick. On the one hand, police practices are often driven by the fear of being rendered physically disabled by some member of the public (Harris 2019; Stoughton 2015). On the other hand, the standard sociological and philosophical accounts of policing present the police role as defined by the production of dis/ability used to incapacitate civilians who might resist or refuse an officer's demands (Bittner 1970).

Policing occurs against the background of power and authority. Power is simply the capacity or disposition to act so as to get what one wants (Morriss 2002). It is a type of ability that one can choose to exercise or not (Morriss 2002; Raz 1988). Authority is normatively justified power: it entails, rather crudely, the claim that one has a right to get what one wants (Raz 1988). Accordingly, to have a *material* power is to have the physical or mental ability to place handcuffs on a suspect or shoot a gun; to assert a *legal* power is to claim that the law justifies these exercises of material power, for example, when making an arrest or apprehending a suspect.

In the United States, the police often improperly conflate their legal authority—which confers a limited power to intervene to restore public order on the street—with each police officer's material ability to use physical force to inflict disabling violence on members of the public. From the police officer's perspective, the state's authority becomes embodied in the physical person of the officer on the street. These officers, however, perceive *themselves* as vulnerable to disabling force posed by people embodied in various ways, and so target these groups—characterized by race, gender, and dis/ability—for the use of violent, disabling force.[2]

So understood, the police regard themselves both normatively and descriptively as super-abled, and so always justified in using disabling force to resist threats to their authority. Policing thus has at its core the *production* of dis/ability. If we are to capture the nature of the police production of dis/ability properly, we need to incorporate but move beyond the insights of theories that treat dis/ability as a static state—such as the social model of dis/ability and

DOI: 10.4324/9781003257196-9

supplement these accounts using various intersectional theories of embodiment that provide a dynamic account of the production of dis/ability in relation to race and gender (but also class, houselessness, and so on).

A dis/ability focus undermines the police-vulnerability justification that dominates current policing theory and practice. Instead, we should turn from a justification predicated on the risk of police injury caused by an ever-present, disabling, violent public, to a justification that accounts for the interests of the people policed in being treated in a dignified and respectful—or at the very least, non-disabling—way.

## Embodiment and dis/ability

When the police encounter members of the public on the street, the threat of force to both prevent and inflict dis/ability is a core feature of the policing enterprise. The dominant account of the police function in the United States identifies violence that causes temporary or permanent dis/ability as definitive of the police role (Bittner 1970). It identifies the police as people who have both the psychological motivation and physical ability to cause temporary or permanent dis/ability to overcome resistance to their demands. On this *disablement model* of policing, producing (and resisting) dis/ability structures how the police comprehend their authority and how they perceive threats to their standing in the community.

Attending to the different ways in which embodiment risks or threatens disablement helps expand the contemporary discussion of ways in which policing and dis/ability interact. Currently, the discussion of policing and dis/ability focuses primarily upon the ways in which the police target people with disabilities, either for removal from public spaces (Morgan 2020; Schweik 2009) or by reacting violently when confronting people with disabilities, and especially mental illnesses (Harriet Tubman Collective 2016). Black people with mental disabilities are particularly likely to be vulnerable to deadly police violence.

The complicated interaction of policing, race, and dis/ability is exemplified by the demand made by the Harriet Tubman Collective (2016), an organization of Black Deaf people and people with disabilities, that the Black Lives Matter movement properly acknowledge "the unspeakable violence and Black death found at the intersection of dis/ability, ableism, audism, and anti-Black racism" as part of the Black Lives Matter policing policy platform (Harriet Tubman Collective 2016, p. 1).

The interrelation of dis/ability, race, and policing is a complex one, especially for Black people. As the Harriet Tubman Collective (2016) and others have noticed, the intersection of race and dis/ability renders people of color who are also disabled peculiarly susceptible to police violence. Although Black Lives Matter was somewhat crass in its discussion of dis/ability (Harriet Tubman Collective 2016), part of the problem is that Black embodiment is *itself* constituted by tropes of impairment and dis/ability in ways that are often not well captured by dis/ability scholars and activists who adopt the currently popular *social model* of dis/ability (Erevelles 2011, 2016; Erevelles & Minear 2010; Harriet Tubman Collective 2018; Lukin 2013; McRuer 2006, 2010).

The social model posits dis/ability as emerging from the relationship between some mental or physical impairment and the social response to that impairment. On the one hand, the social model rejects a *medical model* of dis/ability that characterizes physical and mental impairments as objective, medically determined, and fixed (Davis 2014; Kanter 2011). On the other hand, the social model identifies "normalcy" as a socially constructed category (Belt & Dorfman 2019; Davis 2014; Shakespeare 2016) one that is used both descriptively, to identify an ideal of physical and mental performance, and normatively as a standard to evaluate and marginalize bodies that disturb and disorder that ideal (Garland-Thomson 2009).

According to the social model, society constitutes the category "dis/ability" by imposing (or neglecting to ameliorate) obstacles that non-disabled people need not face (Shakespeare 2013). Social groups[3] oppress people with disabilities by claiming the power to determine whose bodies count and which virtues and vices we are to associate with those bodies. That power is expressed, in part, through the ability to create and enforce norms and practices that valorize or denigrate certain types of people around their physical and mental capacities.

Significantly, however, the social model places an undue emphasis on dis/ability as an *end-state* without properly considering the different ways in which people may be threatened by or vulnerable to impairment. The social model simply interrogates how society helps or hinders the person once impaired by creating obstacles to their inclusion in that society. What the social model does *not* address is *how* different individuals or groups of people become impaired. This process of debility or disablement does not impact all groups equally (Puar 2017). Some social groups are more vulnerable than others to disablement because they are at a higher risk of impairment-producing illness or violence than other social groups (Gilmore 2007; Puar 2017; Ribet 2011).[4] By focusing on only one feature of embodiment, the social model overlooks these other, often gendered and racialized, features of dis/ability (Erevelles & Minear 2010; Harriet Tubman Collective 2018; Puar 2017).

The social model, predicated on a relationship between impairment and society, also assumes that its political demand to remove social obstacles to mitigate the effects of an impairment is the core way to empower people with disabilities as social equals. However, because race and gender are often associated with falsely ascribed physical and mental attributes, there is often no impairment for women or people of color to mitigate, no barrier to remove. Historically, Black people have been mis- or over-diagnosed with various mental and physical impairments (Lukin 2013). To include women or people of color as impaired is precisely one way in which the practice of normalcy has been used, historically, as a tool to dehumanize and subordinate Black people.

As a result, "traditionally, African Americans have been extremely averse to race/dis/ability analogies" (Lukin 2013, p. 311). In an effort to ameliorate their standing in a white-dominated society, Black people have identified Black bodies and minds as the "same" as "normal" ones—as having the same mental and physical capabilities—rather than forming common cause with people with disabilities to overturn this white-and-non-disabled norm (Lukin 2013). On the other hand, people with disabilities have tended to treat the prototypical subject of ableist oppression as a white body and have failed to make common cause with African Americans (Hinton 2017).

In addition, women and people of color are often degraded and dehumanized by being characterized as threateningly *super*-abled—Black people as possessing super-strength; women as possessing a special mental intuition (Fricker 2009); and Asian people as being super-smart. Racism and misogyny thus identify group members as ripe for disablement by removing or downplaying these super-abilities as a necessary feature of restoring the "normal" (or *normate*)[5] (Garland-Thomson, 2017, 2009) order of society or social hierarchy (Fricker 2009).

Accordingly, if we are to preserve some of the important insights of the social model, we need to revise and supplement our concept of dis/ability with a notion of disablement or debilitation that recognizes the different ways in which individuals become—and resist becoming (Hinton 2017)—disabled. That account must include various forms of *embodiment* (Wendell 1996) as socially structured and ripe for disablement.

Embodiment here has a double aspect: it includes both the material facts of a person's body—including size, age, health, musculature, gender, race, hair color, and all their other physical and mental attributes—and the ways they are situated in a particular world, in a particular society, with all the features that go along with that (Young 2005).[6] Embodiment thus addresses the ways in which our material physical and mental attributes interact in given situations with socially constructed positions and practices of social power. These hierarchies of power create entitlements and expectations about how differently embodied members of society will behave toward each other (Young 2005); justify social superiors in their hostility in case their expectations are disappointed; and demand pre-emptive conduct from socially disempowered groups designed to mollify the resentment of their social superiors (Manne 2018).

The differential power to engage in the humanization and dehumanization of different groups is a feature of the intersectional nature of race-and-dis/ability (or dis/ability-and-race) (Erevelles 2011). Intersectionality reveals the ways in which systems of oppression use plural, embodied identities to pull people apart, differentially categorizing the subject as either (in this case) a person with a dis/ability—so obscuring racial discrimination—or a person of color—so obscuring discrimination on grounds of dis/ability.

## The nature of the police

The police are the primary agency authorized to act upon the state's duty to govern in response to actual or threatened public disturbances.[7] The duty to govern exists when there is some social interest that could be resolved by acting, and some person or institution has the resources and ability to do that act. A core feature of the state's duty to govern is to create publicly recognized institutions with special authority, resources, and abilities to address the demand for public services when someone needs to step in and do something. These officials usually also have the authority not simply to organize the public response, but to ensure the response is a public one, on behalf of the state, by excluding (or, if necessary, to deputize) ordinary members of the public from organizing or participating in the response.

We can identify two types of state-based response to situations calling for police action: one grounded in respecting the dignity of the people who are subjects of state intervention and another focused upon the personal authority of the police officers as entitled to use disabling force to preserve and project the authority of the state.

From the governance perspective, state officials gain their authority to act from the interests of all those people with whom the state interacts (Muir 1977; Vorenburg & Bator 1967) and the limits of state authority are established by those subjects' health, safety, and dignity. This model envisages the police as citizens in uniform (Gardner 2013) or street-corner politicians (Muir 1977), embedded in communities and developing strong relationships with community members, able to use various social and cultural skills to defuse and de-escalate situations and ensure cooperation or conformity with their demands (Harris 2019; Vorenburg & Bator 1967).

This model never really caught on in the United States. Instead, the model of authority that structures policing in the United States identifies the distinctive feature of the police as the ability to use physical force or violence to control situations by disabling resistance. Police doctrine now identifies the relevant interests of the police as the officer's concern to avoid threats that could disable or obstruct their ability to intervene in the situations they designate as emergencies requiring their attention. The limit of their authority is established by the actions that the police deem necessary to protect and restore the dignity of the person of the officer (Van Maanen 2015).

### *A nightstick is a weapon with a dis/ability issue at both ends*

According to some of the central definitions of the police role in the United States (Bittner 1970; Kelling & Wilson 1982), producing dis/ability is not simply a contingent consequence of policing. Producing temporary or permanent dis/ability is constitutive of the police role (Bittner 1970). The most influential definition of the police function over the last 50 years has been criminologist Egon Bittner's famous characterization of police authority as "nothing else than a mechanism for the situationally justified use of force in society" (Bittner 1970, p. 39). In dis/ability terms, however, the consequence of using force—whether words, fists, batons, pepper spray, plastic bullets, tasers, or guns—is to temporarily or permanently disable some person.

The police themselves embrace a model of police authority as organized around producing dis/ability (Skolnick and Fyfe 1993) and as distinctively embodied in the person of the police (Van Maanen 2015). The authority of the state is expressed through the ability of the police to physically dominate their surroundings by exercising a "command authority" or "command presence" that communicates "supreme authority, confidence, competence, and the physical ability to back it up" (Barker 1999, p. 69). Because their authority is embodied in their person:

> when the authority of an officer is questioned by a member of the nonpolice public, the officer has three broad responses available to him. He may (1) physically attack the offender; (2) swallow his pride and ignore the offender; or (3) manufacture a false excuse for the arrest of the offender (Van Maanen 2015, p. 149)[8].

The material, physical ability to overpower members of the public, the psychological willingness to inflict disabling violence, as well as the legal permission to incapacitate are essential to the police conception of themselves and the sort of authority they wield. As one officer expressed the notion of command authority:

> [H]ere is the bottom line: if you don't want to get shot, tased, pepper-sprayed, struck with a baton or thrown to the ground, just do what I tell you. Don't argue with me, don't call me names, don't tell me that I can't stop you (Dutta 2014).

The ever-present threat that the *police* present—to use disabling force against civilians—is reciprocated and motivated by the fear the police inculcate in themselves through training and repetition of war stories to encourage the belief that civilians constitute an ever-present disabling threat to police bodily integrity.

> They see themselves, as individuals and as member of an organization, as under unrelenting, violent and illegitimate attack. ... Surrounded by danger, violence, and peril at every turn, officers from the academy onward and well into their careers get constant reminders of the risks to their very lives, every day and everywhere (Harris 2019, p. 204).

Policing practice is thus, in large part, organized around an imperative to resist their own disablement—often by pre-emptively disabling those who are perceived as presenting a threat to the officer.

The dual nature of the threat of disablement—of police disablement by civilians; and of civilians' disablement by police—structures who gets to be a police officer. The threat of and ability to threaten disablement means that the police envisage their authority as made effective through a form of physical power: the ideal or *normate* police officer is one who can physically disable threatening civilians without themselves being physically disabled. This embodied understanding of police authority is not only ableist—it is *super*-ableist, as well as raced and gendered (Cooper 2009). The ideal officer is a warrior (Harris 2019; Stoughton 2015), a muscular man capable of chasing down wrestling a recalcitrant civilian to the ground and placing them in handcuffs, perhaps dispensing some street justice along the way (Kelling & Wilson, 1982; Van Maanen 2015).

The disablement model of policing entails that the police are *disempowered* (and so lose their effective authority) when they cannot use violence to disable others to ensure compliance. This disabling disempowerment occurs when an officer is unable to physically enforce their commands—that is, when they lack the physical or psychological capacity to do so. Police authority, embodied in the ability to physically and mentally enforce commands, is, however, gendered and socio-cultural. The "social work" parts of the job that require psychological or cultural competence and skill are often gendered as female. The ideal of the male warrior cop (Stoughton 2015) renders women police officers vulnerable to gender-biased discrimination from their male counterparts. Because of their perceived mental (Martin 1999) or physical (Prokos & Padavic 2002) inability to overpower civilian men, women officers face heightened pressure to use disabling physical violence during interactions with civilians.

Furthermore, being *racially empathetic* is itself police-disabling. According to implicit-bias expert Song Richardson (2017),

> if officers believe that an individual views them as racist, officers will also likely assume that the individual will not respect their authority or grant them any legitimacy. This assumption increases the likelihood that officers will feel unsafe (Richardson 2017, p. 79).

Faced with this perceived weakness within themselves, racially empathetic police are more likely to escalate encounters with civilians of color and use disabling violence to resolve any perceived slight to their authority. (RichardsonThere is a savage irony here. Disabling police violence produces distrust of the police in minority communities. The police translate this distrust as creating a risk that they will themselves face disabling violence from members of the Black community, which the police then use to justify doubling down on using disabling violence against people of color, producing a vicious cycle of their own making.

The police are also disabled when the civilian is perceived to be super-powered and resistant to police directives. Some civilians figure as categorically resistant to disabling police power: ironically, these are people who are already disabled in a variety of ways. Their physical or mental inability to comply with police commands is their super-power (from the police perspective structured by the disablement model of police authority). It is what justifies the police rapidly escalating up their use of force protocol to use extreme, often deadly force.

Under the disablement model, some of the situations that threaten police authority are encounters in which the police face civilians they regard as *super-powered* and so physically or mentally able to overcome the police. These individuals are pictured as boosted by innate or acquired physical or mental abilities that render them immune to police authority. For example, this "superhumanization bias" (Rutbeck-Goldman and Richardson 2017, pp. 159–160) leads the police to experience Black people as larger, older, more powerful, and more violent than they in fact are, so justifying excessive disabling force.

Superhumanization also enables the police to treat neurodivergent people (people with mental disabilities) or people under the influence of narcotics as super-powered, so justifying harsh, disabling violence. These individuals often do not respond to police commands in the manner the police expect and demand but are instead disordered and disoriented by the command-presence model of asserting authority. A predictable outcome is that the police will *shoot, tase, pepper spray, strike with a baton or throw to the ground*, people who are disabled in these ways precisely because they just cannot *do what the police tell you* (Dutta 2014).

## What the police do

These features of the disablement model and the embodied, command-authority it seeks to project are all the more disturbing given the police's primary role as the first responder to people in need of social services.

There is a general perception that most of what the police do is fight crime: chase down criminals and make arrests. On this widely-shared view, policing is a dangerous, exciting job: the activity, as described by Justice Jackson, of "the officer engaged in the often-competitive enterprise of ferreting out crime" (Johnson v. United States 1948, p. 14).

This picture, however, is quite wrong.

> One of the earliest findings of sociological research on policing, replicated time and time again over the last fifty years, is that—contrary to popular images—most police work does not involve crime or at any rate law enforcement (Reiner 2010, p. 19)[9].

Most calls for help are not calls requiring response to serious criminal activity: for the most part, the police respond to and deal with "medical emergencies, family quarrels, auto accidents, barking dogs, minor traffic violations, and so on" (Wilson 2013, p. 49).[10]

The non-criminal aspects of police patrol have two important features. The first is that the police are often called to resolve conflicts among civilians: their public authority as agents of the state provides a sense of closure for individuals unable otherwise to resolve a dispute (Kleinig 1996). Accordingly, a central skill required for street police is the ability to talk to and negotiate with quarreling civilians. Often these quarrels have a domestic aspect; part of that domestic aspect may include a mental health component, and the decision to denominate a quarrel as a civil or criminal matter is often itself a matter of dispute and police discretion. Nonetheless, the idea that the police solve disputes on the street has long been recognized as a core part of their function, and the police capacity for dispute resolution is a core feature of the job (Muir 1977; Punch 1979). This governance style of authority is itself deeply embodied by the police in terms of gender (Martin 1999) and perhaps race (Vorenburg & Bator 1967).

The second important feature is that the police have, as one of their primary jobs, the provision of emergency services to vulnerable individuals. As a consequence, the role of the police requires them to engage with people who have "no money, no family, no job, no property, no respectability, no health, no skills, and no hope" (Muir 1977, p. 62). The police find many of the people that they encounter discomfiting: some due to the circumstances of their life; others due to houselessness or drug addiction; some because they have mental illnesses; yet more because of race and gender. All these groups, in different ways, upset police expectations about who belongs where (Waddington 2002). Under the dis/ability model of policing, the police respond to their own disappointed, discomfited, and disabled expectations with disabling, degrading force (Van Maanen 2015).

The disturbance and disorder created by people with disabilities bring into focus one way in which policing impacts social expectations about the presence of "divergent" bodies in public spaces. Policing entrenches normalcy in profound ways. One is simply to reinforce ableist understandings of who belongs where. Dis/ability theory presses us to think about relations with the "ordinary" and the "orderly" (Garland-Thomson 2009). Disabled bodies are perceived, from the perspective of normalcy, not merely as "out of the ordinary," but as disrupting society's sense of order. Because so much of modern policing has become "public order policing," that is, about maintaining a sense of who belongs where, dis/ability, along with race, sexual orientation, houselessness, and so on, challenges that sense of belonging.

One function of policing is thus to restore a sense of order by removing disordering bodies from "respectable" places through harassment, degradation, violence, and arrest (Ericson 1982; Waddington 2002). However, even police officers who are not motivated by harassing the disorderly are often significantly discomfited by people with disabilities—which can include not only people with mental disabilities, but the wider group of socially marginal, disordering people, made up of "homeless people, impoverished people, end-stage cancer patients, the comatose, heroin, crack, or methamphetamine addicts" (Davis 2014, p. 4). These, unfortunately, comprise a large portion of the people with whom the police are called upon to interact.

Although there is a paucity of information on these types of encounters between police and civilians (Frankham, 2018; Saleh et al. 2018; Shah, 2019), the little data available on police resort to violence during these interactions are grim (Saleh et al. 2018). Most of the data come from various newspaper reports: the *Portland Press Herald* found that from 2001 to 2012, 42% of the people shot by police had a mental illness (Bouchard 2012). The *Washington Post* found that, nationally, about one-quarter of the people killed by the police were people with a mental illness (Shah 2019). Just as worrisome, a study based on the same data demonstrated that 41% of those calls were initiated by a family member asking the police to help with a mental health crisis (Frankham 2018). Instead of de-escalating the crisis, the police killed the person in distress.

## Policing dignity

The three main events justifying police intervention—criminal law-enforcement; public order dispute resolution; and emergency provision of social services—correspond with broad categories of activity—investigation; mediation; and caregiving. Only the first even implicates the deployment of force: the other two could be—and in the case of emergency services provided by non-police-agencies—often are staffed by officials who lack the police's power to disable and interest in degrading the people they encounter.

In turn, there are three approaches to combating the power of the police to disable the public. The first has been to impose limits on their *legal power* to use disabling force. Whether through judicial reform interpreting the limits imposed by the United States Constitution; through litigation; through legislative or administrative policymaking; or through civilian oversight, there have been numerous efforts over the past century and more to limit the power of the police to harm the public. Yet the same disablement model prevails, and vulnerable groups suffer the same treatment.

Another option that is currently popular has been to impose *material* limits on the power of the police. That option is often presented as removing the *physical* capacity of the police to engage in degrading and disabling treatment, perhaps by disarming the police or preventing them from using dangerous chokeholds or by limiting their encounters with the public. However, physical limitations on policing are not enough, on their own, to prevent state violence against the vulnerable populations currently susceptible to disablement. The *psychological* power—the will or motivation—to use disabling force against disordering people is one that the police share with many members of the public. And all these powers are themselves baked into the current structure of society in the United States, because of the ways that race, gender, class, and so on intersect with dis/ability.

All of this is to suggest that disempowering the police is not enough without a replacement model that respects the dignity and interests of vulnerable populations. Policing does not stand outside society: it is simply one of the most powerful means of reasserting the structures of dominance, oppression, and exclusion relied upon by civilians and police alike to restore order and authority by disciplining and disabling disordering bodies perceived as not knowing their place.

## Conclusion

In a case that was ultimately to make its way to the Supreme Court, Davis v. Washington (1972/1975/1976), the Washington D.C. District Court held that "[t]he ability to swing a nightstick no longer measures a policeman's competency for his exacting role in this city" (p. 17). However, the disablement model of policing has proved harder to shift than the court believed. Dis/ability and dis/ablement are recalcitrant features of oppression in the United States and cut across multiple features of our embodiment. Accordingly, dis/ability must be a core aspect of any platform that seeks to understand and resist the disabling state.

## Notes

1 My thanks to Jamelia Morgan, Frank Rudy Cooper, Alexis Hoag, and the other contributors to this volume for their helpful comments.
2 My account of the relation between dis/ability and power takes some of its inspiration from Macklem and Gardner (2014).
3 I have not specified *which* social groups because different groups use the concept of dis/ability to empower themselves in different ways. They do so, as will become clear, not only over people with disabilities but also over (at least) people of color.
4 Here it is perhaps worth highlighting Ruth Wilson Gilmore's definition of "Racism, specifically, [a]s the state-sanctioned or extralegal production and exploitation of group-differentiated vulnerability to premature death" (2007, p. 28). Puar (2017) and McRuer (2006) echo this definition in different ways.
5 Normate is a deliberately neologistic term designed to highlight the standards whereby people construct themselves in ableist terms as ideal human beings, and then use those standards to discriminate against people with disabilities. As will be clear, I think these standards are plural and shifting; are also raced, gendered, classed, and so on; and change from social role to social role.
6 Young's (2005) discussion of embodiment engages with other feminist thinkers and provides a useful summary and critique of feminist theories of embodiment.
7 The Broken Windows movement (Kelling & Wilson 1982) has done much to consolidate *fear* of disturbance—of the entitlements that go along with property, wealth, and power—as a core justification for using disabling police violence.
8 According to two well-known criminologists, Jerome Skolnick and James Fyfe (1993), "[c]ops, especially, understand that. Indeed, anybody who fails to understand the centrality of [disability -producing] force to police work has no business in a police uniform" (p. 37).
9 Criminologist David Bayley (1994) found that "[v]ery little of the work patrol officers do has to do with crime … [and m]ost of the genuine crime that police are called upon to handle is distinctly minor" (p. 17).
10 British criminologist Robert Reiner (2010) sums up the sociological consensus that the police have a limited impact on crime and disorder in the following terms: "Altogether the police are marginal to the control of crime and the maintenance of order, and always have been" (p. 19). Instead, "the sources of order lie outside the ambit of the police, in the political economy and culture of a society" (Reiner 2010, p. 17).

## References

Barker, J., (1999). *Danger, duty, and disillusion: the worldview of Los Angeles police officers*. Prospect Heights, IL: Waveland Press.
Bayley, D., (1994). *Police for the future*. New York: Oxford University Press.
Belt, R. and Dorfman, D., (2019). Disability, law, and the humanities. In: S. Stern, M. Del Mar and B. Meyler, eds. *The Oxford handbook of law and humanities*. New York: Oxford University Press. pp. 143–161.

Bittner, E., (1970). *The functions of the police in modern society*. Chevy Chase, MD: National Institute of Mental Health Center for Studies of Crime and Delinquency.

Bouchard, K., (2012). Across nation, unsettling acceptance when mentally ill in crisis are killed. *Portland Press Herald* [online]. 9 December. Available from: http://www.pressherald.com/

Cooper, F. R., (2009). "Who's the man?": masculinities studies, terry stops, and police training. *Columbia Journal of Gender and Law*. **18**, 671–742.

Davis, L. J., (2014). *The end of normal: identity in a biocultural era*. Ann Arbor, MI: University of Michigan Press.

Davis v. Washington, (1976). 348 F. Supp. 15 (1972) *rev'd* 512 F.2d 956 (1975) *rev'd* 426 U.S. 229.

Dutta, S. (2014). I'm a Cop: if you don't want to get hurt, don't challenge me. *The Washington Post* [online]. 19 August. Available from: https://www.washingtonpost.com/

Erevelles, N., (2011). *Disability and difference in global contexts*. New York: Palgrave Macmillan.

Erevelles, N., (2016). Becoming disabled/becoming black: crippin' critical ethnic studies from the periphery. In: N. Elia et al., eds. *Critical ethnic studies: a reader*. Durham, NC: Duke University Press. pp. 231–251.

Erevelles, N. and Minear, A., (2010). Unspeakable offenses: untangling race and disability in discourses of intersectionality. *Journal of Literary Cultural Disability Studies*. **4**(2), 127–145.

Ericson, R., (1982). *Reproducing order: a study of police patrol work*. Toronto: University of Toronto Press.

Frankham, E., (2018). Mental illness affects police fatal shootings. *Contexts*. **17**(2), 70–72.

Fricker, M., (2009). *Epistemic injustice*. New York: Oxford University Press on Demand.

Gardner, J., (2013). Criminals in uniform. In: R. A. Duff et al., eds. *The constitution of the criminal law*. New York: Oxford University Press. pp. 97–118.

Garland-Thomson, R., (2009). *Staring: how we look*. New York: Oxford University Press.

Garland-Thomson, R., (2017). *Extraordinary bodies*. New York: Columbia University Press.

Gilmore, R. W., (2007). *Golden Gulag: prisons, surplus, crisis, and opposition in globalizing California*. Berkeley: University of California Press.

Harriet Tubman Collective, (2016). Disability solidarity: completing the "vision for Black Lives". September 7. Available from: https://harriettubmancollective.tumblr.com

Harriet Tubman Collective, (2018). Accountable reporting on disability, race, and police violence: a community response to the "Ruderman White Paper on the media coverage of use of force and disability." 1 June. Available from: https://harriettubmancollective.tumblr.com/

Harris, D. A., (2019). How fear shapes policing in the United States. In: T. Lave and E. J. Miller, eds. *The Cambridge handbook of policing in the United States*. Cambridge, UK: Cambridge University Press.

Hinton, A., (2017). "And so I bust back": violence, race, and disability in hip Hop. *CLA Journal*. **60**(3), 290–304.

Johnson v. United States, (1948). 333 U.S. 10.

Kanter, A. S., (2011). What's disability studies got to do with it or an introduction to disability legal studies. *Columbia Human Rights Law Review*. **42**(2), 403–480.

Kelling, G. L. and Wilson, J. Q., (1982). Broken windows: the police and neighborhood safety. *The Atlantic*, 1–19.
Kleinig, J., (1996). *The ethics of policing*. New York: Cambridge University Press.
Lukin, J., (2013). Disability and blackness. In: L. J. Davis, ed. *The disability studies reader*. New York: Taylor & Francis Group. pp. 308–315.
Macklem, T. and Gardner, J., (2014). Human disability. *King's Law Journal*. **25**, 60–79.
Manne, K., (2018). *Down girl: the logic of misogyny*. New York: Oxford University Press.
Martin, S. E., (1999). Police force or police service? gender and emotional labor. *Annals of the American Academy of Political & Social Science*. **561**, 111–126.
McRuer, R., (2006). *Crip theory: cultural signs of queerness and disability*. New York: New York University Press.
McRuer, R., (2010). Disability nationalism. *Crip Times: Journal of Literary Cultural Disability Studies*. **4**(2), 163–178.
Morgan, J., (2020). Policing marginality in public space. *Ohio State Law Journal*. **81**, 1045–1063.
Morriss, P., (2002). *Power: a philosophical analysis*. 2nd ed. Manchester, UK: Manchester University Press.
Muir, W., (1977). *Police: streetcorner politicians*. Chicago, IL: University of Chicago Press.
Prokos, A. and Padavic, I., (2002). "There oughtta be a law against bitches": masculinity lessons in police academy training. *Gender, Work & Organization*. **9**, 439–459. doi:10.1111/1468-0432.00168.
Puar, J. K., (2017). *The right to maim: debility, capacity, disability*. Durham, NC: Duke University Press.
Punch, M., (1979). The secret social service. In: S. Holdaway and M. Chatterton, eds. *The British police*. London: E. Arnold. pp. 103–114.
Raz, J., (1988). *The morality of freedom*. New York: Clarendon Press.
Reiner, R., (2010). *The politics of the police*. 4th ed. New York: Oxford University Press.
Ribet, B., (2011). Emergent disability and the limits of equality: a critical reading of the UN Convention on the Rights of Persons with Disabilities. *Yale Human Rights and Development Law Journal*. **14**(1), 155–203.
Richardson, L. S., (2017). Implicit racial bias and racial anxiety: implications for stops and frisks. *Ohio State Journal of Criminal Law*. **15**, 73–88.
Rutbeck-Goldman, A. and Richardson, L., (2017). Race and objective reasonableness in use of force cases: an introduction to some relevant social science. *Alabama Civil Rights & Civil Liberties Law Review*. **8**(1), 145–162.
Saleh, A. Z. et al., (2018). Deaths of people with mental illness during interactions with law enforcement. *International Journal of Law and Psychiatry*. **58**, 110–116.
Schweik, S., (2009). *The ugly laws: disability in public*. New York: New York University.
Shah, P. V., (2019). Use of deadly force: people with mental health conditions and encounters with law enforcement. *Harvard Human Rights Journal*. **32**, 207–222.
Shakespeare, T., (2013). The social model of disability. In: L. J. Davis, ed. *The disability studies reader*. 4th ed. New York: Routledge. pp. 215–221.
Skolnick, J. H., (1975). *Justice without trial: law enforcement in democratic society*. 2nd ed. New York, Wiley.
Skolnick, J. and Fyfe, J., (1993). *Above the law : police and the excessive use of force*. New York, Toronto: New York Free Press, Maxwell Macmillan International.
Stoughton, S., (2015). Law enforcement's warrior problem. *Harvard Law Review Forum*. **128**, 225–234.

Van Maanen, J., (2015). The asshole. In: G. Alpert and R. Dunham, eds. *Critical issues in policing: contemporary readings*. 7th ed. Long Grove, IL: Waveland Press. pp. 143–161.
Vorenburg, J. and Bator, P., (1967). *The challenge of crime in a free society: President's Commission on Law Enforcement and the Administration of Justice*. Washington, DC: US Government Printing Office.
Waddington, P. A. J., (2002). *Policing citizens: police, power and the state*. New York: Taylor and Francis.
Wendell, S., (1996). *The rejected body: feminist philosophical reflections on disability*. New York: Routledge.
Wilson, J. Q., (2013). *Thinking about crime*. New York: Basic Books.
Young, I. M., (2005). *On female body experience: throwing like a girl and other* essays. New York: Oxford University Press.

# Part III

# Representation, Liminality, and Resistance

# 8 Reassessing Japanese Radical Feminism from the Vantage Point of Dis/ability

*Anna Vittinghoff*

## Introduction

The 2019 Japanese House of Councillors elections resulted in a historical win for the representation of dis/abled people in Japanese society. For the first time in postwar Japanese history, two candidates with dis/abilities from the *Reiwa Shinsengumi* party, Kimura Eiko,[1] who has cerebral palsy, and Funago Yasuhiro, who has Lou Gehrig's disease, were elected to Japan's upper house. One of the party's main ideological principles is the belief that "… productivity is no way to measure people's value and that it is the role of politics to create a society in which existing is enough to have worth" (Mainichi Shimbun 2019, para. 10).

For people interested in Japanese 1970s leftist politics, this principle sounds strangely familiar. In this period, the Japanese women's liberation movement *ūman ribu* used almost the exact same formulation in their own critique of postwar Japanese societal relations.[2] However, *ribu* was a fringe organization whose moment only lasted from 1970/1 to 1977. The transformation of societal relations they envisaged never materialized, and their transformative ideas are commonly regarded by historians as having failed to penetrate mainstream society. How then did *ribu* ideology make its way from the minds of activists of the radical, loosely organized women's liberation movement almost 50 years ago, to Japanese party politics in 2019?

In this chapter, I develop three linked arguments. First, the experiences of dis/abled people in Japanese society were core to *ribu's* intersectional analysis of social injustices in Japan as seen by *ribu's* assertion that women and dis/abled people were equally devalued by what activists described as the dominant masculine logic of capitalist productivity. Second, I explain how feminists and dis/ability activists, two groups holding supposedly antagonistic ideas about abortion, came together to argue that abortion raised fundamental questions about the government of bodies. That is, abortion was and is not solely a matter of individual liberal rights. Third, I will show that it was through the entrepreneurial activities of the female dis/abled *ribu* activist, Yonezu Tomoko,[3] that *ribu's* theorizing incorporated a feminist critique. This led to *ribu's* social critique being adapted to a range of dis/abled organizations, thus giving it new life in different contexts. Based on a series of interviews I have conducted with

DOI: 10.4324/9781003257196-11

Yonezu since spring 2020, I will argue that her vantage point at the intersection of gender and dis/ability enabled her to articulate and institutionalize new forms of disabled activism which we see reflected in the statements by the politicians of *Reiwa Shinsengumi*.

## The Eugenic Protection Law, its purpose and bio-politics

After World War II, Japan's population initially witnessed a sharp drop as a result of the country's war effort and loss of empire, but this trend was soon reversed, and Japan experienced rapid annual growth rates of 2–5%. The root causes for the baby boom of the late 1940s were the population policies of the interwar years and the subsequent repatriation of Japanese nationals from former colonies (Takeda 2005).

Japan's interwar policies, which were eugenicist and pro-natalist, aimed:

> to ensure perpetual population growth; to surpass the rate of increase and quality of populations of other nations; to ensure for the armed forces and the labour force a quantity of personnel sufficient for a high degree of national security; and to redistribute the Japanese population geographically in order to ensure guidance for the peoples of East Asia (Norgren 2001, pp. 32–33).

Hence, population policy and state interference with people's bodies were central to Japanese imperialism, militarism, and national definitions of productivity.

Key legislation for securing a high productive quality of the population was the 1940 National Eugenic Law (NEL) enacted in 1940. The NEL sanctioned the sterilization of those deemed of low productive value for the empire, such as the mentally and physically dis/abled, banned inter-racial reproduction, and restricted access to birth control to ensure those deemed of high productive value would not limit their reproduction (Norgren 2001).

The costs for Japan of World War II engendered the postwar development of policies limiting population growth. Japan's economy was weakened by the war and the dissolution of its empire resulting in the loss of one-third of the nation's production capacities (Nakamura 1995). Moreover, in 1946, inflation, food shortages, unemployment, and a lack of housing created a severe socio-economic crisis. Officials understood this as a "textbook Malthusian situation," i.e., a surplus population exceeding the limits of the national economic competence (Takeda 2005). The US Occupational Forces, Japanese cross-party politicians, and academics from both the US and Japan agreed that the imperatives of economic reconstruction and the democratization process required a comprehensive policy aimed at curbing population growth (Norgren 2001). Thus, the Eugenic Protection Law (EPL) was promulgated in 1948.

In its language, the EPL echoed the NEL of the interwar years which had emphasized the promotion of a healthy and strong population and the prevention of "biologically inferior offspring" (House of Representatives 1949). Enforcement of the EPL called for state-managed population growth and the sterilization of those Japanese deemed likely to transmit undesirable heritable characteristics. In 1949, the "economic reasons clause" was added, enabling women to have abortions on the basis of economic reasons that might lead to seriously harming the mother's health (House of Representatives 1949; Takeda 2005). Three years later, the requirements for sterilization were extended to those whose spouses suffered from "mental illness and mental deficiency" (Takeda 2005, p. 104).[4] The genesis of the EPL is a demonstration of how population management was inherently connected to economic and socio-economic development of the nation state. Furthermore, through its eugenicist language and ideology, the EPL devalued dis/abled lives and bodies and worked toward their erasure.

We can analyze these laws through the lens of what Foucault calls "bio-politics," which he has described as the power over life and the management of embodied lives on either the individual or group level (Taylor 2011). As Takeda (2005) points out, "… Foucault's concept of bio-power is concerned with human bodies, and more precisely, the management of the population of the nation-state" (p. 13). This regulation of a population by the state is characterized as "bio-politics" (Takeda 2005, p. 46). Bio-politics relies on data from a range of demographic surveys, e.g., the ratio of birth to death within a population and its reproduction and fertility rates, because these indicators are crucial to population control (Tremain 2008). Hence, reproduction becomes a key target for Japanese bio-politics overseen by lawmakers and government officials. In sum, eugenics play an important part in the management of post-World War II Japan's population. But of course, the exercise of this power produces resistance as was the case in Japan from the late 1940s through the 1990s. This resistance is exemplified by *ribu* and the dis/ability movement and their intersection is embodied by Yonezu Tomoko.

## Yonezu Tomoko and the Japanese student movement—catalyst for the *ribu* movement

In many ways, Yonezu's life reflects tensions within postwar Japan. She was born in 1948 and contracted polio in 1951, which left her with a permanent limp. People's general reaction to her dis/ability, their apprehension, and pity were emotionally painful for her (Yonezu 2020). Her parents, agitated by these responses to their daughter, saw her as a burdensome child. Owing to the hostility Yonezu experienced on multiple fronts from a very young age, she realized that the standard life course for Japanese women at the time was not viable because her dis/ability excluded her from mainstream society. Yonezu needed to make an independent life for herself because marriage and the attendant reliance on a breadwinning husband were out of reach. Only later in life did Yonezu come to understand the intersectional nature of the discrimination she experienced.

Having reconciled herself to the life of a non-traditional woman, Yonezu decided to enroll at Tama Arts University to become a designer.

In the late 1960s, the student movement kicked off across campuses in Japan, and Tama Arts University was no exception. Yonezu, who had concerns about her future, was encouraged by the student movement' aspirations for social transformation and she joined the barricades. Yonezu remembers the atmosphere of free discussions and different voices being heard as uplifting. For the first time, she felt comfortable talking about her dis/ability and how she hated the way people stared at her (Schieder 2021). Feeling empowered by this newly found space, she formed her own student group, which is discussed later.

Yonezu was subject to the dualities that characterized female students' existence within the movement. In the first case, women inside the barricades helped the revolutionary cause by engaging in intense physical labor, but it was the pretty, dolled up women who visited and became romantically involved with male students within the barricades (Oguma 2015; Schieder 2020; Yonezu 2020). Women were assigned either one or the other identity but never both. In the second case, more and more female movement activists identified another fundamental difference between themselves and their male comrades. Even if the student movement did not achieve its goals, the professional and personal futures of the men involved in it would remain intact. Women, however, had no job waiting for them and they didn't see any premium in being a "good wife and wise mother." So, as the student movement started to cool down and the male students began to leave their revolutionary activities behind them, female students refused to surrender their emancipatory struggles. This led in turn to the formation of the *ūman ribu* (a Japanese rendering of the English term "women's liberation") movement of the 1970s.

Founding members of *ribu* met one another while organizing for a cultural revolution in the reproductive sphere. On April 2, 1970, Yonezu together with Mori Setsuko and other female students formed the group "Thought Group S.E.X." (*Shisō shūdan Esu・ E—・ Ekkusu*) which explored the relationship between sexuality and disability. In June 1970, the group encountered another group of women having similar ideas at a rally against the US-Japan Mutual Cooperation and Security Treaty (*Anpo*) held at Yoyogi Park in Tōkyō. One of these women was Tanaka Mitsu who later became the main theorist of the *ribu* movement. At the rally, the group distributed a pamphlet titled "The Declaration of the Liberation of Eros" which later became the manifesto of the *ribu* movement. The tract criticized both the existing women's movements and the Marxist New Left groups for their failure to recognize that gender relations and the family system were foundational to the capitalist authoritarian state (Shigematsu 2012). By contrast, *ribu's* aimed primarily to radically transform Japanese society by liberating it from this oppressive patriarchal and capitalist regime. This required the breakdown of gender roles and the dissolution of the family system.

Central to *ribu's* politics of direct action was the Ribu Shinjuku Centre. Founded in May 1972, it was home to several *ribu* groups and their members and served as an important communication hub and safe space for *ribu* activists across Japan. Here Yonzu embraced her disability, girded as she was by the Centre's emotional support and openness and by her newly gained sense of belonging afforded by *ribu*. Taking a constructivist approach to reflection on her life, Yonezu realized that if not for the *ūman ribu* movement, she would have a negative image of herself.

> I understood very well that I am a social being. This is very important. It's not that I personally have a hard life because I'm disabled, but if I have a hard life, it's because of my social circumstances and history. So, you can change the way you think about and see yourself, and to do that you need to change the way society works which is possible. We can change the way people perceive us. I was able to think of it as a social problem, not an individual one. I thought that was a good thing for me (Yonezu 2020).

Owing to Yonezu's involvement in and presence at the fore front of *ribu*, her understanding of dis/ability influenced *ribu's* social critique and, among other things, enabled the movement to develop an intersectional approach to reproduction that was both gendered and anti-ableist. Her conception of dis/ability echoes the embodiment theory outlined by Siebers (2017) and Silvers (2019). Her experiences of her body in the social landscape and her reflections on them led her to the social constructionist conclusion that her dis/ability was a product of her social environment rather than a medical condition. This idea also informed *ribu's* conviction that society needed to create the circumstances where people can live a fulfilled life regardless of their gender, sexuality, race, or dis/ability.

## 1972—revision attempts of the EPL and *ribu's* intervention into bio-politics

As I have argued, after World War II, Japan enacted legislative measures aimed at stimulating economic growth and rebuilding its economy. The legalization of abortions in the immediate postwar years was implemented in the spirit of family planning and to slow population growth after the baby boom years of the early 1940s. Even though the final version of the EPL made abortions legally accessible and was regarded as quite progressive, it operated within a eugenicist ideological framework. That is, reproductive rights were linked with a program of sterilization of so-called undesirables. In the early 1970s, political and economic elites recognized that the rapidly declining birth rate of the last decade would endanger Japan's further economic development and subsequently threaten Japan's international standing (Norgren 2001; Takeda 2005). To reverse this trend, Japan's bio-politics targeted reproduction via the Eugenics Protection Law.

Efforts to revise the EPL in 1972 focused on the removal of the "economic reasons clause" which made abortions widely accessible across Japan.

Additionally, conservative lawmakers planned to add a "foetal conditions clause" that would legalize abortions if prenatal diagnostics of the fetus detected a dis/ability. Dis/ability activists condemned this policy as "eugenic abortion" (Saxton 2017, p. 74). The proposed bill intended to replace the EPL's "economic reasons" with "mental reasons," which *ribu* women considered "... as signifying an ideological shift that would place the blame for abortion on the individual mother instead of improving the societal conditions for giving birth" (Shigematsu 2012, p. 88). The proposed "foetal clause" allowing eugenic abortions also sparked outrage among dis/abled people. In short, the planned expansion of state control over reproduction that encompassed both women's bodily autonomy and the negation of dis/abled life provided the basis for an intersectional alliance between *ribu* and dis/ability activists.

## *Ribu's* opposition to the proposed revisions

Early in *ribu's* campaign against the proposed revisions of the EPL, they focused on preserving the "economic reasons clause" and hence the legal access to abortion for Japanese women (Kato 2009; Mizoguchi et al. 1994). However, *ribu's* rhetorical strategy in demanding legal access to abortion evolved. Rather than emphasizing women's right to abortion, *ribu* demanded reproductive freedom from state control (Shigematsu 2012). Development of this demand emerged from *ribu's* exchanges with dis/ability activists like the radical cerebral palsy activist group *Aoi shiba no kai*[5] and dis/abled people within *ribu*, most prominently Yonezu Tomoko (Shigematsu 2012). *Aoi shiba no kai* emphasized that having a dis/ability should not be seen as a negative and instead argued (similarly to *ribu*) that the determining value of the body within Japanese society was an ethics of productivity (Kato 2009). Rather than address the semantics of *ribu's* evolving framing of their opposition to revision of the EPL, I highlight the tensions inherent in this intersectional approach to reproduction and how this approach was influenced by Yonezu Tomoko.

## *Ribu* and the dis/ability movement

The proposed addition of the selective abortion clause to EPL law would have effectively denied dis/abled people the right to exist. Hence, dis/abled people were part of the movement to oppose the EPL revisions and were present at activist meetings and demonstrations. However, at the time dis/abled people's groups like *Aoi shiba no kai* did not trust women's rights activists whom they saw as harboring an anti-dis/ability bias (Kato 2009). Their suspicions were raised further by a rash of highly publicized cases of women killing their dis/abled children. While it is unclear whether this media frenzy was indicative of an increase in such cases (Castellini 2017), it is safe to say that the heightened media attention combined with the personal experiences of those within the dis/ability movement made these killings a contentious point between the movements.

Yonezu explains that many of the dis/abled people who debated the proposed revisions of the EPL in the early 1970s had almost been killed by their own mothers or had heard stories from someone close to them. This anger was often unloaded on women of the *ribu* movement.

> They saw women as mothers who were trying to kill them, when they were mothers who were supposed to protect them. It was very hard for me because they were pointing that at me and I thought, "I'm not your mother, I'm not trying to kill you, why are you saying that?" Disabled women, in particular, did not have much sympathy for a woman without a disability saying that she should decide for herself whether or not to have a child either. Given that as disabled women they are told not to have a baby, they are forced to have sterilizations, they are told to have an abortion and so they have. They don't have agency over their own bodies. This was very hard for me to hear. I heard the same things in the rallies and demonstrations which made me think "Yes, that's true." In the end, the same way that disabled people are killed or excluded or told not to have children, women are told not to have children or to only have healthy children. The root cause for it is the same, isn't it? Namely the Eugenic Protection Law (Yonezu 2020).

Yonezu's statement highlights the key difference between feminists and dis/ability rights activists on the issue of reproduction as identified by Saxton (2017): "the reproductive rights movement [*represented by ribu*] emphasizes the right to have an abortion; the dis/ability rights movement, the right not to have to have an abortion" (p. 74). To bridge this gap, *ribu* activists sought an alliance with dis/ability activists to challenge the ideology behind the EPL which denied women's agency, able-bodied and dis/abled alike, rather than fighting with one another. However, *ribu* was not advocating on behalf of dis/abled people against the fetal clause. Instead, they incorporated dis/ability-based points of criticism into their framing.

## Incorporating dis/ability into the reproduction debate

For Yonezu, as a dis/abled woman, the discrimination she experienced in Japanese society was profoundly intersectional. She felt ostracized by society not just because she was a woman or just because she was dis/abled, but because she was both. Accordingly, she came to understand that reproductive issues are not exclusively women's issues, rather they are a human issue. However, the men who dominated the dis/ability movement in the 1970s and early 1980s did not concede this point. Reflecting on their attitudes about reproduction over the past decades, Yonezu explains:

> Men and disabled men have not changed much [really]. Nowadays, it is common to use prenatal diagnosis to check the foetus and the fertilised eggs

> to make sure they are healthy, so the child will be born without any disabilities. Disabled men often say that when it comes to this issue it is about women wanting to choose their children. However, this is not a women's or a men's issue per see. I do not want it to be a just a women's issue, men are involved in having children too. Furthermore, women have realised that the discrimination against disabled people and the discrimination against women are interconnected and intersecting. Hence, I strongly believe that men who are reflecting on the discrimination against disabled people should also think about how the two are connected (Yonezu 2020).

Yonezu's observation on men's attitudes not only shows the gendered nature of the reproductive discourse within the movement but also hints at the gendered role allocation within Japanese society. Childbearing and nurturing children are widely attributed to women. Being a woman and motherhood are equated with one another. *Ribu* saw the idealization of women as mothers as an ideological device of the nationalist capitalist state—one that incorporated women into the capitalist machinery and regulated their reproductive capacities through the patriarchal family system for the benefit of capitalist production (Shigematsu 2012).

Japanese cultural definitions of womanhood marginalized dis/abled women in two ways. First, their bodies were not deemed appropriate vessels for childbearing. In other words, women's bodies were understood either as maternal or non-maternal and valued as productive or unproductive accordingly. It followed that considerations of gender alone could not deliver a satisfying answer to questions raised by the abortion debate. Issues related to reproduction are entwined with issues related to dis/ability and questions about potential eugenic ulterior motivations. Legislation governing women's bodies not only restricted women's bodily autonomy but also manipulated the population to make it more productive in service to the existing power structure. The consequences for dis/abled Japanese were lethal and underscore the necessity of an intersectional analysis of reproductive rights.

In the early 1970s, during the first attempts to revise the EPL, discourses on reproduction advanced by *ribu* and dis/abled women were antithetical to one another. For *ribu*, bio-political interventions into women's bodies in the form of the denial of abortion rights represented the imposition of motherhood on every Japanese woman. *Ribu* realized that women's role in postwar Japan was reduced to the production of healthy offspring who would later become components of the capitalist machinery. *Ribu* also argued that the state imposed this responsibility on women without providing the social infrastructure required to raise children (Mizoguchi et al. 1994). The social compact for women was entirely one sided. As we have seen, dis/abled women were denied motherhood by a bio-politics that characterized their bodies deficient and inappropriate for reproduction. Thus, motherhood was defined within parameters of productive capacity.

Given these circumstances, it is unsurprising that the alliance between *ribu* and the dis/ability movement on the issue didn't arise naturally. As Yonezu explains:

> There was the common perception that disabled women should not have children. So, when people who have been deprived of the opportunity to have children, who have been sterilised, who have had their wombs removed, when disabled women want to recover from those violations of their human rights, they don't think too much about not giving birth. They wanted to be able to have a baby (Yonezu 2020).

Dis/abled activists' presence and participation within this debate highlight how the Japanese discourse on reproduction went beyond consideration of bodily autonomy based on gender and sexuality. When reproduction is examined through the lens of dis/ability, the mechanisms of bio-power become visible, as do the interests they serve. What the women's rights and its gender-based arguments failed to uncover was that reproduction is not merely about having or not having children, whether or not to terminate an unwanted pregnancy. Reproduction is also subject to state bio-power exerted over the population through the medium of women's bodies and for the benefit of capitalist production. It highlights the intersectional nature of reproduction—an insight that moved reproductive discourses from liberal concepts of self-determination to a much deeper societal critique of the social order and the system of powers at play.

## 1981—calls to revise the EPL resurface again

In 1977 the Ribu Shinjuku Centre closed for good. This marked the formal end of the *ribu* movement. Two years earlier, in June 1975, Yonezu, Mori, and Sayama Sachi[6] co-founded a printshop called *Aida Kobo*. The printshop became Yonezu's new home until 1982 and a venue for former *ribu* members and activists coming by for the occasional chat (Yonezu 2020). It was there that a close friend of Yonezu alerted her to a short article on the front page of the evening edition of the *Yomiuri Shimbun* which announced a question-and-answer session in the National Diet (Japan's bicameral legislature) discussing the expungement of the "economic reason clause" from the EPL (Yomiuri 1982, p. 1). The article reported that the Minister of Health and Welfare Morishita Motoharu (1922–2014) stated his intentions to curb the legal access to abortions at a meeting of the Health and Welfare Committee (Yomiuri 1982). Yonezu and other activists experienced feelings of déjà vu. Being able to retrieve some of the materials from the 70s, Yonezu made a leaflet about it and distributed it among people who were still actively campaigning for women's issues.

Why was there a renewed interest on the part of the Japanese government to revise the EPL in 1982? In 1980 the overwhelming majority of the Liberal Democratic Party (LDP) in both houses of the National Diet ushered in a conservative era, especially in terms of social policy. That same year Japan's fertility rate fell below the population replacement level of 2.08 (Schoppa 2011). Conservative law makers blamed the declining birth rates on the increased participation of women in the labor market. They accused women of abandoning their role as mothers and caregivers for individual fulfillment. In 1980, Premier Minister Ōhira Masayoshi's cabinet (1978–1980) published the "Policy to Strengthen the Foundations of the Family" (*Katei kiban jujitsu seisaku*) which promoted the traditional family unit as the main foundation of Japanese society and upheld women's role as caregivers for children and the elderly (Norgren 2001). This set the tone for the upcoming scaling back of social welfare in Japan and the attendant shifting of responsibility from the state to the individual and of social caretaking from the state to women.

## Opposing revision attempts after *ribu*

Alarmed by these renewed revision attempts, Yonezu and representatives of other activist groups founded the "82 Liaison Group to Block the Revision of the Eugenic Protection Law" (*Yūsei hogohō kaiaku soshi renrakukai*), which after 1996 (the year the EPL was changed) became "SOSHIREN—From Women's Bodies." Members ranged from former *ribu* activists and veteran campaigners from the 1970s to a younger generation of activists such as university students and part-time workers who had not participated in the 1970s struggles. In the beginning, the group focused on keeping the EPL the way it was, and only later did activists consider writing completely new legislation regulating reproduction.

After the first gathering of the 82 Liaison Group in November, which included 1100 people across 40 organizations, attendees published a pamphlet outlining their arguments. This pamphlet featured a mechanical girl doll on the cover whose movements were controlled by someone else, symbolizing how women's bodies are controlled by the state (the image can be viewed here). The pamphlet cover featured this statement, "A human woman would not be able to keep quiet after being treated like this. I'm a living woman, and I'm going to fight back. – Fight against the Revision of the Eugenic Protection Law." The pamphlet sold very well and provided important financial support for the group's activities.

The pamphlet also stated that during the debates surrounding constitutional reform in 1980, conservative lawmakers were not focusing exclusively on the Constitution's war-renouncing Article 9; they also hoped to overturn Article 24 which called for the dissolution of the pre-war family system and the formal establishment of equality at law between men and women within the family. These actions, or so the argument went, hearkened back to the Meiji Constitution of 1889 which established the family system as the foundation of social mobilization for Japan's war efforts and it codified the gendered division of labor. For the 82 Group, proposed constitutional revisions such as the "Policy to Strengthen the Foundations of the Family" would revive the abolished family system in support of militarism and the Japanese economy (82 Liaison Group to Block the Revision of the Eugenic Protection Law 1982). As a result, women's work, which would restrict them to housework, childcare, and caring for the elderly, would effectively bar them from the economy and politics (82 Liaison Group to Block the Revision of the Eugenic Protection Law 1982). With these arguments activists framed government efforts to revise EPL, itself part of the broader conservative agenda to dismantle social welfare, as the reinstatement of the gendered division of labor. The results would be that "... women are at home (behind the leadership) and men are at work (on the battlefield)" ('82 Liaison Group to Block the Revision of the Eugenic Protection Law 1982, p. 5). State intervention focused on women's roles and bodies was a critical piece of the government's social engineering.

In addition to Yonezu's group of activists, there were four other blocs which compromised the resistance to the EPL revision attempts and all opposed the deletion of the "economic reason clause" from the law, participating activists ranging from well-established groups and medical professionals to grassroots women's groups and organizations involved with maternal and child health (Amemiya 1994; Norgren 2001; Yonezu 2021). A broad consensus among Japanese women buttressed the legitimacy of women's groups in the campaign. Soon political leaders concluded that women's sentiments and activism were serious threat to the political status quo. Activists' political leverage combined with the very well-organized opposition to proposed revisions (especially in local council assemblies) were instrumental in the government's decision to abandon their plans for revising policy (Norgren 2001).

Rather than concentrating on who led the revision attempt and how it was defeated, my investigation interrogates efforts by allied activists to challenge revision of the EPL and the rhetoric that infused their mobilization. Once again, women's rights activists and dis/ability activists engaged one another to craft an intersectional analysis of salient issues.

As of 1982, proposed changes to the EPL focused on eliminating the economic reasons clause and did not include a fetal clause. Unsurprisingly, the movement's vanguard consisted of women's organizations. Still, dis/abled people were not absent from campaign protests, and they often participated in rallies and demonstrations organized by Yonezu's group. Dis/ability activists did so because they feared that the government might eventually reinstate eugenic abortions as had happened during the 1970s, they often joined rallies or demonstrations of Yonezu's group. Nonetheless, dis/abled organizers remained distrustful of women's groups seeking to preserve the EPL as written. Dis/abled people continue to speak out against the fetal clause by invoking their knowledge of and experiences with maternal killing. It is important to mention that at this point in time there was no specific advocacy or activist group for women with dis/abilities. This only changed in 1986 with the establishment of the DPI Disabled Women's Network, an organization with which Yonezu is still involved. Yonezu recalls that dis/abled people, especially male leaders of the dis/ability movement, had fundamental disagreements with women's rights activists and these had to be overcome:

> ... I don't know if we really understood each other. You know, the men in the disabled people's group were very much opposed to the women's group, likening themselves as if they were unborn babies, or as if they were little

> children who had been born with disabilities and who might be killed by their parents. It was very difficult to overcome that and to have a discussion (Yonezu 2020).

These communication hurdles were mostly overcome by the formation of personal friendships and continuous dialogues between members of both groups, including that between Yonezu Tomoko and *Aoi shiba no kai* leader Yokota Hiroshi. Even so, ideological tensions persisted throughout the development of an intersectional analysis and articulation of a joint political position on reproduction.

Over time, what began in 1982 as a coalition led by a steering committee of organizational liaisons gradually yielded deepening trust and personal relationships among meeting attendees. The committee adopted the idea first advanced by the *ribu* movement that state policies governing population growth subordinated women and that state control of reproduction affected all individuals. This development demonstrates that *ribu's* challenge to state bio-power endured through the 1980s as did arguments against state intervention in reproduction and government control of women's bodies. This legacy persisted in the person of Yonezu Tomoko.

The announcement that there would be no revision or amendments to the EPL in 1983 did not mark the end of the group. Although the law continued to be problematic and was understood as such by activists like Yonezu, it also represented the only option for a legal abortion for Japanese women at a time when the Penal Code still criminalized the termination of a pregnancy. Consequently, activists embraced a new goal: replacement of the EPL and decriminalization of abortion. One of the reasons for the urgency for new legislation was that under the EPL, sterilization of mentally and/or physically dis/abled people was still allowed and practiced. As a matter of fact, between 1948 and 1996, more than 16,500 people were sterilized without their consent, as sanctioned by Articles 4 and 12 of the EPL which upheld involuntary sterilization (Tsuchiya 1997). During the 1980s, more victims of sterilization emerged within the dis/ability movement as a result of the burgeoning independent living movement in Japan. Hence, the EPL's highly discriminatory nature and eugenic language against dis/abled people catalyzed the writing of a new legislation during the 1990s.

As discussed earlier, the EPL was not the only legislation that governed reproduction. The Maternal and Child Health Care Act also upheld population control. Although the law does not feature any explicitly eugenic language, its call for women to give birth to "healthy" children was implicitly eugenicist. In 1983, concurrent with activists' mobilizations to oppose revision of the EPL, the Central Child Welfare Council, an advisory body to the Minister of Health and Welfare, began to consider the future of the Maternal and Child Health Care Act. SOSHIREN publicly highlighted how the Act worked in tandem with the EPL and the Penal Code's criminalization of abortion to subordinate women and the dis/abled (Yonezu 2021). This argument fueled continuing challenges to bio-power by movements of women and the dis/abled.

## Conclusion

While I cannot reconstruct the actual process whereby the present-day progressive Reiwa Shinsengumi party developed their critique of capitalist productivity as the sole determinant of people's value in Japanese society, I have documented the origins of this social criticism in the 1970s reproduction debate. Central to its formulation were the *ribu* movement and dis/ability activists who elevated debates over reproduction to an expansive critique of power relations and values in postwar Japan. Indeed, it was only through the constructive exchange of ideas and experiences by *ribu* women and dis/abled people that the reproduction debate significantly intervened in Japanese bio-politics. Key to this was the recognition by activists of the profoundly intersectional nature of reproduction and its functioning as a mechanism for state control of bodies. Further, the campaigns of the 1970s and 1980s remind us that reproduction must be interrogated through the intersecting lenses of gender and dis/ability. Further, analysis of Yonezu Tomoko's life and activism illumine the process by which the ideas and politics of the *ribu* transcended the movement itself and infused Japanese politics through the 2019 elections. Finally, this chapter challenges conventional wisdom among academics that Japan's 1968 and liberation movements—the Japanese New Left and its successors—ended in failure. Indeed, dis/ability challenges us to think more carefully about how we evaluate Japan's radical moments and to tease out historical connections that otherwise remain invisible.

## Notes

1 Throughout this chapter, I will use the Japanese word order for names, surname first followed by the first name.
2 From here on I will refer to the *ūman ribu* movement as just *ribu*.
3 Yonezu Tomoko is also known for protesting the exclusionary exhibition practise of Leonardo DaVinci's Mona Lisa at the Tokyo Metropolitan Art Museum in 1974 in the so-called "Mona Lisa Spray incident" where she sprayed red paint at the artwork's security glass case. She subsequently was detained by the police. However, this chapter will focus on the equivalences Yonezu and the *ribu* movement drew between women and dis/abled people regarding reproduction only.
4 Since 2018, 25 victims of forced sterilizations under the now defunct law came forward and sued the Japanese government over this human rights violation (Hovhannisyan 2020; legal team of the victims of the Eugenic Protection Law 2021).
5 For more detailed information on *Aoi shiba no kai*, see Chapter 9.
6 Sayama Sachi joined the Group of Fighting Onna in 1971 and was one of the founding members of the Ribu Shinjuku Centre (Shigematsu 2012). Sayama Sachi is a pseudonym she uses as an activist (Yonezu 2021).

## References

82 Liaison Group to Block the Revision of the Eugenic Protection Law, (1982). *Fight against the revision of the Eugenic Protection Law*. Tokyo: Aida Kōbō Printshop.

Amemiya, K. K., (1994). *The road to pro-choice ideology in Japan: a social history of the contest between the state and individuals over abortion*. Ann Arbor, MI: University Microfilms.

Asahi Shimbun, (1982). Untitled article. 30 June. p. 1.

Campbell, J. C., (1992). *How policies change: the Japanese government and the aging society*. Princeton, NJ: Princeton University Press.

Castellini, A., (2017). *Translating maternal violence: the discursive construction of maternal filicide in 1970s Japan*. London: Palgrave Macmillan.

Chronology: The History of Disabled People (and Their Movement) in Japan, (2021). arsvi.com [online]. Available from: http://www.arsvi.com/d/d00h-e.htm

Davis, L. J., (2017). *The disability studies reader*. 5th ed. New York: Routledge.

Estevez-Abe, M., (2008). *Welfare and capitalism in postwar Japan: party, bureaucracy, and business*. Cambridge, UK: Cambridge University Press.

House of Representatives, (1949). *Yūsei Hogo Hō [The Eugenic Protection Law]*. Tokyo: National Diet of Japan.

Hovhannisyan, A., (2020). The testimony of a victim of forced sterilization in Japan: Kita Saburō. *The Asia-Pacific Journal: Japan Focus*. **18**(7.2), 1–11.

Kato, M., (2009). *Women's rights? The politics of eugenic abortion in modern Japan*. Amsterdam: Amsterdam University Press.

Mainichi Shimbun, (2019). *Candidate with ALS guaranteed to win seat in Japan upper house* [online]. Available from: https://mainichi.jp/english/articles/20190721/p2a/00m/0na/004000c

Mizoguchi, A., Saeki, Y. and Miki, S., (1992) *Shiryō Nihon ūman ribu-shi: Volume 1, 1969–1972*. Tokyo: Shōkadō.

Mizoguchi, A., Saeki, Y. and Miki, S., (1994). *Shiryō Nihon ūman ribu-shi: Volume 2, 1972–1975*. Tokyo: Shōkadō.

Mizoguchi, A., Saeki, Y. and Miki, S., (1995). *Shiryō Nihon ūman ribu-shi: Volume 3, 1975–1979*. Tokyo: Shōkadō.

Nakamura, T., (1995). *The postwar Japanese economy: its development and structure*. Tokyo: University of Tokyo Press.

Norgren, T., (2001). *Abortion before birth control: the politics of reproduction in postwar Japan*. Princeton, NJ: Princeton University Press.

Oakley, D., (1978). American-Japanese interaction in the development of population policy in Japan, 1945–52. *Population and Development Review*. **4**(4), 617–643.

Oguma, E., (2015). Japan's 1968: a collective reaction to rapid economic growth in the age of turmoil. *The Asia-Pacific Journal*. **13**(1), 1–31.

Saxton, M., (2017). Disability rights and selective abortion. In: L. J. Davis, ed. *The disability studies reader*. 5th ed. New York: Routledge. pp. 72–88.

Schieder, C., (2021). *Coed revolution: the female student in the Japanese New Left*. Durham, NC: Duke University Press.

Schoppa, L., (2011). *Race for the exits: the unraveling of Japan's system of social protection*. Ithaca, NY: Cornell University Press.

Shigematsu, S., (2012). *Scream from the shadows: the Women's Liberation Movement in Japan*. Minneapolis, MN: University of Minnesota Press.

Siebers, T., (2017). Disability and the theory of complex embodiment: for identity politics in a new register. In: L. J. Davis, ed. *The disability studies reader*. 5th ed. New York: Routledge. pp. 310–329.

Silvers, A., (2019). Feminist perspectives on disability. In: E. N. Zalta, ed. *The Stanford encyclopedia of philosophy* [online]. Available from: https://plato.stanford.edu/archives/fall2019/entries/feminism-disability/

Takeda, H., (2005). *The political economy of reproduction: between nation-state and everyday Life*. Oxon, UK: Routledge Curzon.
Taylor, C., (2011). Biopower. In: D. Taylor, ed. *Michel Foucault: key concepts*. Durham, UK: Acumen. pp. 41–54.
Tremain, S., (2008). *Foucault and the government of disability*. Ann Arbor, MI: University of Michigan Press.
Tsuchiya, T., (1997). Eugenic sterilization in Japan and recent demands for apology: a report. *Newsletter of the Network on Ethics and Intellectual Disability*. **3**(1), 1–4.
Yomiuri Shimbun, (1982). 15 March. unknown page number.
Yonezu, T., (2020). In person interviews with Yonezu Tomoko. 5 and 8 March. Tokyo.
Yonezu, T., (2021). Follow-up interviews via e-mail with Yonezu Tomoko. 9 April. Tokyo.

# 9 *Sayōnara CP*: The First Filmic Representation of the Japanese Dis/ability Rights Movement

*Anne-Lise Mithout*

The documentary film *Sayōnara CP* (1972) was at the same time the first movie shot by the director Hara Kazuo and the first documentary dealing with the Japanese Dis/ability Rights Movement. It made a breakthrough in the on-screen representation of people with disabilities because it not only depicted their lived experiences but also their struggle for emancipation. The movie was a collaboration between Hara Kazuo and the group Aoi shiba no kai, a pioneering association in the Japanese Dis/ability Rights Movement. Until then, dis/ability in Japanese culture had long been equated with "unhappiness": people with disabilities were represented primarily as objects of pity. Aoi shiba no kai, a self-advocacy group of people with cerebral palsy, strongly opposed this view and challenged the social perception of dis/abled people in many ways during the 1960s and 1970s. *Sayōnara CP* is a powerful vector for their message because it conveys a realistic vision of dis/abled people's struggle for empowerment. Yet, at the same time, the relation between the able-bodied director Hara Kazuo and Aoi shiba no kai members is ambiguous and several of his choices raise questions which are discussed later. Hara indeed looks at Aoi shiba no kai with a male ableist gaze, though he also questions his own position as an able-bodied director filming people with disabilities.

This chapter aims to analyze the film's visual representations of Aoi shiba no kai's activist message, their significance for Japanese society at that time and their unresolved contradictions (especially in terms of ableism and gendered representations). The study explores the relation between the on-screen representation of dis/abled bodies and the construction of dis/ability as a social phenomenon, a relation that works in two directions. First, the purpose of documentary movies is to present reality: a filmmaker chooses the documentary genre rather than fiction in order to express a supposedly objective perspective on a subject. *Sayōnara CP* is thus made to approach the reality of life with a dis/abled body in Japanese society. Yokota Hiroshi's dis/abled body is filmed at length in various situations and used to convey the association's political message. Second, filmic representations, even in documentaries, are social products, constructed by factors such as the filmmaker's and producer's beliefs or the material conditions of shooting. Therefore, the movie expresses a socially situated voice and can, in turn, be analyzed as a social reality. In a context

DOI: 10.4324/9781003257196-12

where filmic representations of people with disabilities are often infused with ableism, the fact that an able-bodied director films dis/abled bodies is not inconsequential.

My primary research material was the movie itself; yet, in order to analyze its meanings for the filmmaker and Aoi shiba no kai, I have also used Hara Kazuo's writings on the movie, gathered in his book *Camera Obstrusa* (Hara 2009), in which he details his trajectory as a filmmaker, the process of shooting *Sayōnara CP* and the motivations for his cinematographic choices. I have also analyzed various Japanese sources revolving around Aoi shiba no kai, including the writings of Yokozuka Kōichi, one of Aoi shiba no kai's leaders featured in the movie.[1]

As far as I am aware, there is little academic literature discussing this movie. Japanese scholars have analyzed the screenings of and debates revolving around *Sayōnara CP* and their role in the Dis/ability Right Movement (Sadatō 2007; Yamashita 2004), but not the content of the movie itself. There is one paper in English (Elliott 2015) that discusses it from the perspective of film studies, but as the author does not speak Japanese, her access to contextual sources was limited. Therefore, this chapter aims to fill this gap.

First, I present the association Aoi shiba no kai and its campaign for dis/abled people's self-advocacy. Then, I analyze how bodies are used in *Sayōnara CP* as vectors pointing to social problems related to dis/ability. Finally, I discuss Hara Kazuo's ambiguous gaze and the political significance of his cinematographic choices.

## Aoi shiba no kai: the first self-advocacy group of dis/abled people in Japan

A few advocacy groups had defended dis/abled people's rights in Japan before Aoi shiba no kai, yet their scope was limited to certain categories of disabilities (mostly the blind and wounded veterans). Though they campaigned for their rights, their claims were limited to their specific situations and they did not intend to speak for all "dis/abled people." For people with mental disabilities or so-called "severe" disabilities (including cerebral palsy), groups of family members were the main spokespeople (Hori 2014).

When Aoi shiba no kai started to take action, it was thus the promoter of a radically new type of activism. Aoi shiba no kai[2] was created in 1957 by former students of a special school located in Tokyo, all of them living with cerebral palsy. At first, they engaged in political discussions through a journal but, over the next 10 years, local branches were created throughout the country, especially in Kanagawa Prefecture in 1966, where *Sayōnara CP* was shot. In 1963, it established the first independent living community in Japan: *Mahārāva mura* (*Mahārāva*[3] village). The "village" was located on the lands of a Buddhist temple in a mountainous area. Thirty people with cerebral palsy lived there, in a non-medical environment, for six years; some of them married and had children in the village. The community finally disbanded but, in spite of its ending, this experiment had a strong impact on community members. For them and others, the village was proof that people with so-called "severe" disabilities could lead an independent life outside of medicalized facilities, against the flow of institutionalization promoted by the Ministry of Health and Social Welfare and public opinion at that time (Mithout 2021). Independent living was indeed the association's main motto, but Aoi shiba no kai's actions took a wide range of directions to raise public attention on dis/ability-related issues. Its members' goal was to challenge mainstream conceptions of dis/ability and to assert dis/abled people's rights to express and represent themselves.

The association's fight was especially directed against "eugenic thinking." Indeed, in postwar Japan, the Eugenic Protection Law (Yūsei hogo hō) (1948) aimed at "preventing the birth of offspring of poor quality from a eugenic point of view" (Article 1). This law authorized the sterilization of people with certain types of conditions presumed to be hereditary. Aoi shiba no kai's members objected strongly to the expression "offspring of poor quality," and the awareness of that they, too, were "beings that should not exist" guided their movement. Even though Japan's postwar eugenic policies were very different from those implemented in Nazi Germany,[4] Aoi shiba no kai emphasized the underlying threat of murder for infants born with disabilities. Fueling their discourse was the case of infanticide of a dis/abled baby that was heavily covered in the media in 1970. During the trial, a group of parents of dis/abled children had initiated a movement supporting the mother and finally, the mother received a milder sentence than the minimum sentence for murder, and the court upheld the view that the child's dis/ability was a mitigating circumstance.

Aoi shiba no kai's members were shocked by the sentence (Yokozuka 2007, p. 12). One of Aoi shiba no kai's leaders, Yokozuka Kōichi (see later), discussed this case and used it as a basis for radically criticizing the social welfare system. He argued that dis/ability policies were the expression of "the egotism and discriminatory thoughts of parents and society" (Yokozuka 2007, p. 101).

Yokozuka's condemnation of "parents" stands out. Aoi shiba no kai championed the idea of dis/abled people's self-advocacy and, consequently, its members criticized associations of parents that at the time were the main spokespersons for people with "severe" disabilities and yet were upholding views infused with ableism and eugenics (Hori 2014). Yokozuka attributed these ideas to Japanese culture, which strongly associated dis/ability with the idea of unhappiness. The parents' associations laid the ground for the exclusion of dis/abled people from society, for their neglect, and for infringement on their human rights. Therefore, Yokozuka argued that self-assertation is the only way for dis/abled people to resist oppression and to reclaim their identity as individuals entitled to equal rights with able-bodied members of society. He defined people with disabilities as "irrational beings" intent on resisting a society based on rationality and profitability and which threatens their right to exist. He argued, "if we let them think that it is natural to kill dis/abled people, one day we might get murdered too. We have to acknowledge that we are those who get murdered" (Yokozuka 2007, pp. 82–86, 97). Aoi shiba no kai's program was thus based on the consciousness of being a group of people unwelcome in society. This consciousness is the core of their movement, as expressed in their manifesto:

> We identify ourselves as people with Cerebral Palsy (CP). We recognize our position as "an existence which should not exist," in modern society. ... We refuse love and justice. We condemn egotism held by love and justice. ... We believe that an endless confrontation is the only possible course of action for us, and we act on this belief (quoted in Yoritaka 2012, p. 70).

Guided by these principles, Aoi shiba no kai mobilized in various ways: through demonstrations, pamphlets, meetings with other social movements, and negotiations with the Ministry of Health and Social Welfare. Throughout these actions, the organization spoke out in the name of all dis/abled people and successfully asserted the capacity of people with so-called "severe" disabilities to speak for themselves.

The making of *Sayōnara CP* by Hara Kazuo was a byproduct of dis/ability rights activism. In the early 1970s, Hara Kazuo was a photography student working as a helper in a special education school in Tokyo. He was also involved in different left-wing groups and social movements which proliferated during that decade[5] (Hara 2009). Hara met members of the Kanagawa branch of Aoi shiba no kai and spent time with them in Mahārāva Village. Inspired by Ogawa Shinsuke's documentary films, which filmed different social movements throughout the 1960s, Hara began shooting short films and set out to create a documentary about Aoi shiba no kai. To make the movie, he collaborated with two prominent members of the Kanagawa branch of Aoi shiba no kai: Yokota Hiroshi (1933–2013) and Yokozuka Kōichi (1935–1975).

Yokota and Yokozuka, young men living with cerebral palsy, collaborated with Hara. Both men had spent a large part of their childhood confined at home due to the lack of special education facilities in prewar Japan. However, they had been part of the Mahārāva experiment and had come to occupy leading positions in Aoi shiba no kai. They agreed to take part in the movie and defended it because, they asserted, "it was different from those social welfare films that directed a sympathetic gaze upon them from a distance, looking at them from a privileged position" (Hara 2009, p. 92). Hence, Aoi shiba no kai and Hara Kazuo's goals were converging.

## Exposing bodies, exposing problems?

Bodies occupy a major place in Hara Kazuo's cinema, as well as in Aoi shiba no kai's discourses. In a society where dis/ability is associated with shame (Katō 2010), dis/abled bodies are neither normalized nor hidden (Asaka 1993). Therefore, asserting one's dis/ability as an identity means embracing one's body as it is, and exposing dis/abled bodies through film would expose problems related to the social maltreatment of dis/ability, problems that would remain hidden as long as dis/abled people remain invisible.

### *Challenging conceptions of the "normal body"*

Aoi shiba no kai urged people with disabilities to take to the street to reclaim their right to exist. The activist Yokozuka elaborated:

> Trains, buses, footbridges, station stairs and other types of architectural constructions, entire cities ignore our existence and the fact that we are living there. So I thought our movement should begin with going out in the city. That is exposing us as we are, that is strong self-assertion (Yokozuka 2007, p. 63).

In order to claim their right to accessibility, Aoi shiba no kai members challenged conceptions of the "normal body": bodies that can stand, walk, climb stairs in the built environment. Appearing in the public space was for Aoi shiba no kai a way to draw public attention to the inaccessibility of infrastructures, especially for wheelchair users. Hara Kazuo shared this vision of the body as a way to expose social problems. As a helper in a special education school, he encouraged dis/abled students to go to a train station and ask passers-by to carry them through the stairs, his goal being to raise awareness about the issue of accessibility (Hara 2009). Yet, for the film, he decided to take this idea one step further:

> How … can this problem of standards for the body that are then imposed upon people with disabilities be destroyed? … A wheelchair might be necessary for them in their daily lives, but in order for them to confront their own bodies, they had to reject their wheelchairs (Hara 2009, p. 71).

That is why people with disabilities featured in the movie are not using wheelchairs. Yet, there are various types of cerebral palsy and each has different effects on individual mobility. Yokozuka Kōichi had difficulties walking but could stand. Conversely, Yokota Hiroshi could not stand at all, for him, not using a wheelchair meant crawling with his knees and hands on the floor.

The use of body performance as a political action is clearly visible in one of the first scenes of the movie. The scene shows Aoi shiba no kai members collecting money in the street. Images show Yokota walking on his knees and distributing pamphlets, next to a donation box where people come and put money. Most people shown as donors are in fact children: adults give them coins and make them put the money in the box. The sound associated with these images is not real-time audio recording; it is a composition of extracts from interviews with donors explaining why they gave money. Mostly they report that they "feel sorry" for Aoi shiba no kai members. Expressions such as "*kawaisou*" ("poor thing") and "*ki no doku*" ("unfortunate, pitiful") are repeated numerous times. The scene emphasizes the feeling of pity experienced by able-bodied people when they see a dis/abled person. Yokota appears at the beginning of the scene, but then the camera focuses only on donors, especially children. But while off-screen, Yokota's presence is invoked through donors' spoken comments about his body. In this way, Hara's camera captures the visual impact of Yokota's body on abled-bodied passers-by and highlights the fact that Yokota is never perceived as physically "normal," that he cannot go unnoticed in the public space. This scene reinforces the radicality of Aoi shiba no kai members appearing in the streets and being seen by the non-dis/abled public; it creates an event and attracts public attention. Making dis/abled bodies visible breaks a cultural taboo. For Hara, filming able-bodied people's reactions to Yokota's body were a way to reveal that though onlookers' perceptions were not directly negative, they were based on feelings of pity and on the belief that dis/abled people were not equal with other Japanese.

One of the final scenes of the movie also exposes Yokota's body in an even more radical way; Yokota appears completely naked while sitting on his knees in the middle of a road. The camera stays still and there is no sound for almost one minute. Finally, the image is mixed with a recording of Yokota's voice saying, "We set out to make this film to show that we can't do anything. But I was hoping I could do something to make a different kind of movie,"[6] and the film switches to Yokota with his clothes on. The scene is in a way the highlight of the movie. Hara wrote about it:

> When we first met Yokota, he'd said that he'd spent his whole life concealing his body, but that now he wanted to expose it, to completely bare himself. ... At first, Yokota had romanticized the idea of getting naked in front of the camera. But the reality was that he could only get naked after he was backed into a corner and had nowhere else to go. That's ultimately what it takes to liberate oneself (Hara 2009, p. 88).

The quotation raises questions about Hara and Yokota's relationship as I will discuss later. Yet, it highlights the meaning of the scene, and maybe of the whole movie. As Erving Goffman has shown, managing the social stigma of having a dis/abled body is a permanent burden for people with disabilities in their daily interactions (Goffman 2009). In the public space, people with visible disabilities are subject to persistent stares even though staring at dis/abled people is socially prohibited (Garland-Thomson 2009). Therefore, body performance is a mode of expression familiar to many people with disabilities, be it in their daily life or in an artistic context (Sandahl & Auslander 2005). In the performing arts, nudity is used as a way to challenge visual representations of dis/ability. Davis (1997) has shown that in classical arts, nudity is associated with beauty, even in the case of statues with missing limbs such as the Vénus de Milo. Conversely, dis/ability carries a sense of being "grotesque," therefore, dis/abled bodies are simultaneously objects of curiosity and taboo. Performers such as the dis/abled feminist performer and writer Mary Duffy expose their nude bodies in order to challenge viewers' conceptions of what is appropriate looking and beautiful (Garland-Thomson 2000). Similarly, Yokota decenters ableism by appearing naked. As Garland-Thomson (2009) has argued about female body performers:

> [Yokota] purposively enlists and manipulates the staring dynamic to mount a critique of dominant cultural narratives about disability. By boldly inviting the stare in [his] performance, [he] violates the cultural proscription against staring, at once exposing [his] impairments and the oppressive narratives about disability that the prohibition against staring attempts to politely silence (Garland-Thomson 2009, p. 33).

While the performers discussed by Garland-Thomson were all female, and thus her analysis partly focuses on how their work challenges the "male gaze" (Mulvey 1975), Yokota challenged the ableist gaze and gender norms in comparable ways. In prewar Japan, masculinity had been strongly associated with the military. Japan's modernization policy in the Meiji (1868–1912) and Taishō (1912–1926) periods revealed a hygienist preoccupation, and by upholding the ideology of the "national body," it strongly tied physical health to national power (Frühstück 2003). With the introduction of conscription, male bodies were submitted to various evaluations and measurements, and elements such as height, weight, and the ability to perform physical exercise were constructed as key to a positive masculine identity. In the postwar period, though the military system was entirely dismantled, images of men as soldiers remained deeply rooted in the popular imagination, as can be seen by the prevailing characterization of Japanese corporate workers as past-time warriors. In Japan, in the 1960s, male nudity was relatively less shown than female nudity, and, when it was, it was strongly estheticized. See, for example, the photographs of the writer Yukio Mishima exposing his athletic body and posing with a loincloth and a sword, constructing a form of military eroticism. Yokota's physical exposure was entirely at odds with this image and, consequently, it is significantly disruptive. By revealing his body as it is, with his atrophied muscles, Yokota confronts the normalized conception of masculinity as physical strength. The scene particularly affected the audience when the movie was screened. As Hara recalled, "Among people with cerebral palsy, Yokota Hiroshi was a hero. 'He's so cool,' they'd say. Especially when he took off his clothes in the end" (Hara 2009, p. 93).

Hara's challenging of ideas about the "normal body" in the documentary also interrogated "the normal way of speaking" because some Aoi shiba no kai members had difficulties pronouncing words due to their cerebral palsy, and their speeches are not easily understood by audience who are unaccustomed to listening to people with elocution difficulties. Yet, Hara chose to present the movie with no subtitles, so that the audience has to make an effort to listen and get used to his subjects' pronunciation.

### *Challenging the medicalization of dis/ability*

In *Sayōnara CP*, exposing dis/abled bodies is a political act that not only challenges body-normativity but also highlights the issue of dis/abled people's living conditions. This aspect of the film aligned with the views of Aoi shiba no kai whose members were highly critical of the medicalization of dis/ability and policies that led to dis/abled people's segregation into special institutions. Yokozuka equated special institutions with prisons (Yokozuka 2007); people living there are deprived of their individuality and freedom. Expanding on this idea, he wrote that, when he went to the street by himself, he often heard people wondering: "Which institution does he belong to?"; or even "Which institution did he run away from?" (Yokozuka 2007, p. 103). He even compared institutions to concentration camps (Yokozuka 2007).

Since its beginning, Aoi shiba no kai promoted independent living, as shown with the experiment of Mahārāva Village. Consequently, *Sayōnara CP* features people with disabilities living outside medical facilities and in their own houses. A scene that will be discussed later takes place at Yokota's house, with his wife and children gathered round. Another scene shows a garden party: several people are in a large garden filled with tangerine trees. They pick tangerines on the trees, eat them, discuss their taste, and laugh. Aoi shiba no kai's members' children are present too. The camera moves from one person to another, showing smiling faces and conveying the merry atmosphere of this moment. Nothing extraordinary happens during the scene, and the very ordinariness of the situation is striking; the scene is aimed at showing people with cerebral palsy having fun and casually spending time with their children and friends. These scenes undercut the common perceptions of dis/ability as a tragedy, of dis/abled people's lives as full of sorrow, and of dis/abled people needing medical assistance in an adapted environment. Aoi shiba no kai's members appear as ordinary adults socializing in an ordinary garden.

The matter of dis/abled people forming families and having children is explored in detail in the following scene. Indeed, marital life and conceiving children entail having sex. Yet, dis/abled people's sexuality was then (and is still) a taboo. On the one hand, dis/abled women were commonly perceived either as asexual or as easy prey for abuse, and their desires and ability to consent to sex are rarely acknowledged (Asaka 1993). On the other hand, dis/abled men are often seen as having either no desires or monstrous and uncontrollable desires (Giami et al. 1983). In Japan, the saying "don't wake up the sleeping child" (*neru ko wo okosu na*) expresses the idea that sexual matters must not be discussed with dis/abled people so as not to give them desires that they do not naturally feel and that they would not be able to fulfill. This belief led to a deficit of sex education in special schools (Mithout 2018; Ningen to sei kyōiku kyōkai 2001).

To return to the scene, a group of Aoi shiba no kai male members answer Hara's question about their first sexual relations. Two of them explain that they went to a red-light district, one clearly says that he raped a girl, and two others report that they had a girlfriend (one of them mentions that he was 28 at that time, while the others had their first sexual experience when they were 16–18). They all express their feelings about these experiences very openly; three of them explain more or less clearly that, the first time, they could not have an erection; the one who raped a girl expresses regrets. All of them recalled youthful feelings of frustration over being excluded from the realm of love and sexuality: "thinking of sex was taboo," "I suppressed it for so long." Their families' message to them was that they would never be seen as suitable partners by the opposite sex, and that even if they were, they would not be physically able to have intercourse.

The report of having committed a rape is striking for two reasons: it reveals not just the intensity of frustrations felt by dis/abled men, an intensity that can turn into violence, but also the existence of a social context of gendered relations that makes rape a possible choice for a frustrated man. Indeed, as will be discussed later, Hara's representations of gendered relations in the movie are rooted in sexism and the almost casual discussion of rape as a form of sexual encounter, one that is on an equal footing with other forms of sexuality, reveals the overwhelmingly masculine perspective of the group and the filmmaker, and their striking lack of consideration for women as subjects (the position of women in the association will be discussed later).

In sum, though, this scene is groundbreaking because it deals with a subject hardly ever discussed in the Japanese media and movies of that time, namely, dis/abled people's sexuality and reproduction. As mentioned earlier, in the 1970s, Japanese society was living under a eugenic regime: the Eugenic Protection Law, passed in 1948, authorized the sterilization of people with certain kinds of disabilities.[7] Therefore, showing on screen dis/abled people openly discussing their sexual and reproductive lives was breaking a taboo. In all these aspects, the movie uses images of dis/abled bodies and discourses about physical disabilities to expose various social barriers to dis/abled people's social participation and relationships and disrupts widespread discriminatory beliefs. However, some of Hara's choices in making this movie are questionable, as seen by his casual handling of rape. His radicality is not entirely free of ambiguities and contradictions.

## Hara Kazuo's gaze: from ableism to abuse?

Just like representations of women in the arts are mainly constructed by the "male gaze" (Mulvey 1975), representations of people with disabilities created by non-dis/abled artists are often the products of an "ableist gaze." Ableism is

> a network of beliefs, processes and practices that produce a particular kind of self and body (the corporeal standard) that is projected as the perfect, species-typical and therefore essential and fully human. dis/ability, then, is cast as a diminished state of being human (Campbell 2001, p. 44).

Movies made by able-bodied filmmakers not only tend to present characters with disabilities as radically and ontologically different from non-dis/abled characters, but these films also "isolate disabled characters from their able-bodied peers as well as from each other" (Norden 1994, p. 1). Hara's gaze, though guided by a willingness to challenge common perceptions of dis/ability, does not avoid all the pitfalls of ableism.

### *Creating a freak show?*

*Sayōnara CP* was shot at a time when perceptions of the exploitation of dis/abled bodies were changing. In Japan, representations of dis/ability have long been associated with the idea of *misemono*, that is, "things to be shown." Street performances were an important part of urban popular culture in the early modern period: it encompassed exhibitions of exotic animals, flowers, inventions, or human performances such as music, dance, theater, or exceptional strength (Markus 1985). Exhibitions of people with non-standard bodies were also common.[8] In a context where many of those performances took place during shrine festivals, those exhibitions were often promoted as religious lessons, as disabilities were believed to be a form of punishment for sins committed in a previous life (Hur 2020, p. 61). Such exhibitions were banned from the streets in 1873, both on humanitarian grounds and as a result of a new conception of public morality (Markus 1985). Yet, "freak shows"[9] did not disappear before the second half of the 20th century. The economic exploitation of people with disabilities became reprehensible as a legislation regarding dis/abled workers' employment emerged in 1960, and the exhibition of a dis/abled person on stage in an "inappropriate environment" was forbidden in 1970 by the Basic Law on people with disabilities.

Therefore, in 1972, when *Sayōnara CP* was shot, the idea of showing dis/abled bodies to an audience was perceived as an infringement on human rights. One scene reveals that when Hara was filming the movie, he was accused of creating a freak show. Indeed, he films Yokota making a poetry performance on a street in Tokyo. Yokota is kneeling on the ground. After writing his name and drawing a circle around himself with a chalk, he starts reciting his poems. A crowd is standing around him and listening. At some point, the camera stops, and the voice of a police officer says "This is a freak show. Please stop." Hara (2009, p. 85) explains that, while he was reloading the camera, Yokota was taken away by the police. Hara and his producer had to go to the police station and argue with officers so that Yokota could be released.

In his book, Hara writes that, at first, Yokota was very pleased with the adventure, as he felt that he had created a situation that required police intervention. But Hara replied: "You say so excitedly that so many people gathered to see you when you started reading poetry—but in fact, they gathered because of the movie camera." After Hara said this, Yokota was crushed and said he wanted to quit the movie. In this episode, one can see the ambiguity of Hara and Yokota's relationship. Even though Hara is embracing Yokota's ideas of challenging perceptions of dis/ability through body performance, he affirms that Hara is the one creating the event with the camera, while denying Yokota's ability to attract interest. His dismissal of Yokota's part in the film can be interpreted as an expression of ableism.

Even more revealing is another scene when Yokota expresses his desire to quit the movie. Yokota has been filmed crawling out of a train while the door closing warning signal is sounding. He has a narrow escape, is visibly scared, and falls on the platform. In the next scene, he explains that his family wants him to stop walking on his knees and to again use a wheelchair. It must be stressed that Yokota's not using a wheelchair in the movie is Hara's idea, and not something that Yokota would normally do. Yokota's wife strongly disagrees with Hara's idea because she finds the act of crawling humiliating for her husband (see later). Yet, Hara and his producer insist (as well as other Aoi shiba no kai members) and finally Yokota agrees to keep crawling in front of the camera.

The visual representations of dis/ability created by Hara are simultaneously a challenging of ableism and a product of it. However, Hara tries to provide a counter-mechanism to the ableist gaze: some scenes feature Yokozuka holding a camera and approaching people in the street, taking close-up pictures of them. This "reverse gaze" (Hara 2009, p. 76) mechanism was inspired by an exercise that Hara had to do as a photography student: getting close to an unknown person in the street and taking a close-up of them. He asked Yokozuka to perform this exercise, so as to capture reactions of passers-by to being suddenly approached and photographed by a dis/abled person. Hara's idea was to reverse the stare that people with disabilities receive from passers-by every time they go out. In that sense, he expresses reflexivity regarding his own ableist gaze as a filmmaker creating performances with people with disabilities:

> The premise at the start of the film was the conflict between the healthy and the disabled. As the camera operator, and as a person who wanted to express himself, I stood on the side of the healthy, opposite the disabled subjects of my film. This was extremely clear when I aimed the camera at them; there was no question about it. The real problem was thus how to contradict or negate this dichotomy (Hara 2009, p. 76).

### *Looking at the individual rather than the group*

Hara established his method for making documentaries in opposition to the previous generation of Japanese documentary filmmakers, represented by the director Ogawa Shinsuke. While documentaries made by Ogawa Productions focused on communities, Hara focused on individuals (Hara 2009). He adopted this method again in his second movie, *Extreme Private Eros*, which focuses on his ex-wife.

In *Sayōnara CP*, Hara's focus on individuals is visible throughout the film. Most scenes focus either on Yokota or Yokozuka and tackle their relations with non-dis/abled people through individual interviews or "events" such as the poetry reading or the photography exercise. Yet, this focus can be surprising, to the extent that Aoi shiba no kai was a group of people with cerebral palsy with strong community ties. Activities such as peer discussions and group protests played a major part in the life of the association, which had started, as noted, as an independent living community. Therefore, the focus on individuals was not necessarily the most natural choice to capture the originality and radicality of the movement. The lack of representations of peer relations between people with disabilities can be seen as another expression of Hara's ableist gaze.

Indeed, the film contains very few group scenes where people with disabilities interact with one another. The first is the garden party scene, discussed earlier. The second is the one where several Aoi shiba no kai members discuss their first sexual experiences. Through a group scene, the filmmaker mediates the group interview. The situation is not that of a peer discussion: each participant narrates his own story, with the camera focusing on his face, and no reactions from other participants are seen or heard, and thus no group conversation is created. Hara's choice to film individuals results in silencing group dynamics. It also obliterates the political principles of the movement.

Hara's choice is questionable from the perspective of dis/ability studies. The narrative of "disability as a personal tragedy" (Oliver 1990) is one of the most common conceptions of dis/ability, and the whole point of the social model of dis/ability was to contradict it by highlighting the role of social and environmental factors in the process of disablement (Shakespeare 2010). Psychology has also played a role in emphasizing the management of the consequences of impairment at an individual level (Sullivan 1991). Therefore, movies dealing with dis/ability have long been anchored in the conception of dis/ability as isolation (Norden 1994, p. 3). Given this, Hara's approach to documenting dis/ability is not as disruptive as he claims. Consciously or not, while trying to challenge prejudices and stereotypes about dis/ability, he chose to use a way of filming dis/abled people deeply rooted in one of the most persistent stereotypes: that of dis/abled persons as isolated individuals. This choice is all the more surprising that the whole point of the Japanese Dis/ability Rights Movement was to take people with disabilities out of isolation and create a sense of belonging and community. Yet, the depiction of dis/abled people as isolated individuals and the stereotypes that ignore the existence of peer relations are still very common today, for example, in contemporary Japanese television drama (Mithout 2020).

### *Looking at dis/abled men*

The last point that can be raised about Hara's choices is the issue of gendered representations. Indeed, rather than a movie about "dis/abled people," *Sayōnara CP* is a documentary about "dis/abled men". All the members of Aoi shiba no kai who appear on screen are male, except one: Yokota's wife, who appears in one scene.

Yokota's wife, Yoshiko, could have been a very interesting character. She too has cerebral palsy (yet her mobility is less impaired than her husband's). She is married and has given birth to a child, a very rare situation for a dis/abled woman at that time. She could have given her opinion, especially during the scene about love and marriage, where she could have provided a different perspective on those subjects.

Yet, she is not interviewed. One can understand why during the scene where she appeared: her relationship with Hara seems very conflictual. Indeed, she strongly disapproves of Hara's choices in making the film, especially his insistence on making her husband crawl. The scene begins with Yokota explaining to a group of Aoi shiba no kai members that his wife will divorce him if he continues walking on his knees, and that he has to stop making the film. At first, his comrades say things like "You're the man in the family, you're the one to make rules." But then one of them says that they have all put money in the movie and that stopping the shooting now would be "cheating." Yokota is visibly insulted by this argument and starts fighting with him. As the meeting takes place at Yokota's home, his wife and son are present in the room at this moment. Yoshiko repeatedly asks Hara to leave. She seems very angry and says things like "How dare you in my home? … It's unlawful entry. I'll get someone." She turns her back on Hara in order to avoid the camera, but Hara keeps filming. Finally, she goes to the sleeping room, where Yokota and their son follow her. Yokota begs her to calm down and says "I don't want Hara to see us like this." Finally, Yoshiko says to other Aoi shiba no kai members: "You're not a woman. Let me ask you. I didn't want to bring this up but, what about your own family? … You want to break up a family to continue this film?"

This scene is violent as it expresses all the tensions revolving around the film, between Yokota and his wife, between Hara and Aoi shiba no kai members, and among Aoi shiba no kai members. Yoshiko appears as doubly isolated from the other participants: because she is the only one expressing harsh criticism towards Hara, and because she is the only woman. The scene suggests that those two elements are connected: she wants to stop the film because she perceives it as a threat to her family, while her role as a woman is to protect her family. This assumption is deeply anchored in the belief that women have the responsibility of maintaining a harmonious household (Bernstein 1991; Gordon 1997). Therefore, she accuses Aoi shiba no kai members of not understanding her position because they are men. Their disagreement on the film is thus expressed under the form of a gendered conflict. As Yoshiko is the only dis/abled woman in the film, she is made to represent a "female perspective." On the opposite, male Aoi shiba no kai members express various opinions during the film and their positions in debates are not connected to their gender. As a result, Yoshiko is made to embody her gender, instead of expressing her own personal opinions and experiences like other participants do. It thus seems that, in this movie focused on "individuals," the underlying definition of an individual is in fact "a man."

However, this should come as no surprise in a movie shot during this period. The invisibility of women was common to all social movements in the 1960s: female activists were confined to subaltern tasks such as cooking for their male counterparts, who were conducting the core of political activities. This situation fed activist women's frustration and led to the emergence of feminist movements in the 1970s (Mackie 2003). The same phenomenon existed in the Japanese Dis/ability Rights Movement, as Aoi shiba no kai was a male-dominated group until the mid-1970s to early 1980s, when women progressively began to access more leadership positions in the movement. The emergence of female voices had a strong impact on the movement, with a change in methods (for example, collaborations with feminist movements) and more attention given to some subjects that were neglected by male leaders, such as marriage, reproduction, eugenic sterilizations, and sexual violence (Mithout 2022). This shift started when a female branch of Aoi shiba no kai (*CP Onna no kai*) was created, in 1974, two years after the movie was shot. Vittinghoff's contribution, in this volume, provides a more detailed account of the twists and turns of the relations between feminist movements and the dis/ability right movement.

## Conclusion

The aim of this chapter was to discuss both the originality and the ambiguities of *Sayōnara CP*. There is no denying that this film was a milestone in the representation of people with disabilities, as it enabled Aoi shiba no kai members to speak in their own voices and to express their political goals. Its focus on dis/abled bodies was at the same time a way of challenging common conceptions of dis/ability and a method for deconstructing the filmmaker's own "ableist stare" (Boyd 2016), even though in a limited and imperfect manner. Its flaws are partly due to the director's own choices, and also reflect the state of society at that time, especially in terms of gendered relations.

Because of its radicality, the movie was at first screened mainly in universities, among left-wing student groups. Yet, it progressively reached a larger audience. It thus made a breakthrough in the cinematic representations of dis/ability. But its main achievement was probably the impact it had on people with disabilities themselves: by showing people with disabilities expressing their individualities, it provided dis/abled spectators with images of empowerment.

## Notes

1 This material is used more extensively in Mithout (2021).
2 Which means "Green grass society," to convey the idea that "grass stays green no matter how many times it is stepped on."
3 "Mahārāva" meaning "loud cry" in Sanskrit.
4 As they were aimed to eliminate certain types of disabilities in future generations, not to murder living people.

5 Social movements were booming in Japan in the 1960s: student movements, movements opposing the war in Vietnam, protests against the Okinawa Reversion Treaty, various communist movements (Chapter 8).
6 He implies that, for Aoi shiba no kai members, the purpose of the movie was to show that people with disabilities are blocked in their life by social and architectural barriers, and to offer an image of dis/abled people as willing to take an active part in society. He is referring to the common representations of people with disabilities in Japanese cinema at that time, as pitiful, passive, and unhappy and he is expressing his wish to challenge this image through *Sayōnara CP*.
7 Among the victims were people with cerebral palsy; see Toshimitsu (2016).
8 These exhibitions reinforced the taboo on dis/ability (as discussed earlier) because they contributed to highlighting dis/ability as an extraordinary (monstrous or sacred) phenomenon, thus setting it apart from ordinary life.
9 Freak shows somehow similar to that of the Western world existed in Japan in the late 19th, early 20th century.

## References


Asaka, Y., (1993). *Iyashi no sekushī torippu*. Tokyo: Tarōjirōsha.

Bernstein, G. L., (1991). *Recreating Japanese women, 1600–1945*. Berkeley, CA: University of California Press.

Boyd, N., (2016). The warped mirror: the reflection of the ableist stare in David Lynch's The Elephant Man. *Disability & Society*. **31**(10), 1321–1332.

Campbell, F. K., (2001). Inciting legal fictions: 'disability's' date with ontology and the ableist body of law. *Griffith Law Review*. **10**(1), 42–62.

Davis, L. J., (1997). Nude Venuses, Medusa's body, and phantom limbs: disability and visuality. In: D. T. Mitchell and S. L. Snyder, eds. *The body and physical difference: discourses of disability*. Ann Arbor, MI: University of Michigan Press. pp. 51–70.

Elliott, L. L., (2015). *In what ways was Kazuo Hara's representation of The Green Lawn Movement in his debut film, Goodbye CP, a radical new form of representing disabled characters on screen?* London: Dissertation for Bachelor of Arts, Central Saint Martins College of Arts & Design.

Frühstück, S., (2003). *Colonizing sex sexology and social control in modern Japan*. Berkeley, CA: University of California Press.

Garland-Thomson, R., (2000). Staring back: self-representations of disabled performance artists. *American Quarterly*. **52**(2), 334–338.

Garland-Thomson, R., (2009). Dares to stares: disabled women performance artists and the dynamics of staring. In: C. Sandahl and P. Auslander, eds. *Bodies in commotion: disability and performance*. Ann Arbor, MI: University of Michigan Press. pp. 30–41.

Giami, A., Humber, C. and Laval, D., (1983). *L'ange et la bête: représentations de la sexualité des handicapés mentaux chez les parents et les éducateurs*. Paris: Editions du CTNERHI.

Goffman, E., (2009). *Stigma: notes on the management of spoiled identity*. New York: Simon and Schuster.

Gordon, A., (1997). Managing the Japanese household: the New Life Movement in postwar Japan. *Social Politics: International Studies in Gender, State & Society*. **4**(2), 245–283.

Hara, K., (2009). *Camera Obtrusa: the action documentaries of Hara Kazuo*. Los Angeles: Kaya Press.

Hori, T., (2014). *Shōgaigaku no aidentiti—Nihon ni okeru shōgaisha undo no rekishi kara*. Tokyo Seikatsu shoin.
Hur, N-l., (2020). *Prayer and play in late Tokugawa Japan: Asakusa Sensōji and Edo Society*. Leiden, the Netherlands: Brill.
Katō, M., (2010). Cultural notion of disability and prenatal testing in Japan. In: M. Sleeboom-Faulkner Margaret, ed. *Frameworks of choice: predictive & genetic testing in Asia*. Amsterdam: Amsterdam University Press. pp. 125–144.
Mackie, V., (2003). *Feminism in modern Japan: citizenship, embodiment and sexuality*. Cambridge, UK: Cambridge University Press.
Markus, A. L., (1985). The carnival of Edo: Misemono spectacles from contemporary accounts. *Harvard Journal of Asiatic Studies*. **45**(2), 499–541.
Mithout, A.-L., (2018). Récupérer le sexe qui m'a été volé: la sexualité comme affirmation de soi chez Asaka Yūho. *Genre, Sexualité et Société* [online]. **19**. doi:10.4000/gss.4200
Mithout, A.-L., (2020). Disabled heroins: representations of women with disabilities in Japanese television drama. In: D. Garrisi and J. Johanssen, eds. *Disability and the media in Asia*. New York: Routledge. pp. 114–134.
Mithout, A.-L., (2021). Aoi shiba no kai: un mouvement de personnes handicapées face à l'eugénisme. *Cipango: French Journal of Japanese Studies*. **24**, 129–162.
Mithout, A.-L., (2022). Entre mouvements féministes et mouvements de personnes handicapées: confrontation ou convergence des luttes?. *Japon Pluriel*. **13**, 313–320.
Mulvey, L., (1975). Visual pleasure and narrative cinema. *Screen*. **16**(3), 6–18.
Norden, M. F., (1994). *The cinema of isolation: a history of physical disability in the movies*. New Brunswick, NJ: Rutgers University Press.
Ningen to sei kyōiku kyōkai – Shōgaiji sākuru (2001). *Shōgaiji (sha) no sekushuariti wo hagukumu*. Tokyo: Ootsuki shoten.
Oliver, M., (1990). *The politics of disablement*. New York: Palgrave Macmillan.
Sadatō, K., (2007). Ōsaka—Kōbe no shōgaisha jiritsu seikatsu undo no genten. *Core Ethics*. **2**, 129–139. Available from: https://www.r-gscefs.jp/pdf/ce02/sk01.pdf
Sandahl, C. and Auslander, P., eds., (2005). *Bodies in commotion: disability and performance*. Ann Arbor, MI: University of Michigan Press.
*Sayōnara CP*., (1972). *Directed by Kazuo Hara*. Tokyo: Shisso Production.
Shakespeare, T., (2010). The social model of disability. In: L. Davis, ed. *The disability studies reader*. New York: Routledge. pp. 266–273.
Sullivan, M., (1991). From personal tragedy to social oppression: the medical model and social theories of disability. *New Zealand Journal of Industrial Relations*. **16**(3), 265–272.
Toshimitsu, K., (2016). *Sengo Nihon ni okeru josei shōgaisha e no kyōseiteki na funin shujutsu*. Kyoto: Ritsumeikan University Press.
Yamashita, Y., (2004). Kenjōsha to shita shōgaisha kaigo ni kakawaru to iu koto: 1970nendai shōgaisha kaihō undo ni okeru kenjōsha undo no shisō wo chūshin ni. *Shukutoku daigaku shakaigakubu kenkyū kiyō*. **38**, 51–61. Available from: http://www.arsvi.com/2000/031013ys.htm
Yokozuka, K., (2007). *Haha yo! Korosu na*. Tokyo: Seikatsu Shoin.
Yoritaka, T., (2012). Nihon ni okeru shōgaigaku no genryū to shite no Aoi shiba no kai. In: M. Hori, ed. *Kyōsei no shōgaigaku—haijo to kakuri o koete*. Tokyo: Akashi shoten. pp. 48–77.

# 10 *Voltron: Legendary Defender* and Compulsory Able-Bodiedness

*Lauren Rouse*

## Introduction

*Voltron: Legendary Defender* is an animated Netflix television series that tells the story of "Defender of the Universe" Voltron. Voltron is a 100-meter tall robot warrior composed of five lion mechas.[1] The lions and Voltron are separate entities but Voltron cannot function without the lions. Each of the lion mechas has a pilot called a Paladin. The five Paladins bring to the team different personalities, bodily strengths, and weaknesses. Their attributes amplify when they work together to form Voltron.

This chapter will focus on one Paladin, Shiro. He has a prosthetic arm and post-traumatic stress disorder (PTSD). He is also same-sex loving. His trauma came from being kidnapped by alien forces and sold to a gladiator-esque fighting ring. Despite his dis/ability, this character embodies natural leadership qualities, such as being charismatic, inspirational, and trustworthy. He acts calmly and is in control during crisis. His dis/ability does not drive the plot. This contrasts with how characters with dis/abilities are often treated in media, in that their dis/ability must have relevance to the plot. Because of this, fans feel compelled to make dis/ability relevant to the plot by creating fan fictions drawn from the original canonical media.

Representations of Shiro's dis/ability vary in fan fictions: some writers replicate common dis/ability tropes, while others heal Shiro's trauma through involving him in romantic relationships. Some writers disregard his dis/ability and trauma altogether by reimagining Shiro as an able-bodied character with no past trauma. They do so by not tagging the work, thus failing to draw attention to his dis/ability in the canonical work. These normalizing tactics are similar to previous representations of dis/ability (Bérubé 2018; Mitchell & Snyder 2014; Quayson 2007; Schalk 2018). Several fan fictions also heteronormatize Shiro by placing him in same-sex relationships that are meant to normalize him. By deemphasizing dis/ability and ignoring trauma, fan narratives reinforce hegemonic identity politics by subjecting disabled characters to compulsory able-bodiedness (McRuer 2006) and homonormative domesticity, both force to bodily and social norms. I argue that normalizing homonormative representations would undermine subjugated knowledge about disabilities, which are functions of fan fictions.

DOI: 10.4324/9781003257196-13

## Background

Fan fiction (known as fic) is produced by amateurs. Fic continues, retells, rearranges, or completely scraps canonical[2] media works. Fic often reframes narrative in the canon, placing characters in plotlines not found in mainstream television shows, movies, and comic books. Henry Jenkins suggested that "fan critics pull characters and narrative issues from the margins; they focus on details that are excessive or peripheral to the primary plots but gain significance within the fan's own conceptions of the series" (2012, p. 155). Further, "fanfiction [is] widely more biodiverse than the canonical works that it springs from" (Jamison 2013, p. xiii). Fic uses a variety of tropes, kinks, relationships, sexual fetishes, and a whole host of other, non-sex-related tropes.[3]

Even though fandom could be a liberatory space and a subversive rejection of mainstream media (Bacon-Smith 1992; Jenkins 2012), this space is dominated by white males. Racism and anti-Blackness in this space are unwelcoming to fans of color; media accessibility and assumed ableism have presented roadblocks to the disabled community; pervasive sexism and misogyny gatekeep this space from women, non-binary, trans*, and gender non-conforming fans. Thus, there is a rise in awareness of fandom not being a safe space for fans who do not identify as abled-bodied heterosexual white males. Despite the advancements, dis/ability continues to be an unexplored area in the scholarship of fandom.

Scholars of fan studies need to acknowledge how dis/ability impacts fandom. One way to do so is to "borrow the discourse of disability studies—of embodiment, recalcitrance, normativity, and access—as the primary screen through which to view all fanworks, regardless of their engagement with disability explicitly" (Clemons 2019, p. 253). Through examining the intersections of underrepresented identities, scholars may "[show] the power imbalances and failures of systems to grant personhood; [which in turn] help … locate possible re-enabling strategies available in fannish practices" (Clemons 2019, p. 253).

This chapter responds to Clemons' work by examining how fans appropriate or dismiss dis/ability in *Voltron* fic. First, I will give a brief overview of the television show and the character Shiro. Then, I will introduce the methodology. Next, I will analyze several fics to see how fans use tropes to construct Shiro's ability by erasing his dis/ability or curing it with him engaging in heteronormative relationships. From there, I posit that fans socially construct Shiro's disabilities, which allows him to embody the noble crip trope. However, replicating these tropes reinforces heteronormative ideology and fails to diversify the representations of dis/ability in relation to other identities.

## *Voltron: Legendary Defender*

The eight seasons of *Voltron: Legendary Defender* tells the stories of how Paladins of Voltron save the galaxy from the Galra Empire. The five Paladins of the lions that make up Voltron are Takashi "Shiro" Shirogane, Keith, Katie "Pidge" Holt, Lance, and Hunk. The lions choose the Paladins; only one can be the official pilot at a time. At the beginning, the lions are separated from each other because the former pilot of the Red Lion hid them across the Galaxy during an attack. In the first episode, the Paladins find the Blue Lion before setting off across the Galaxy to find the rest of the lions and form the fabled Voltron.

In season 1, Shiro is written as the natural leader of the Paladins because of his age, rank, temperament, and abilities. He is older than the other Paladins and outranks them. He is known for his patience, kindness, endurance, and perseverance. He copes with the trauma of being kidnapped and forced to fight in a gladiator arena. Further, he is known for his almost unheard-of piloting abilities. In addition, Shiro is a skilled hand-to-hand combatant. Lastly, his prosthetic arm enables superhuman strength and durability.

In the first two seasons, Shiro's dis/ability was not relevant to the plot. Even though he experienced traumatic flashbacks and chronic pain from his prosthetic, these moments do not drive the plot. For example, when Voltron fights a Robeast in season 1, the combat triggers a traumatic memory of him fighting the same type of mecha in the gladiator ring. At first, he struggles to communicate with his team because of PTSD. But a sound triggers Shiro to realize that his dis/ability does not hinder his skill: "That sound! I recognize it from my time in Zarkon's prison! I know how to beat him!" Past trauma taught Shiro how this team could defeat the robot. The show did not hide his dis/ability, and fans and media critics initially received it positively.

However, as the series goes on, his disabilities are undermined. In some episodes, other characters talk over Shiro when he wants to discuss his dis/ability; in others, his dis/ability was forgotten. For example, in season 8, Shiro enters an arm-wrestling competition that reminds him of his gladiator fighting days. Fans expected this would be a significant moment because of his trauma, but this scene is over almost as quick as it begins, there is no hint at his dis/ability or trauma. The undermining of his dis/ability co-occurs with changes in his trauma triggers: in earlier seasons, the triggers are similar; in later seasons, these are more flexible, depending on what the plot demands.

## Methodology

In this section, I explain how I chose the sample for analysis. First, I searched for fics on the *Voltron: Legendary Defender* fandom on a fic hosting site called Archive of Our Own (AO3). In April 2020, the dataset had about 75,000 fics. I narrowed down the results by using the parameters "kudos," "Include Relationship," "Completed," and "English." For the "include relationship" parameter, I chose two types of pairings: Shiro/Keith, because it was the most popular among fans and Shiro/Adam, because it was the least popular and was a canonical relationship. I chose the top five fics with 5,000 words or above in each relationship pairing. Lengthier fics would allow for in-depth character development. Next, I looked at the tags.

### *Tagging*

Fic writers tag their works on AO3. Tags are author-generated, fic writers decide whether or not to tag specific parts of the story. Tags contribute to the overall paratextuality, materials supplied by the authors, editors, printers, and publishers about the main text of a fic. Some examples are story synopsis, non-fiction description, and poems. Tags set up a frame for readers to read a story in a specific way (Leavenworth 2015).

Some tags could be "BDSM," "Modern Era," or "UK Education system." These tags inform about the story content and allow readers to draw inferences. For example, the tag "Modern Era" informs readers that the story takes place in an alternative universe fic where canonical characters are placed in a different setting. In this era, they use cell phones and computers. The "BDSM" tag means that sex scenes follow the BDSM (bondage, discipline, dominance and submission, sadomasochism) etiquette. This tag warns users who may be uncomfortable with sex scenes or BDSM content. Finally, "UK Education System" tells readers where a particular story is set.

Tagging may allow for what Mitchell and Snyder (2014) call "narrative prosthesis." They argued that prosthesis is often used to solve the dis/ability problem in narratives. The function of the prostheses serve both literary and body functions:

> A body deemed lacking, unfunctional, or inappropriately functional needs compensation, and prosthesis helps to affect this end. … To prostheticize, in this sense, is to institute a notion of the body within a regime of tolerable deviance. If disability falls too far from an acceptable norm, a prosthetic intervention seeks to accomplish an erasure of difference all together; … the minimal goal is to return one to an acceptable degree of difference (p. 7).

As a literary prosthesis, tagging erases dis/ability via a "quick fix," hence affording the audience the ability to consume the media without constant vigilance about the character's dis/ability. For visual media, tagging alleviates viewers' discomfort as they no longer need to determine if they should look at the disabled body or decide what their moral standard of dis/ability is. A literary prosthesis makes dis/ability non-existent.

Literary prosthesis through tagging is common in the Voltron fandom: while there are 49,000 tagged fics with Shiro on AO3, only 0.0007% were tagged with #canondisabledcharacter, 0.04% tagged with #PTSD, 0.052% tagged with #trauma, and 0.00018% tagged with #trauma and #canondisabledcharacter. This invisibility of dis/ability is not uncommon across other fandoms.

Gray (2010) noted that popular fics in the "relationship pairing" parameter are very impactful because they serve as an unofficial guide for the tagging, plotlines, and characterizations of other fics. For example, if a popular fic gives a character one *specific* characteristic (such as an eye color description), other authors may replicate that tag/characterization within the fandom, eventually becoming "fanon" (fan-made canon). Fanon allows for the replication of tropes, characterizations, genres within a relationship pairing and, therefore, fandom. All of these pairings can provide a space to reinforce negative stereotypes as well as sexist, racist, or ableist tropes.

## *Close reading: disability tropes and plot-telling*

In this section, I analyze how dis/ability was used as a trope—or plot-telling device—and how tropes build the fic narratives and genres which eventually impact how fandom interprets certain characters. While some tropes were brought from the original canon (for example, Hunk in *Voltron* is loving and big-hearted), others were introduced by fans.

Three major recurring tropes are as follows: first, the pity trope; second, the handicapped badass; and third, the noble crip. The first trope—the pity trope—is about the helplessness of being disabled. In these fics, Shiro's partner infantilizes him and stops him from taking care of himself. The focus on how the partner cares for Shiro means they *really* care for him. The second trope is the handicapped "badass." This is similar to Shiro's canonical portrayal. His mechanical arm allows for him to do things that no human can do. He is a superhuman with it. The third trope is the noble crip and requires more explanation.

I coin the term noble crip to combine the "noble" savage trope from romantic literature and the super "crip" trope of heroes who overcome their dis/ability. The noble crip is the "Other" in the story even though the noble savage is a juxtaposition to Otherness in early American literature.[4] The noble crip who has overcome life difficulties is an outsider to the norm. I argue that the process of overcoming difficulties is embodied in heteronormativity. Since heteronormativity is rooted in gender binary and assuming sexual and marital relations between the opposite sex (Waner 1991), it implies futurity. To explain, heteronormativity has an intrinsic link to historical forms of reproduction; therefore, heteronormativity means futurity.

### *Shiro, "noble crip"*

None of the sample fics addresses the implications of Shiro's dis/ability. In the canon, he lost an arm and has PTSD but is characterized as an incredible marksman, fighter, leader, and thinker. In the canonical show, Shiro embodies the noble crip trope, as he is still an outsider and seen as the Other. He does not belong to the norm because his prosthetic was a weapon given to him, allowing him to survive fights in Galra gladiator competitions. Since the arm is not part of him but an object, it poses a challenge to his humanity and subjectivity. Comparatively, Erevelles (2011) addresses this objectivity among soldiers who have served in Operation Iraqi Freedom:

> [they] are the new posthuman subject who is intimately interconnected with modern technologies of war that are infused with the ability to reason and think without being interrupted by emotions, guilt, or body limitations. … the cyborg soldier, in almost every way, is in constant battle against the normal human male body (2011, p. 111).

Drawing on this idea, Shiro is a cyborg in two ways: first, he is one through his prosthetic arm; second, in him being a part of a lion robot linked by consciousness in military situations. Having the prosthetic arm and being part of the lion make Shiro's body becoming "whole" again. Having a "whole" body allows him to overcome his dis/ability. However, his able-bodiedness is only temporary; in time he returns to being disabled again. When this happens, he is still seen as the "Other."

Unlike in the canonical work, Shiro in the fics has permanently and unproblematically overcome his dis/ability because fans choose to ignore his dis/ability. Nonetheless, this literary erasure does not mean readers will accept him as the norm because they could still make reference to his dis/ability in the television show. In other words, background characterization and fic's paratext remind readers that Shiro exists outside the norm of able-bodiedness; intertextuality between canonical text and fan fictions prevents him from fully embodying the able-bodiedness set up in fics. Because of this inbetween-ness between the erasure of dis/ability in fics and fans' recalling of the canonical work, Shiro can simultaneously exist as an abled body that has overcome a dis/ability AND the Other with a disabled body. In this sense, he is at the intersection and within the trope of the noble crip: that his background characterization cannot be erased even if fans choose to ignore it in their fics.

## Shiro/Keith: lovers and brothers in arms

In the canonical work, Shiro has the intersectional identity of being disabled and gay. Viewers learn about his dis/ability early on but they only learn about his sexuality in later seasons when they are introduced to his fiancé and his marriage to another man. Fans have built on Shiro's sexuality vis-à-vis dis/ability.

The three dis/ability tropes—pity, the handicapped badass, and the noble crip—are used in fics about the Shiro/Keith relationship. The relationship between Shiro and Keith is very contested in the fandom. "Antis" (fans who dislike a certain relationship or pairing because of moral or personal reasons) believe that in the canonical work, Shiro and Keith, often referenced as "brothers," are more like coworkers: one as a commanding officer, and the other his inferior. Some believe Shiro is more like a father-like figure to Keith so a same-sex, underaged relationship is pedophilic. At the start of the series, Shiro is in his mid-20s while all the other Paladins are thought to be older teens. However, since they knew each other before the story begins, Shiro and Keith could have been underaged when they began their relationship. (Shiro is thought of to be almost 18 when he meets a much younger Keith, thought to be as young as 11, but probably 14 or 15.)

Fans did not alter too much of Keith's background. In the canonical show, Keith was orphaned at a young age. He is seen as a rebel who is prone to violence and has trouble connecting with others. He views Shiro as a mentor. In fics, Keith suffers from the emotional trauma of being abandoned by his parents. However, in the case of modern alternate universes (AUs),[5] he is fostered or adopted. He also tends to be a victim of child abuse and/or sexual assault. The trauma experienced by Keith and Shiro may be seen as soulmate markings.

In soulmate markings, AU characters are marked so that they can discover each other and become soulmates. A marking can be a tattoo with words or a birthmark. In this fic, soulmates receive identical markings on their bodies. For example, if one soulmate receives a bruise, the other will also receive the same bruise of the same shape. Sometimes the markings just appear on the body, other times they are inflicted by themselves or by their soulmates. In this motif, the trauma of receiving an injury is a "signifier of ritual insight; [and labels] disability as inarticulable and enigmatic tragic insight" (Quayson 2007, p. 53).

Subjecting a soulmate to a trauma before receiving the same one instills the need for one soulmate to rescue another from their disabling past and bring that partner to the able-bodied present. This return to the able-bodied present is in conjunction with the hypernormative structure (McRuer 2006). In soulmate AUs, it is inevitable that markings will connect the two characters. It is also inevitable that one soulmate would remove another from a traumatic situation. Because the end goal of such AUs is to eliminate past trauma through finding a soulmate, this goal reinforces able-bodiedness as one's body becomes whole again after finding a soulmate. In the Shiro/Keith pairing, fics attempt to "cure" mental/cognitive disabilities by pairing an able-bodied character with a disabled one. Shiro is disabled, but Keith is able-bodied; Keith was abused by his parents, but Shiro has a loving family.

In the fic, Keith experiences intense pain due to parental abuse; so Shiro deliberately crashes his car into a tree:

> He was numb to the entire affair.
>
> All he could think about was how losing a limb felt to someone who hadn't yet lost one. He wondered if the gash across his nose would scar the other person, or if it would fade like bruises did.
>
> The cybernetic arm was a complicated operation. He wondered what it felt like to his soulmate. What was he putting the other through? That person who had already suffered so much was being subjected to it without any pain medication, any buffer between them and the surgery.
>
> It was strange. The arm felt like his by all accounts, and yet not. It responded a little slower than his flesh arm, but that was to be expected

> since it was brand new. ... For goodness' sake, he could still feel things with it, although his sense of touch had been muted somewhat. It felt like wearing gloves, almost.[6]

In the aforementioned description, the readers only see Shiro's dis/ability by him feeling Keith's abuse. The soulmate connection allows Shiro to (re-) experience a dis/ability and to renew feeling about it. In this description, no physical pain is inflicted on Shiro by another person on Shiro but he receives it through Keith. By experiencing it, he turns to the way that his dis/ability might affect others. He notes that his new prosthetic is *almost* as normal as his real arm, that he is still whole, that he can still be normal. The juxtaposition of normalcy versus abnormalcy reinforces the narrative of able-bodiedness. In Shiro's mind, if he embodies a just-enough-of-a-normal body, his soulmate will accept him. Because the wholeness of Shiro's body matters, fans tell each other that it is important to be able-bodied in order to be loved by a soulmate.

Shiro/Kieth fics belong to the hurt/comfort genre (H/C) which reinforces heteronormativity. H/C is "a [fic] genre that involves the physical pain or emotional distress of one character, who is cared for by another character. The injury, sickness or other kind of hurt allows an exploration of the characters and their relationship" ("Hurt/Comfort-Fanlore" n.d.). Central to this H/C genre is the care received after trauma; the traumatized character receives comfort from a romantically involved character, and eventually returns to an abled body when the care work is done. When H/C genre is a foundation for these fics, writers show that society does not want a disabled body and it can be healed through another person's care.

## Shiro/Adam: bury your gays

Like the Shiro/Keith pairing, the Shiro/Adam pairing is contested in the fandom, mostly because of how the pairing was handled in the canon. Fans accused showrunners of queerbaiting them because Shiro's sexuality was only revealed in season 7, the second to last season. In addition, at the end of the season, Adam died in a fiery crash after fighting against the enemy and shortly reuniting with Shiro. Therefore, many fics in this pairing attempt to "right" the supposed wrongdoings, namely, killing off Adam and hiding the relationship of Shiro and Adam. These fics are known as "fix-it" fics.

In these "fix-it" fics, many understand what Shiro's dis/abilities are through Adam's eyes. Adam, as the spouse, is forced into a caretaker position, insinuating the role of the ethics of care within fandom (*Care Ethics*, n.d.).[7] As Gilligan (2013) argues: Care Ethics "requires [carertaker's] paying attention, seeing, listening, responding with respect" (p. 23). Society undervalues care ethics even though it is important to members of the disabled community.

When fics have a character performing these tasks, it brings Care Ethics to light by highlighting the gendered labor of care in the current, patriarchal, US society. However, the radical addressing of Care Ethics in fics is overshadowed by potential conflicts in the story when the spouse uses "safety" as a reason to undermine another person's self-autonomy. For example, Adam wants to keep Shiro safe by denying him bodily and self-autonomy:

> Adam argues that it is a sign that Shiro should slow down, while Shiro strongly argues back against any lightened schedule. That's when Adam knows that he is going to lose this fight repeatedly, until Shiro goes so far; Shiro is Icarus and flying to close to the sun.

In this fic, Adam maintains that Shiro's terminal illness—muscular dystrophy—means he should abandon all work, but Shiro disagrees. However, Adam does not respond with respect or listen to Shiro's objection, thus violating the principle of Care Ethics.

Heteronormativity dominates the Shiro/Adam pairing through futurity. Kafer (2013) explored futurity in *Feminist, queer, crip*: "disability is seen as the sign of no future, or at least of no-good future … not only do we accept that couples don't want a child with Down Syndrome, we know that anyone who feels otherwise is 'crazy'" (p. 3). This fic introduces Shiro's muscular dystrophy and notes Adam's immediate turn to disparaging the future:

> It's just that Adam thinks about the illness a lot. When he wakes up, when he eats, when he goes to sleep. When he waits for Shiro to come back from the hospital and hopes in vain for better news about a degenerative curse. …
>
> Adam doesn't know how, where, or for how long Keith and his antics can fit between these entities. He wonders whether he himself can still fit anyhow, anywhere, any longer as well. He wants nothing more than to stay, but there is so much energy spent on Shiro's part to juggle it all, it is unlikely this can go on for long.

Adam's denial of Shiro living with a dis/ability is a denial of the future: he expects Shiro to die from this disease. Adam does not think Shrio has a future because he will not be able to fly, complete his work, and fit into the normate[8] box. All these mean he is metaphorically dead. When Shiro leaves for a mission, Adam is again struck by his partner's mortality, stressing that going into space may kill him. Adam has a fear that dis/ability will make Shiro fail at work, reinforcing an able-bodied, capitalist narrative that an economically productive person needs an abled body (Chapters 5 and 6).

## Conclusion

Fan studies scholarship has noted that fan fiction is transformative and sets out to provide a better space for those who read and write it. However, this is unrealistically utopian. Even though social media platforms and fics allow the underrperesented to talk back, fics continue appropriating tropes about dis/

ability and heteronormativity. Beyond blatant ableism in physical fan spaces and online dis/ability, misogynoir detrimentally affects Black women's experiences in fandom spaces; Gamergate and Comicsgate add to mainstream racist, sexist, and homophobic movements.[9] Fandom is not the "safe" space initially thought to be or touted by white fans. In this chapter, I have shown that tropes are only one small tool that reinforces hegemonic ideology through fandom.

One could argue that some *Voltron* fans are merely replicating the ways that dis/ability is expressed in the show to their fics. Because of the pervasive able-bodied narratives in Western media, it is not surprising that fans do not go out of their way to research dis/ability to better understand their characters. For example, some depictions of Shiro's muscular dystrophy show that fans have little understanding of how the disease varies among patients and how it progresses.

Voltron fan fiction and fandom, like all others, do not exist in a cultural vacuum: fandom is and has never been apolitical. Scholars cannot claim that fandom is liberatory or a safe space when it routinely disregards, harasses, and attacks readers who belong to marginalized communities. By ignoring Shiro's dis/abilities and entrenching him in canonical and fanonical heteronormativity and able-bodiedness, fans do a disservice to their own fandoms and to themselves. Ultimately, expanding upon ideas about dis/ability in these fics can allow for fans to embody non-ableist, non-hegemonic discourses about dis/ability and queerness, which in turn benefits us all.

## Notes

1 Mecha is a common genre in anime or manga (Japanese animation and comics). The main character is a giant robot that is partially or completely controlled by human pilots. Mechas are typically humanoid in shape, although their parts may be biomorphic.

2 Canon or canonical works are the original media works. For example, the films *Avengers*, *Black Panther*, and *Thor*; television shows *WandaVision*, *Falcon and the Winter Soldier*, and *Agents of Shield* in the Marvel Cinematic.

3 Fandom often splinters around a media text. Fans who write on Archive Of Our Own (AO3) might decidedly ignore other parts of that media object's fandom, creating separate fandoms around the same media text. According to Jenkins (2012), men tend to participate in fandom through ranking every character while women are more likely to participate by creating transformative works. Despite the differences, they still enjoy the same text (Jenkins 2012).

4 For example, the titular character in Aphra Behn's Oroonoko embodies this trope. Oroonoko was an Indigenous person enslaved to white colonizers, but he overcame his "destitute" beginnings and acted like the British to the point where his rulers overlooked his background.

5 Alternate universes are a genre of fic that takes the characters and some aspects of their canonical worlds to another setting. Some popular AUs are Hogwarts AU, where the characters of one series become students and professors at Hogwarts. Another kind is AUs where science fiction and fantasy characters are put into modern-day settings in the West, such as living in New York or London.

6 The quotations from fan fiction throughout the essay are what Annette Markham (2012) calls an "ethical fabrication," a representative quotation that is constructed to convey what the data are like. It protects the writer's identity online.
7 The ethics of care is a philosophical theory that states that there is "moral significance in the fundamental elements of relationships and dependencies in human life" (Care Ethics n.d.).
8 According to Garland-Thomson (1997), "the normate is the imagined everyman whose self-determination, independence, rational thinking ability, and physical sturdiness makes American democracy philosophically possible. The disabled figure–the cripple, the invalid, the idiot–comes to represent everything that the normate is not" (p. 8).
9 Gamergate is an online harassment campaign that targets women in the video game industry. Comicsgate is a campaign that opposes diversity in the superhero comic book industry.

## References

Bacon-Smith, C., (1992). *Enterprising women: television fandom and the creation of popular myth*. Philadelphia, PA: University of Pennsylvania Press.

Bérubé, M., (2018). *The secret life of stories: from Don Quixote to Harry Potter, how understanding intellectual disability transforms the way we read*. New York: New York University Press.

Care Ethics, (n.d.). *Internet encyclopedia of philosophy*. Available from: https://www.iep.utm.edu/care-eth/.

Clemons, A., (2019). Enabling/disabling: fanfiction and disability discourse. *Canadian Journal of Disability Studies*. **8**(2), 247–278. doi:10.15353/cjds.v8i2.500.

Erevelles, N., (2011). *Disability and difference in global contexts: enabling a transformative body politic*. New York: Springer.

Garland-Thomson, R., (1997). *Extraordinary bodies: physical disability in American culture and literature*. New York: Columbia University Press.

Gilligan, C., (2013). *Joining the resistance*. 1st ed. Malden, MA: Polity.

Gray, M., (2010). From canon to fanon and back again: the epic journey of supernatural and its fans. *Transformative Works and Cultures*. **4**. doi:10.3983/twc.2010.0146.

"Hurt/Comfort-Fanlore", (n.d.). *Fanlore.org*. Available from: https://fanlore.org/wiki/Hurt/Comfort.

Jamison, A., (2013). *Fic: why fanfiction is taking over the world*. Dallas, TX: BenBella.

Jenkins, H., (2012). *Textual poachers: television fans and participatory culture*. New York: Routledge.

Jenkins, H., (2018). Fandom, negotiation, and participatory culture. In: P. Booth, ed. *A companion to media fandom and fan studies*. New York: Wiley. pp. 11–26. doi:10.1002/9781119237211.ch1.

Kafer, A., (2013). *Feminist, queer, crip*. Indianapolis, IN: Indiana University Press.

Kurvet-Käosaar, L., (2013). What only fiction can do. In: G. Rippl et al., eds., *Haunted narratives: life writing in an age of trauma*. Toronto: University of Toronto Press. pp. 316–320.

Leavenworth, M. L., (2015). The paratext of fan fiction. *Narrative*. **23**, 40–60. doi:10.1353/nar.2015.0004.

Markham, A., (2012). Fabrication as ethical practice. *Information, Communication & Society*. **15**(3), 334–353. doi:10.1080/1369118X.2011.641993.

McRuer, R., (2006). *Crip theory: cultural signs of queerness and disability*. New York: New York University Press.

Mitchell, D. T. and Snyder, S., (2014). *Narrative prosthesis: disability and the dependencies of discourse*. Ann Arbor: University of Michigan Press.

Quayson, A., (2007). *Aesthetic nervousness: disability and the crisis of representation*. New York: Columbia University Press.

Schalk, S., (2018). *Bodyminds reimagined: (dis)ability, race, and gender in black women's speculative fiction*. Durham, NC: Duke University Press.

Schönfelder, C., (2013). Renegotiations of longing and belonging: exile, memory, and nostalgia. In: G. Rippl et al., eds., *Haunted narratives: life writing in an age of trauma*. Toronto: University of Toronto Press. pp. 297–304.

Waner, M., (1991). Introduction: fear of a queer planet. *Social Text*. **29**, 3–17.

# 11 Corrective Lens: Dis/abilities and the Materiality of Media

*Micky Lee*

## Introduction

Media studies scholars have not paid much attention to dis/abilities as a difference comparable to race, gender, and class. This oversight may be explained by a belief that dis/abilities are pathological, thus not a socially constructed difference (Alper et al. 2015; Ellcessor & Kirkpatrick 2017). Nevertheless, since the 2000s, there has been a surge of media scholarship on dis/abilities. Some studies examined media representations (Ellis 2019), online subjectivity (Adkins et al. 2012; Boellstorff 2019), and digital media accessibility (Ellcessor 2016; Ellis & Kent 2011; Ellis et al. 2017). This surge may be explained by the increased interactivity of media: the media have changed from something that the audience watch to something with which they interact. Because interactive media require audience participation, they create new ways for the audience to experience the media as technologies and meaning-making systems (Alper et al. 2015).

However, the tensions between social constructionist and embodiment approaches have not been adequately explored in media studies scholarship (see Chapter 1 for the definitions of both approaches). For example, even though the media could include a wider range of representations of dis/abilities, representations alone do not increase media accessibility because media producers have little control over how different bodies experience the media. Even if telecommunication policies require media companies to provide accessible content such as audio description and closed captioning, accessible content does not lead to the same media experience because each modality requires a different cognitive capability and provides a different sensory experience. Therefore, media studies scholars should expand their interests beyond representations and media accessibility by paying attention to the relationship between the body and technologies. Some questions to ask are as follows: How do media technologies change the body? If they do change the body, then what is meant by a normal body? Is the understanding of a normal body changing along with that of technology? If yes, then how is the body socially constructed when it is technologically modified?

DOI: 10.4324/9781003257196-14

To answer these aforementioned questions, media studies scholars need to forefront the relations between the body and technology by paying attention to how the materiality of technologies actively shapes the body. For example, the definition of normal eyesight—"normal visual acuity measured at a distance of 20 feet"—disembodies the body ("Visual acuity" no date ). This definition has overlooked a range of materials with and through which the patients experience the world during an eye examination, such as the glossy paper of the chart and the fluorescent light. This is not to suggest that the paper texture and type of light will lead to a misdiagnosis, but the ability and experience of reading out rows of letters is not isolated from other sensory inputs. Ellcessor et al. (2017) argue that a range of material, social, and cultural institutions construct and reproduce a "normate" subject position. Often people who identify as able-bodied do not take into consideration how their bodies have come to be normal or might have been measured and diagnosed to be abnormal.

In this chapter, I look at two assistive technological devices: eyeglasses and Google Glass. I argue that both are media for the following reasons: first, assistive technology provides users a vantage point because like any mass media—television, film, the Internet—they do not neutrally reflect the world, but enable viewers to experience the world through them; second, one definition of medium—the material through which something is conveyed—highlights the different materials that compose all technological devices; third, materials used in devices shape users' subjectivity, such as the shape of eyeglasses frames widening or limiting the field of vision; lastly, devices actively shape the body and demand it to accommodate them, thus altering the body. In one example, the weight of eyeglass frames and the pressure of their arms permanently shape the flesh and bone behind the ears. In other examples from across time, extensive exposure to today's electronic screens (Myopia [Nearsightedness] no date) and the new availability of daily newspapers in 18th-century Britain have caused myopia in the population (Eighteenth Century Spectacles, no date).

A key question that explores the tensions between social constructionist and embodiment approaches is how the materiality of the media foregrounds the body when it interacts with technologies (Ellcessor et al. 2017). Galis (2011) suggested that dis/ability is experienced in everyday life and through different subject positions and that this dis/ability experience is linked to a socio-material configuration; one in which technologies, bodies, and culture are entangled. I assert that assistive technology does not enhance or correct the body. Instead, it shapes, molds, and trains the body: some of these bodily limits are spatial, others are temporal. Assistive technology is best seen as devices that challenge these limits, which in turn call the question of what bodily normalcy is. In other words, if the body is *always* a limit to a human, then what does an abled/disabled body mean?

Furthermore, I argue that a focus on the materiality of the media will challenge a temporal linearity assumed in both medical and social constructionist models of dis/abilities. The ideology of temporal linearity assumes that advancement in human knowledge and changes in attitude will move the human race forward. An attention to the materiality of media disproves these assumptions and necessitates taking an embodiment approach to dis/abilities. To explain briefly, humans are embodied to do things, we rely on both natural and human-made environments to achieve social purposes. Human experience is always enabled and limited by the environments built with various materials. But the assemblage of materials shapes human actions which in turn re-assemble the built environment. A good example is that people in a wheelchair could not move onto or off the sidewalk, so curb cuts were invented. In the following, I first review the literature on dis/abilities and technologies from a media studies perspective.

## How media studies scholars conceptualize dis/abilities and technologies

Writings on media technologies and dis/abilities can be categorized into two groups: the first one concerns how technologies increase accessibility for users, and the second one asks how technologies create users' subjectivity. Some studies adopt an embodiment approach, but few pay attention to the materiality of the media.

Media studies scholars commonly agree that technology is not neutral, its design is embedded with ableist norms (Bitman & John 2019; Ellcessor 2016; Ellis 2019; Goggin & Newell 2003; Ledder 2019). These norms very often intersect with the gender, race, class, and geographical location of technology designers (Ellcessor 2016). For instance, even though digital media are believed to break down barriers by allowing users with dis/abilities to function (thus pass) as able-bodied, digital media design perpetuates such norms (Goggin & Newell 2003). For example, most digital media for the disabled are poorly designed and unintentionally exclusive; these technologies may in fact disable users because they allow for few modalities of information input (Paterson 2017).

Drawing on feminist scholarship (Wajcman 1991), Goggin and Newell (2003) argued that technology is a form of social knowledge, practices, and products that are outcomes of power struggles between social groups. Technology is not merely tool; it also constructs dis/abilities (Goggin & Newell 2003). Adding to this, Gilmore (2019) has suggested that media technologies shape bodily and cultural practices, such as hearing and listening.

Some scholarship focuses on national telecommunications policies about media inclusivity and accessibility. Media access is a central experience for audiences with dis/abilities (Ellis 2019). Digital technologies enable audiences with dis/abilities to personalize content such as audio description, captions, signing, spoken subtitles, clean audio, and simultaneous interpretation (Ellis 2019). However, telecommunications policies are often embedded with ableist norms (Ellis 2019; Goggin & Newell 2003) and neoliberal economic ideals (Goggin & Newell 2003). Regulators see the whole audience as autonomous individuals who can inform the market of their needs and wants even though the market tends not to recognize the full citizenship of this audience

(Goggin & Newell 2003). However, when technology is intentionally designed with inclusivity, it could provide a positive environment for content creators with dis/abilities (see Johnson (2019) on the live streaming site twitch.tv).

Inclusive technologies are often an afterthought of the market (Gilmore 2019). For example, online streaming services are less subject to regulations than traditional broadcasters, so they are exempt from providing captioning (Ellis 2019). Companies often use financial constraints to explain why they are not able to provide accessible media (Ellis et al. 2017). Lastly, there are different kinds of accessibility, including those to online cultural production, political participation, and social collaboration (Ellcessor 2016).

Some studies focus on the potentials and shortcomings of the Internet. The Internet offers a number of advantages for people with dis/abilities: expanding users' social capital (such as interpersonal connections) and cultural capital (such as cultural, subjective, and affective dimensions of online capital) (Davis & Boellstorff 2016); allowing users with dis/abilities to share information, form self-help groups, and be rid of prejudice. However, shortcomings are plentiful. For example, the online world reinforces the boundaries between the abled and disabled body (Cole 2011), differentiates online practices (Shpigelman & Gill 2014), and endorses unfriendly user interface (Ellis & Kent 2011).

The second group of literature examines how digital media enable users to form a new kind of subjectivity by drawing on embodiment theories. Self-driving cars, Google Glass, AirPods, and Second Life require scholars to rethink the boundaries between humans and technology, online and offline worlds, the body and the mind (Davis & Boellstorff 2016; Gilmore 2019; Goggin 2019). For example, digital technology enables teenagers with intellectual dis/abilities to develop an aesthetic agency through creation of an alternative inclusive space within which participants can negotiate the meaning of intellectual normalcy (Adkins et al. 2012).

Digital technologies create an economic subjectivity for users with dis/abilities when they engage in a platform economy in which they form an entrepreneurial subjectivity and inclusive citizenship (Goggin et al. 2019). An online entrepreneur is implied to be risk-taking and economically productive, both qualities essential to an ableist selfhood (Boellstorff 2019). In addition, digital work is believed to increase individuals' worth in the labor market. When workers can pass as abled-bodied, they can bypass inequity, exclusion, and implicit bias in the workplace. Lastly, they can choose an online identity that challenges bodily normalcy, such as a hybridized human-mythical creature avatar (Davis & Chansiri 2019). However, Elman (2018) warns that wearable devices, such as those for fitness, may reinforce the belief that an economically productive person is able-bodied.

The above-reviewed studies show that digital technologies do not compensate for or normalize bodies, they also do not make bodies irrelevant in an online environment. Instead, technologies may increase the capacities of people with varying dis/abilities and allow them to experience the body and technology in new ways. Very often, these experiences are co-constituted by gender, race, and class. These studies have laid a good foundation for the remainder of the chapter to further inquire how technologies have enabled bodies of varying abilities to experience the environment. In the next section, I argue how media studies scholars can intervene in a study of technology and dis/abilities by focusing on materiality.

## Materiality in assistive technology

Materiality of the media refers to their physical properties, such as the raw and human-made materials used in technological hardware, the infrastructure to which the devices are connected (such as electricity and WI-FI), and physical properties of the medium (such as sound waves transmitted through the air and radiated light) (Lievrouw 2014). By examining materiality, scholars necessarily acknowledge that studies of media are not limited to immaterial representations or users' subjectivity, they also include an examination of technical devices on which media are watched and the technological infrastructure within which digital signals are transmitted.

Considering the materiality of media will bring to the forefront the central place that the body plays in using technical devices. Previous literature has stated that technical devices were designed for a physically, psychologically, and cognitively abled body: one that has the ability to perceive light and color, move the hand and fingers with dexterity, manipulate the interface with cognitive capability, and stay focused in a cacophony. Dis/abilities provide a lens for scholars to examine how a body experiences the media through interacting with technical devices and infrastructure in specific time and space. The limits of the body and the enabling functions of technology will call into question what bodily ab/normalcy is.

I use eyeglasses and Google Glass as two examples of assistive technology. The Assistive Technology Industry Association (ATIA) defines assistive technology as "products, equipment, and systems that enhance learning, working, and daily living for persons with disabilities" ("What is AT?" no date). Assistive technology can be hardware—such as equipment—and software—such as computer programs. Some are low tech—such as the white cane—while others are high tech—such as optical readers. Learning materials and curriculum aids are also assistive technology (Visual acuity, no date). In this chapter, I follow the lead of Goggin and Newell (2003) and define assistive technology as a set of knowledge and an assemblage of technical devices. However, I add to this definition by highlighting the role of the body as it interacts with technology and vice versa.

## The slash: myopia, between ability and dis/ability

Myopia is the medical term for nearsightedness, a vision condition caused by an elongated eyeball or an overly curved cornea that makes refracted light focused in the front of the retina, making distant objects blurry. Myopia is a common vision condition, affecting approximately 30% of the US population (Visual acuity, no date ) and 80% of the population in some parts of East Asia (Orszag 2018). It is projected that in 2050 half of the world's population will be myopic (Ossola 2016).

Myopia provides a good case study to examine the slash (/) between ability and dis/ability. As this chapter's introduction stated, the term "dis/abilities" acknowledges that both ability and dis/ability are not constant conditions, but processes of being and becoming. The slash signifies an in-between, ambiguous space that refuses to be labeled. Myopia illustrates this space: it is caused by a bodily characteristic deemed defective, but not legally defined as a dis/ability[1]; a remedy—the eyeglasses—marks the body as different but is commonly worn.

Eyeglasses are not as stigmatized like other assistive technologies because the wearers are often viewed positively.[2] Eyeglass wearers are perceived to be more intelligent and belong to a higher social class. They enhance positive perceptions of African Americans, making them appear to be friendlier, more attractive, and less threatening (Whitbourne 2016). Moreover, eyeglasses became fashion accessories in the 1940s when women were encouraged by advertisers to match eyeglasses with outfits. Later, when European designers entered the markets, the placement of their logos on the arms of the eyeglasses became fashionable (Ward 2005).

## Myopia and eyeglasses: first, there is a problem, then there is a solution?

Both medical and social constructionist models of dis/abilities subscribe to a temporal linearity. As argued earlier, they believe that medical knowledge will advance and societal attitudes will change; cures will be found to eliminate bodily defects and people with dis/abilities will be accepted. However, the histories of ophthalmology and eyeglasses technology show that medical and technological developments were not linear or interconnected at all: the recognition of poor eyesight did not immediately lead to the invention of eyeglasses; frames and lenses were invented and used before humans understood light refraction in human eyes; and lenses and frames were two separate instruments independently developed. Thus, social attitudes toward eyeglasses did not experience gradual or uni-directional change. The separate developments are better characterized as disconnected and multi-directional; and what better explains them is the availability of different materials that afforded humans the ability to experiment with eyeglass technology.

The first pair of round spherical lenses were invented in 4th century BC in today's Tunisia. The first frames were however found in the north most region of the Americas. These frames had no lenses, they only had narrow slits. They protected Native Americans' eyes from the glare reflected from the snow. The habitants used readily available materials (such as animal bones and hide) to make the frames. They also modified the designs to suit specific daily needs.

They used these frames for four millennia before switching to commercially manufactured sunglasses (Eskimo Goggles no date).

The next group that was active in making frames were the Italians in the late 13th century. However, how lenses refract light in human eyes was not fully understood until the mid-15th century. In other words, spectacles were invented before humans had a correct understanding of myopia. Florence emerged as a glass production center in the 15th century because of the abundance of sand and local oak for furnaces (Eskimo Goggles no date). The relatively high quality of blown glass made possible the manufacturing of concave and convex glasses (Smith 2014). Later, eyeglasses were mass produced for patients with presbyopia (far-sightedness) or myopia.

Despite the advancement in glass technology, medical "men" had misunderstood light refraction. They recognized that concave and convex lenses improved vision but did not understand refraction was a merely physical phenomenon. They believed that the mind controls vision, and the visual spirit passed from the brain to the lens to give vision to humans. This misbelief explained that lenses compensate for blocked spirits by enlarging the visual angle, allowing for a larger view.

The visual spirit theory was rejected by Johannes Kepler who believed that light refraction is strictly a physical phenomenon in which the lenses are optical instruments that simply refract light. Despite this new theory, the old belief persisted. Physicians continued to condemn lenses for being deceptive and unnatural, saying that they make objects larger and closer than they actually are (Smith 2014). They preferred "scientific" potions such as turtle's blood and powdered bat's head to cure the body (Knight 2018). This preference suggests that medical "men" preferred fixing the body rather than appending a scientific instrument that fools the body. To them, eyeglasses did not change the *real* nature of the body, they only gave a false illusion that it is well.

The invention of eyeglasses did not lead to a mass adoption of eyeglasses among myopics. Some of them chose professions that did not require healthy eyesight; others deliberately chose professions that required nearsightedness. In fact, myopics intentionally interbred so that their offspring would excel at copying scripts or being illustrators (Gannon 2019). Similar to Native Americans using animal bones and hide to make frames and Florentians using sand to make glass, people with nearsightedness made use of their defective eyes to fit into certain professions.

Social attitude toward spectacled people also changed, but it was directed toward the types of eyeglasses more than myopia. In the 17th century, society negatively perceived eyeglasses because of the association with old people (Eskimo Goggles no date ). At that time, lenses were prescribed based on wearers' age rather than eyesight (Smith 2014). It was not until the 18th century when lenses were classified into focal lengths. The style of the eyeglasses also created social differentiation. In France, when eyeglasses became more commonplace, the higher class deemed them unfashionable and chose the monocle instead. Lastly, even though corrective lenses first appeared in the 15th century, it was not until post-WWII when eye patients in Britain were more ready to accept eyeglasses (Eskimo Goggles, no date).

To conclude this section, the *longue durée* of glass technologies and ophthalmology show that humans did not invent corrective lenses because they understood what myopia is. The invention of assistive technology also did not persuade all myopics to acquire eyeglasses. These facts show that the development of medical and technological knowledge was not linear. In addition, how Native Americans and Florentians invented frames and lenses suggests that humans transformed readily found materials in their environments and experimented with probable uses. In turn, eyeglasses expanded some bodily limits to experience environments.

## Superhuman abilities for a body with limits

In the previous section, I used the example of myopia to show that a linear temporality does not describe the development of eyeglasses technology and medical knowledge. In this section, I will use Google Glass as an example to further show how technology enables the body to experience time and space in a new way. This device configures time and space to unsettle a linear temporality and challenge how a body experiences time and space because it conflates time and space, making them into fragments of life that can be manipulated by users. This device is supposed to be so intelligent that it renders all human bodies able to expand their limits. Now people can access the Internet's information with a voice command. The superhuman intelligence embodied by Google Glass wearers could in fact be perceived as not normal.

Google Glass is a wearable, Internet-connected device in the form of spectacles. It is a mix of a smartphone and an augmented reality technology. Google conceptualized it as a consumer technology, but the device failed to gain traction. An oft-cited reason for its failure is the concern of privacy; wearers can take pictures or record conversations without others noticing it (Eveleth 2018). Google Glass then was marketed as an industrial product—a hands-free tool that allows for uninterrupted work[3] and social communication (Glass help, no date; Kothari 2017). The tiny camera at the top right corner of the right lens takes pictures and videos of what the viewers see. The right lens serves as a projection screen for digital information. The microphone picks up voice commands for e-mailing and Internet surfing. Privileging the voice as information input means wearers do not need to drop their tools and manipulate the computer.

### *Wearable technology: questioning bodily normalcy*

Google Glass was not designed for those who identify as having dis/abilities, but advocates believed that it could be beneficial for those populations. For example, it helps those with visual impairments to navigate the environment (Christopherson 2013; Della Cava 2013; "How will Google Glass help disabled people" 2013). According to the writings of non-profit organizations for people with dis/abilities,[4] Google Glass compensates for bodily dis/abilities by expanding human capacities that are limited by the body. For example, the camera of Google Glass is said to be very intelligent because it can deduce what information the wearers seek from sensing the head motions. Google Glass's facial recognition application can accurately deduce human emotions. This device also benefits all for it can do real-time interpretation in multiple languages (Christopherson 2013; "Google Glass apps for people with disability" 2014; "Google Glass helps people gain independence" no date ; National Business and Disability Council 2016; Weiss 2013).

Google Glass benefits wearers with varying abilities and extends their bodily abilities. That is, Google Glass does not differentiate abled bodies from dis/abled because it is intended to enhance the whole of humanity's cognitive and emotional intelligences.

The device also raises questions about the normalization about body parts and their assumed functions. For example, those with abled bodies have been trained to use touch (such as clicking the mouse, typing on the keyboard, or touching the screen) to input information on a computer. Google Glass however trains users to use sounds as information input; thus calling into question whether all body parts can be utilized for information input (Goggin 2017). In a way, Google Glass normalized the extraordinary bodies of the "supercrips," such as those who used their feet to feed themselves.

By highlighting and correcting for humans' bodily limitations, Google Glass shows that abled and disabled bodies are on the same playing field. It also tells users that no single human being is as intelligent as the device. Of course, *what* is intelligent is not the device but artificial intelligence generated through Internet connectivity. However, Google Glass makes the users an embodiment of superhuman intelligence. Its wearability makes it part of the body. The embodiment of superhuman intelligence does not cure the body or restore normalcy. Instead, it questions the boundary between normalcy and deficiency by blurring the boundary between human and machine, between limits of the human body and collective human intelligence. However, in some situations, Google Glass may be understood to make one abnormal or even handicapped. For example, one widely expressed fear is that wearers will become so distracted by information that they will be more prone to road accidents. The same fear is expressed about those who are deemed to be cognitively and mentally impaired.

Lastly, Google Glass challenges an assumed linear time-space relation by recreating space and time into multiple two-dimensional planes that wearers can manipulate. Users can retrieve any digital file of the past and the future by juxtaposing them together. For example, they can see future appointments by placing them next to an old e-mail. How Google Glass organizes information on a two-dimensional plane has implications for the assumed linear temporality of the medical and social constructionist models of dis/abilities. Google Glass disembodies the wearers from both immediate time and space, making the material environment less relevant to the body and its experience. For example, the map application gives verbal direction so wearers can rely less on bodily senses to move through space.

## Conclusion

This chapter examines two assistive technological devices—eyeglasses and Google Glass. The former allows people with myopia to focus images on the retina, the latter enhances humans' ability to gather and view information across time and space. Both devices illustrate the slash between ability and dis/ability, the space between normalcy and deficiency. This space is illustrated by myopia being a bodily defect that is not legally recognized as a dis/ability and by eyeglasses marking a difference yet being commonplace. Myopia and eyeglasses illustrate both medical and social constructionist models of dis/abilities. I have shown that we can critique this space by asking what the boundary is between body and technology and whether assistive technology compensates bodily defects.

In this chapter, I specifically looked at how the materiality of media technologies creates a sense of time and space for the wearers and challenges a linear temporality assumed in both medical and social constructionist models. Like all media technology, assistive technology expands and alters our experience with time and space. Media technologies that record humans' thoughts have displaced time and expanded space (Carey 2018): augmented media layers virtual space over "real" space. Even analog technologies transport one from an immediate surrounding to others (Ong 2002). If we take into account that the human body has limits, then all experience is bounded by both time and space. Without media technologies, humans are always disabled from doing certain things and fulfilling certain purposes.[5]

The case study of Google Glass further illustrates that assistive technology neither compensates for nor normalizes the body (Adkins et al. 2012). More than eyeglasses, Google Glass blurs the boundary between humans and machines. This piece of technology embodies superhuman abilities for the wearers. This is not unlike Hayles' (1999) concept of a posthuman, in particular "[its] body [is] the original prosthesis we all learn to manipulate" and "[the human being] can be seamlessly articulated with intelligent machines" (p. 3). To Hayles, the posthuman is neither purely biological nor mechanical, neither informational nor material, but "a collection of heterogeneous components, a material-informational entity whose boundaries undergo continuous construction and reconstruction" (p. 3). In another iteration, Goodley et al. (2019) believe that contemporary times have defied any separation of material from discursive properties, where life—biological, social, technological, algorithmic, computational, human, inhuman, and geopolitical—is tangled and interwoven. For those who wear Google Glass, they are not a human being equipped with a piece of computer, but an assemblage of flesh and metal, bone and plastic. Donna Haraway may have mused about the same thing: the cyborg concept is believed to challenge the assumed given, organic nature of female embodiment.

The cyborg rejects the dualism between body and mind, an abled and disabled body, the human and the machine (Haraway 1991). Both eyeglasses and Google Glass demonstrate that the post-human is becoming more of a cyborg.

## Notes

1 Myopia is not legally defined as a dis/ability. The Supreme Court of the United States has dismissed a case in which the plaintiffs filed a complaint against United Airlines for deeming them unsuitable to be global airplane pilots (SUTTON V. UNITED AIR LINES, INC. (97–1943) 527 U.S. 471 (1999) 130 F.3d 893, affirmed). The court argued that with corrective measures, their eyesight is identical to individuals without myopia. In addition, the court argued that myopia does not limit one's major life activities, so cannot be classified as a dis/ability.
2 Perception of eyeglasses wearers varies across gender, race, class, and age. Young children who wear glasses may be stigmatized, so are people of color in urban areas.
3 Glass help. *Glass*. Retrieved from: https://www.google.com/glass/help/.
4 The organizations are as follows: AbilityNet (UK) that supports people with all kinds of dis/abilities to use technology to achieve personal and professional goals; Disabled World, an independent news source about health and dis/ability; Media Access Australia that aims to increase web and digital accessibility for people with dis/abilities; National Business and Disability Council that provides resource or dis/ability employment and best practices; Wheel:Life that is an information source for populations who travel with a wheelchair.
5 I need to caution that this chapter is not making a case that all bodies are equal because we all use media. I suggest that we all experience media differently because of different materialities and bodies. This chapter is also not making a claim that there is no hierarchy among bodies. This is instead to say we need to reject that there are only abled bodies and dis/abled bodies.

## References


Adkins, B. et al., (2012). Digital technologies and musical participation for people with intellectual disabilities. *New Media and Society*. **15**(4), 501–518.

Alper, M. et al., (2015). Reimagining the good life with disability: communication, new technology, and humane connections. In: H. Wang, ed. *Communication and "the good life"*. New York: Peter Lang. pp. 197–212.

Bitman, N. and John, N. A., (2019). Deaf and hard of hearing smartphone uses: intersectionality and the penetration of ableist communication norms. *Journal of Computer-Mediated Communication*. **24**(2), 56–72.

Boellstorff, T., (2019). The opportunity to contribute: disability and the digital entrepreneur. *Information Communication and Society*. **22**(4), 474–490.

Carey, J., (2018). *Communication in history*. 7th ed. New York: Routledge.

Christopherson, R., (2013). Why Google Glass is a clear winner for the blind [online]. *Abilitynet*. Available from: https://abilitynet.org.uk/news-blogs/why-google-glass-clear-winner-blind.

Cole, J., (2011). GimpGirl grows up: women with disabilities rethinking, redefining, and reclaiming community. *New Media and Society*. **13**(7), 1161–1179.

Davis, D. Z. and Boellstorff, T., (2016). Compulsive creativity: virtual worlds, disability, and digital capital. *International Journal of Communication*. **10**, 2096–2118.

Davis, D. Z. and Chansiri, K., (2019). Digital identities: overcoming visual bias through virtual embodiment. *Information, Communication and Society*. **22**(4), 491–505.

Della Cava, M., (2013). Beyond a gadget: Google Glass is a boon to disabled. *USA Today* [online]. 22 October. Available from: https://www.usatoday.com/story/tech/2013/10/22/google-glass-aids-disabled/3006827/.

Ellcessor, E., (2016). *Restricted access: media, disability, and the politics of participation*. New York: New York University Press.

Ellcessor, E., Hagood, M. and Kirkpatrick, B., (2017). Introduction: toward a disability media studies. In: E. Ellcessor and B. Kickpatrick, eds. *Disability media studies*. New York: New York University Press. pp. 1–30.

Ellcessor, E. and Kirkpatrick, B. eds., (2017). *Disability media studies*. New York: New York University Press.

Ellis, K. et al., (2017). Access for everyone? Australia's "streaming wars" and consumers with disabilities. *Continuum: Journal of Media and Cultural Studies*. **31**(6), 881–891.

Ellis, K., (2019). *Disability and digital television cultures: representation, access, and reception*. New York: Routledge.

Ellis, K. and Kent, M., (2011). *Disability and new media*. New York: Routledge.

Elman, J. P., (2018). "Find your fit": wearable technology and the cultural politics of disability. *New Media and Society*. **20**(10), 3760–3777.

Eighteenth Century Spectacles, (n/a). *Virtual spectacles gallery*. Available from: https://www.college-optometrists.org/the-college/museum/online-exhibitions/virtual-spectacles-gallery/eighteenth-century-spectacles.html.

Eskimo Goggles—the first eyewear? (no date). *The College of Optometrists*. Available from: https://www.college-optometrists.org/the-college/museum/online-exhibitions/virtual-spectacles-gallery,html.

Eveleth, R., (2018). Google Glass wasn't a failure. It raised crucial concerns. *Wired* [online]. 12 December. Available from: https://www.wired.com/story/google-glass-reasonable-expectation-of-privacy/.

Galis, V., (2011). Enabling disability: how can science and technology studies inform disability studies. *Disabilities and Society*. **26**(7), 825–838.

Gannon, M., (2019). How did nearsighted people manage before glasses were invented? *Live Science* [online]. 14 April. Available from: https://www.livescience.com/65229-nearsighted-people-before-glasses-invented.html.

Gilmore, J. N., (2019). Design for everyone: Apple AirPods and the mediation of accessibility. *Critical Studies in Media Communication*. **36**(5), 482–494.

Glass Help, (n/a). *Glass*. Available from: https://www.google.com/glass/help/.

Goggin, G., (2017). Disability and haptic mobile media. *New Media and Society*. **19**(10), 1563–1580.

Goggin, G. (2019). Disability, connected cars, and communication. *International Journal of Communication*. **13**, 2748–2773.

Goggin, G., Fisher, K. and Li, B., (2019). Introduction: disability participation in the digital economy. *Information Communication and Society*. **22**(4), 467–473.

Goggin, G. and Newell, C., (2003). *Digital disability: the social construction of disability in new media*. Lanham, MD: Rowman and Littlefield.

Goodley, D., Liddiard, K. and Runswick-Cole, K., (2019). Provocations for critical disability studies. *Disability and Society*, **34**(6), 972–997.

"Google Glass apps for people with disability trialled by Telstra", (2014). *Media Access Australia* [online]. 2 May. Available from: https://mediaaccess.org.au/latest_news/digital-technology/google-glass-apps-for-people-with-disability-trialled-by-telstra.

"Google Glass helps people gain independence as a futuristic assistive technology device", (no date). *Wheel:Life*. Available from: https://www.wheel-life.org/google-glass-helps-people-gain-independence-as-assistive-technology-device/.

Haraway, D., (1991). *Simians, cyborgs and women: the reinvention of nature*. New York: Routledge.

Hayles, N. K., (1999). *How we became posthuman: virtual bodies in cybernetics, literature, and informatics*. Chicago: University of Chicago Press.

"How will Google Glass help disabled people?", (2013). *Living with disability* [online]. 6 December. Available from: https://livingwithdisability.info/google-glass-disabled-people/.

Johnson, M. R., (2019). Inclusion and exclusion in the digital economy: disability and mental health as a live streamer on Twitch.tv. *Information Communication and Society*. **22**(4), 506–520.

Knight, S., (2018). The spectacular power of Big Lens. *The Guardian* [online]. 10 May. Available from: https://www.theguardian.com/news/2018/may/10/the-invisible-power-of-big-glasses-eyewear-industry-essilor-luxottica.

Kothari, J., (2017). A new chapter for Glass. *Blog for X*. 18 July. Available from: https://blog.x.company/a-new-chapter-for-glass-c7875d40bf24.

Ledder, S., (2019). On dis/ability within game studies: the discursive construction of ludic bodies. In: K. Ellis et al., eds. *Interdisciplinary approaches to disability: looking towards the future*. Vol. 2. London: Routledge. pp. 30–44.

Lievrouw, L. A., (2014). Materiality and media in communication and technology studies: an unfinished project. In: T. Gillespie, P. J. Boczkowskim and K. A. Foot, eds. *Media technologies: essays on communication, materiality, and society*. Cambridge, MA: MIT Press. pp. 23–51.

Myopia (Nearsightedness), (no date). *American Optometric Association*. Available from: https://www.aoa.org/patients-and-public/eye-and-vision-problems/glossary-of-eye-and-vision-conditions/myopia.

National Business and Disability Council, (2016). *Technical assistance guide on wearable technology for people with disabilities*. New York: The Viscardi Center.

Ong, W., (2002). *Orality and literacy: the technologizing of the word*. New York: Routledge.

Orszag, P., (2018). Dramatic global increase in nearsightedness related to time indoors. *The Spokesman-Review* [online]. 12 May. Available from: https://www.spokesman.com/stories/2018/may/12/dramatic-global-increase-in-nearsightedness-relate/.

Ossola, A., (2016). Outdoor light can slow or reduce nearsightedness. *Popular Science* [online]. 7 April. Available from: https://www.popsci.com/outdoor-light-can-slow-or-reduce-nearsightedness/?src=syn.

Paterson, M., (2017). On haptic media and the possibilities of a more inclusive interactivity. *New Media and Society*. **19**(10), 1541–1562.

Shpigelman, C. and Gill, C. J., (2014). Facebook use by persons with disabilities. *Journal of Computer-mediated Communication*. **19**(3), 610–624.

Smith, A. M., (2014). *From sight to light: the passage from ancient to modern optics*. Chicago: University of Chicago Press.

Visual acuity: what is 20/20 vision? American Optometric Association, (n/a). Available from: https://www.aoa.org/healthy-eyes/vision-and-vision-correction/visual-acuity?sso=y.
Wajcman, J., (1991). *Feminism confronts technology*. University Park, PA: Pennsylvania State University Press.
Ward, S., (2005). Eyeglasses. In: V. Steele, ed. *Encyclopedia of clothing and fashion*. Detroit, MI: Thomson. pp. 432–434.
Weiss, T. C., (2013). Google Glass: revolutionary uses for persons with disability. *Disabled World* [online]. 25 October. Available from: https://www.disabled-world.com/assistivedevices/computer/glass.php.
"What Is AT?", (no date). *Assistive Technology Industry Association*. Available from: https://www.atia.org/home/at-resources/what-is-at/#what-is-assistive-technology.
Whitbourne, S. K., (2016). 6 messages your glasses may be sending people. *Psychology Today* [online]. 13 February. Available from: https://www.psychologytoday.com/us/blog/fulfillment-any-age/201602/6-messages-your-glasses-may-be-sending-people.

# Part IV

# The Political Embodiment of Personhood

# 12 Dis/ability and Race in American History: Rhetoric and Reality in the Civil War and Post-Emancipation South

*Jenifer L. Barclay*

At an 1863 rally at Philadelphia's National Hall, Representative William D. Kelley—a white Radical Republican from Pennsylvania—gave a fiery speech, urging black men to join the Union army. Linking respect and racial equality to military service and framing dis/ability as a mark of manly courage, he asked:

> After two hundred years of unmitigated oppression, Providence has opened the way for Africo-Americans to prove his manhood to the world, and command the respect and gratitude of those of his fellow-citizens whose cupidity and prejudice have enslaved and degraded him. Will you not spring to arms and march to the higher destiny that awaits your race, though it may require your mangled bodies to strew the glorious pathway? (Kelley 1863, p. n/a)

Further drawing on the rhetoric of manhood and dis/ability, Kelley called on black community members, mothers, and unmarried young women to pressure black men into service. "Old men" who accumulated wealth "despite the[ir] disabilities" should disinherit "able-bodied sons" who refused to serve. Mothers should encourage sons to enlist and prove that her "pangs of maternity … gave birth to a *man*." Finally, if "spruce young dandies" who avoided military service should propose marriage, young women should rebuff such cowardly men and proclaim that they "would rather marry the wooden leg and empty jacket sleeve of the war-torn hero." According to the speech's transcript, the audience met this advice with cheers as well as laughter (Kelley 1863). Reduced to the absent presence of his amputated limbs, this imagined black veteran traded the metaphorical dis/ability of color—used to "enslave and degrade" him—for an embodied dis/ability that, to the audience, ironically marked him as a manlier, worthier husband.

Kelley's remarks illustrate how dis/ability is both embodied and socially constructed. On the one hand, life as a black veteran and amputee was a particular experience shaped by racism, ableism, and masculinity. On the other hand, social perceptions and definitions of dis/ability change over time, reflecting its discursive fluidity. By the 19th century, professional medicine

DOI: 10.4324/9781003257196-16

pathologized dis/abled bodies and Americans projected disparaging ideas about dis/ability onto entire groups of people to justify their unequal social status (Baynton 2001). Before the war, pro- and antislavery advocates linked blackness to pejorative ideas about dis/ability as a way to bolster their very different claims about enslaved people as either innately suited for or victimized by the institution of slavery (Barclay 2021). As Kelley's speech demonstrates, dis/ability can be conveniently redefined. During the Civil War, national political discourse transformed wartime dis/abilities into symbols of manliness, bravery, and sacrifice that rallied (or goaded) men into service (Clarke 2002). Ideas about and representations of dis/ability, however, feed into and contrast with the complexities of dis/abled people's lived experiences (Siebers 2008). And, whether socially constructed or embodied—whether invoked as rhetoric or experienced as lived reality—dis/ability and ableism intersect with and uphold other categories of identity like race and gender (and their concomitant expressions of power like racism and sexism) (Collins 2000; Crenshaw 1989).[1] These interlocking relationships shaped the lives and representations of dis/abled black men who served in the United States' racially segregated Colored Troops (USCT) as well as those of dis/abled black people who navigated freedom and the postwar South. The years that encompass these dramatic changes—the Civil War (1861–1865), the waves of emancipation that unfolded until Congress passed the Thirteenth Amendment in 1865, and the period of Reconstruction (1865–1877)—provide an important historical window into how dis/ability is socially constructed and embodied. During these tumultuous times, dis/ability was a potent discursive tool that conveyed social and political anxieties and dramatized shifts in structural power and social hierarchies. Along with emancipation, however, the war also produced dis/abilities among freedpeople and black veterans that were exacerbated by racial injustice.

## No whit less brave: race, dis/ability, and military service

The Civil War wrought a tremendous toll for all soldiers. Estimates posit that the number of deaths ranged from 752,000 to perhaps as many as 851,000 (Hacker 2011). Beyond those who lost their lives, combat dis/abled thousands more. New more potent weaponry like the rifled musket and the spread of infectious diseases in camps left many soldiers with physical, psychological, and sensory dis/abilities. Physicians performed thousands of amputations over the course of the war, making amputees some of the most noticeable of all dis/abled veterans. The visibility of war amputees combined with the advent of photography and an expansive prosthetics industry made dis/ability far more commonplace in American society (Nielsen 2012). As physician Oliver Wendell Holmes observed in 1863, "It is not two years since the sight of a person who had lost one of his lower limbs was an infrequent occurrence. Now, alas! there are few of us who have not a cripple among our friends, if not in our own families" (Holmes 1863, p. 574). Given their ubiquity and the circumstances of their disablement, Americans often romanticized "the figure of the war veteran" even though "manhood and impairment coexisted in uneasy conjunction" (Schweik 2009, p. 149). This more ennobled view of dis/ability vis-à-vis veterans sometimes applied to black men but was complicated by the ways that racism intersected with masculinity, the politics of veterans' pensions and fears of malingering, and the gradual retrenchment of prewar racial dynamics (Logue & Blanck 2010; see also Blight 2001).[2]

For free blacks and refugee slaves who fled plantation life and enlisted in the Union forces, battlefield injuries and accidents often resulted in dis/abilities. The US Army assigned black soldiers dis/abled in combat to units responsible for less dangerous or demanding military labor, similar to the all-white Invalid Corps established in 1863 (later renamed the Veteran Reserve Corps). The Invalid Corps was organized into two battalions—the first for soldiers who carried weapons and guarded prisoners, barracks, or other targets and the second for those with more significant impairments who served as cooks and medical personnel (Handley-Cousins 2019). Nondis/abled servicemen ridiculed the Invalid Corps as the "Cripple Brigade" and noted that the initials I.C. also stood for "Inspected, Condemned," a label that the Army "applied to rotten meat, faulty rifles, and rotting ammunition." Nonetheless, members of the Invalid Corps provided essential labor and carried out dangerous actions. Enlisted men "protected warehouses and railway lines, squelched antiwar uprisings ... and enforced the unpopular draft" (Nielsen 2012, pp. 80–85) "Colored" regiments similar to the Invalid Corps likewise employed dis/abled black soldiers in war-related work.

In the fall of 1863, John Eaton—the former general superintendent of contrabands in the Freedman's Department in Tennessee and Arkansas—became colonel of the 9th Louisiana Volunteers organized near Natchez, Mississippi. His colleague, Samuel Thomas, took command of the 7thLouisiana Volunteers, also "composed of such men as may be incapacitated for active service in the field but who are otherwise fitted for ordinary garrison duty." These units later became the 63rd and 64th regiments of the USCT (Eaton 1907, pp. 108–109). In these units, dis/abled black soldiers—informally referred to as a "Home Guard" or "colored invalid corps"—guarded garrisons and supply houses, patrolled local areas, and carried out police duties to maintain order under martial law (Bentley 1955; Gerteis 1973; see also Foner 1988). In southern regions under Union control, white guerillas attacked freedmen and "determined to prevent the growing of cotton at all hazards" by burning cotton gins, "carrying off" blacks, and committing other "outrageous cruelties" (Yeatman 1864, p. 7). Dis/abled black soldiers in these units provided critical protection to laborers on local plantations and, by extension, the region's fragile economy. In his 1907 memoir, Eaton affirmed the significance of their service, noting that history was more likely to forget these men than the black troops who "thrilled the country" when they fought at Port Hudson and Milliken's Bend. As he explained:

> ... the humbler duty of safeguarding the plantations from assaults which were often vindictive and particularly cruel, the task of protecting the

> women and children, the aged and infirm—these were services which devolved upon men debarred by physical capacity from the more heroic campaigns endured by their brothers, but no whit less devoted to the Union, no whit less brave in their loyalty to the cause that had freed them (Eaton 1907, p. 112).

Eaton's remarks capture interlocking sentiments about masculinity and able-bodiedness that defined heroism and erased the legacy of dis/abled black Union soldiers. According to Eaton, the service of dis/abled black soldiers who guarded freedpeople and of nondis/abled black soldiers who fought in major engagements both epitomized heroism, devotion, and bravery. Yet in neither case did black men's service, no matter how heroic, garner them full citizenship.

Americans read the dis/abled bodies of black and white soldiers differently during and after the war. Combat evidenced bravery, independence, discipline, and self-sufficiency, traits associated with mid-19th-century ideals of manliness. Complementing "true" women's piety, purity, submissiveness, and domesticity, this vision of manhood linked able-bodiedness, rationality, and restraint to whiteness, deriving meaning from its contrast to white womanhood (Welter 1966). Men and boys were encouraged to "build a strong, manly 'character' as they would build a muscle, through repetitive exercises of control over impulse" (Bederman 1995, p. 11). Military service concentrated this version of manhood, linking soldiers' courage, independence, rationality, self-control, and stability to manliness and the status of soldier-citizen. Despite "rhetoric that fashioned war wounds into patriotic sacrifices and wounded men into heroes" (Handley-Cousins 2019, p. 30), the presence of dis/ability nevertheless generated anxiety about soldiers' manhood. The 19th century Americans, after all, viewed people with dis/abilities as dependents who lacked self-control, especially the insane, epileptic, and feebleminded. Yet since manhood "is a continual dynamic process … through [which] men claim certain kinds of authority, based upon their particular type of body" (Bederman 1995, p. 7) which in turn intersects with socially constructed ideas about race and dis/ability, wartime dis/abilities ultimately shored up white men's status as citizens. Most whites, however, did not perceive black men's military service as "a means for earning citizenship," but rather as "a way of paying back the favor of freedom." In other words, "soldiering provided freedpeople some of the manly attributes required of free men," but would not alone "result in the full inclusion of African Americans in the body politic" (Emberton 2012, p. 380). While the wartime dis/abilities of black men who served in the USCT may have marked them as brave, they did not mark them as citizens because of the confluence of racism and ableism in their lives. In the war's aftermath, dis/ability similarly mediated various representations of freedpeople and shaped their lives in profound ways.

## Reconstruction and relief: dis/ability and in/dependence in freedom

As the Civil War ended and the Thirteenth Amendment officially banned slavery, Americans faced the prospect of reconstructing the war-torn South and incorporating millions of freedpeople into the nation. The US Army, the Bureau of Refugees, Freedmen, and Abandoned Lands (or Freedmen's Bureau), and northern aid societies played key roles in this effort, but each had different interests. Official records and personal correspondence from these groups document the impact of emancipation on freedpeople and the nation's inadequate response to the thousands of elderly, dis/abled, and dependent freedpeople rendered most vulnerable by this cataclysmic change. These sources also reflect tensions in how various groups represented freedpeople and constructed black dis/ability in freedom. Northern volunteers who worked on behalf of charitable organizations drew attention to the abject poverty, squalid conditions, and lack of basic care that many elderly and dis/abled freedpeople experienced. This practice was, in many ways, an extension of abolitionists' use of pitiful depictions of black dis/ability to rouse support for emancipation prior to the war. It was also an effective fundraising strategy that tugged on people's heartstrings. Federal officials and agents of the military and Freedman's Bureau, on the other hand, prioritized the South's transformation from slavery to waged labor. As a result, they often downplayed freedpeople's needs and depicted them as capable, able-bodied laborers worthy of freedom.

As Union victory loomed on the horizon, the federal government created policies to reconstruct the South. The Freedmen's Bureau, established in March 1865, orchestrated these efforts by providing freedpeople with food, clothing, and medical care and establishing schools, hospitals, and orphanages. It assumed custody of confiscated lands and assisted freedmen with negotiating labor contracts. In the chaos of wartime and the postwar years, enslaved people moved from slavery to freedom, from plantations to contraband camps attached to Union troops, or to southern cities. Freedpeople with dis/abilities faced distinct challenges in navigating these upheavals. Many could not flee plantation life because of the embodied realities of their physical, sensory, or psychological impairments. Of those who secured emancipation, not all experienced freedom as overwhelmingly and immediately positive.

For some enslaved people with dis/abilities, freedom remained elusive long after formal emancipation. While their nondis/abled counterparts "could run toward freedom at the sound of the first Union gunshot, the disabled were forced to remain on the plantation and … within the institution of slavery" (Downs 2008, para. 7). Former slaveholders continued to enslave them or simply neglected to inform them of the end of slavery. Hannah, a blind woman who remained enslaved in Louisiana's Natchez district, worked in her former slaveholder's "garden and … home despite the ending of the institution of slavery." Two other blind slaves on a nearby plantation faced a similar fate (Downs 2008). In 1867, a white woman in Chattanooga with three young children and on her deathbed relied on "an old, helpless, lame, colored woman" (Tate 1867, p. 136). The well-known performer Thomas Green Bethune, known as Blind Tom, also endured a similar experience. Bethune was renowned in the United States and abroad for his talent as a composer and pianist. His blindness and the fact that he was considered "idiotic" rendered his skills even more impressive to mid-19th century audiences.[3] Though the Thirteenth Amendment technically freed Bethune, he remained under his former slaveholder's guardianship until the 1880s (Southall 1999).

Other enslaved people with dis/abilities left plantations on their own accord or were forced out by former slaveholders.[4] Reports from Union commanders and Freedmen's Bureau officials noted the dis/ability status of many who fled to army camps. Since they were unable (or perceived as being unable) to labor, this presented a problem for the federal government. Refugees drew on the military's resources and interfered with its activities. In Tennessee and Arkansas, 113,650 refugees sought asylum behind Union lines in 1864. Almost 10,000 received federal aid, 75% percent of whom were "the aged, the children, the hospitalized, and the crippled" (reported in Genovese 1972, p. 538). After emancipation, federal documents recorded additional scores of dis/abled freedpeople throughout the South. From September 1866 to September 1867, there were "1,400 blind freedmen; 412 'deaf and dumb'; 1,134 'idiotic or imbecile'; 552 'insane'; [and] 251 'clubfooted'" in Washington, DC alone (Downs 2012, p. 126). To provide care to sick, injured, dis/abled, and elderly freedpeople, the Freedmen's Bureau established hospitals, asylums, and home colonies (or farms) "for the aged and infirm freedmen and motherless children unable to perform labor" (Yeatman 1864, p. 7).

While the Freedmen's Bureau assisted elderly, dis/abled, and dependent freedpeople, it emphasized and valued freedpeople's physicality and ability to labor. Pay scales used to compensate freedpeople for their labor on plantations and in Bureau settlements reflect this emphasis. Similar to the ableist "hand system" that slaveholders once used to measure enslaved people's labor capacity, Freedmen's Bureau officials linked freedpeople's wages to their physical abilities. Age, health, and soundness determined their ranking on a scale from the highest-ranked "number one hands" to the lowest "number three hands." "Persons suffering from physical defect or infirmity" were outside of the scale. Officials determined freedpeople's abilities and rate of pay on an individual basis according to their perceived capacity to labor ("Rules and regulations" 1864). The Bureau's "preference for and accommodation of" nondis/abled freedpeople tore former slave communities apart by "separating dis/abled relatives from their able-bodied parents, siblings, and loved ones" (Downs 2008, para. 8). Freedpeople with and without dis/abilities lost their support networks as well as the community-centered labor and social cohesion so often provided by dis/abled community members (Barclay 2021). Because Congress created the Freedman's Bureau to assist former slaves' transition to freedom, it was ultimately far more concerned with "creat[ing] a healthy labor force"—a preference that also skewed its records toward the experiences of nondis/abled freedpeople (Downs 2012).

During and in the immediate aftermath of the war, thousands of displaced former slaves never came under the immediate care of federal officials. Among them were those already living with dis/abilities and those who became dis/abled in the horrific conditions brought on by the dislocation of emancipation and the nation's inadequate response.[5] Of those who flocked to southern cities, sought shelter in abandoned homes and barns, wandered roads and fields looking for food, shelter, safety, and employment, or went in search of distant family members, the number with dis/abilities—let alone the specific details of their experiences—remain unknown. Military and Freedmen's Bureau agents, however, were not the only Americans who encountered freedpeople and documented the effects of emancipation on their lives. Northern benevolent and charitable organizations also sent representatives to the southern states who recorded scattered details about the lives of former slaves, particularly those who were dis/abled.

Northern relief organizations like the American Missionary Association, American Freedmen's Union Commission, National Freedmen's Relief Association, and other state and local groups often drew their ranks from former abolitionists. As a result, many viewed the plight of freedpeople through the familiar lens of pity and focused on dis/abled and elderly former slaves. They initially prioritized education, but quickly recognized the dire health circumstances that freedpeople faced since many lacked food, shelter, clothing, healthcare, and other basic necessities.[6] Many freedpeople experienced chronic ill health, dis/abilities, and death stemming from the poor material conditions of their former enslavement and their newfound freedom (Downs 2012). In their correspondence to their organizations' administrators and supporters, northern volunteers often singled out the struggles of aged and dis/abled freedpeople as well as those who became dis/abled because of disease, starvation, exposure, and poverty.

By emphasizing the additional challenges that dis/abled, aged, and dependent freedpeople faced, northern volunteers roused the emotions and solicited the financial support of those who long saw themselves as selfless advocates for oppressed southern blacks. Their biting commentary often targeted former slaveholders' callousness and drew attention to former slaves' hardships when "benevolent" slaveholders abandoned their "black family." Working on behalf of the American Missionary Association in Chattanooga in 1867, one northerner explained:

> There are still fiends in human shape south of us in Alabama and Georgia who after reaping the fruit of sixty and seventy years of hard labor [from their slaves] and after selling and scattering the[ir] children—God only knows where—bring these poor lame and blind old creatures and drop them in this city, caring not whether they live or die (Tate 1867, p. 136).

This passage highlights the embodiedness of dis/ability that resulted from bondage and was intensified by freedom. Also, by illuminating former slaveholders' heartlessness toward elderly and dis/abled former bondspeople, it constructs dis/ability as pitiful and dis/abled people as dependent.

Similar themes emerge in Josephine Griffing's "Appeal on Behalf of the Freedmen of Washington, D.C." A former abolitionist and women's rights advocate, Griffing worked for the National Freedman's Relief Association (NFRA) of the District of Columbia, a city that absorbed 25,000 freedpeople between 1865 and 1866. Griffing described this wave of humanity to distant northerners as "a host of miserable women, with large families of children, besides old, crippled, blind and sick persons" who sought refuge in the city when they were "driven out of Maryland" by former slaveholders. Imploring the "friends of humanity" to donate funds and goods, she punctuated descriptions of freedpeople's hardships with the spectacle of dis/ability. For instance, she explained how "hundreds of old persons and children were without shoes and stockings, and being badly frost bitten, several had their limbs amputated … and are crippled for life" (Griffing 1865, pp. 174–175). Griffing's discussion captures how some Northern aid workers mobilized dis/ability rhetoric to secure support in the face of widespread suffering, insufficient federal intervention, and the looming return of political power to state governments.[7]

As federal reconstruction policies evolved and Freedmen's Bureau resources waned, relief workers increasingly called on northern supporters. During a drought and famine from 1866 to 1868, the Freedmen's Bureau cut aid to those considered impoverished but able-bodied, limiting relief only to hospital patients and orphans.[8] This decision impacted all freedpeople, but charitable workers shared the experiences of those who were dis/abled, elderly, and dependent to criticize and call attention to the failures of local institutions and federal agencies. One *American Missionary* account described the "general despondency" of Beaufort, North Carolina residents when their crops failed. For many, this was "the most severe misfortune they … ever met," yet the Freedmen's Bureau withheld "rations from hundreds of disabled men, women, and orphan children." When a local family brought an elderly freedman to town "to deliver him to the wardens of the poor," they refused him. The family then tried to obtain rations for him at the local Freedmen's Bureau office but were denied. Finally, they:

> lifted the helpless victim of more than a hundred years from the boat, and laying him down on the shore, left him to his fate. A poor colored man took him in for a few days, 'till his own last crust was exhausted, and then carried him to the same place, and laid him down to wait the passing of another Samaritan ("A Superintendent" letter 1867, p. 272).

This powerful narrative conveyed the grim realities freedpeople faced without family, community, or government support as well as the extreme need for funds to care for dis/abled and elderly freedpeople.

Some of the most striking testimony about aged, dis/abled, and dependent freedpeople came from Griffing. A national figure Griffing organized the efforts of the NFRA in 1862 and advocated for the creation of the Freedmen's Bureau. Long after the Freedmen's Bureau shuttered its doors in 1872, she continued to appeal to Congressmen, northern philanthropists, and sympathizers across the nation for donations. Assisting freedpeople in the nation's capital, Griffing distributed government rations, clothing, blankets, and other supplies at the NFRA's office and from army wagons that traveled throughout the city. She called on supporters to donate cloth, yarn, bedding, household utensils, furniture, and money as well as lumber, nails, and glass to build housing "for the old and the crippled" (Griffing 1865, p. 175). In her years as a relief worker, Griffing visited "hundreds in the alleys and old stables, in attics and cellars, and in almost every place where shelter could be found" and personally knew many freedpeople (Stanton et al. 1889).

In a letter to women's rights activist Lucretia Mott in 1869 or 1870, Griffing wrote about her visits to aged and dis/abled freedpeople who huddled without food or heat in shanties and described those who sought shelter and sustenance at the NFRA offices. Among those who lived in run-down shacks was Aunt Clara, a freedwoman in her seventies. Griffing described her as "stone blind" and "so paralyzed that the slightest touch on the arm or hand made her spring and cry like a child." Another freedwoman, Milly, lived nearby and was "also stone blind and sick and helpless." Milly's husband, Henry, cared for her until he developed a "hip disease" that left him paralyzed and unable to walk. Griffing noted that "for eleven weeks [he] has not walked a step." She also wrote about Johnny Scraper who "sat in rags, paralyzed from the top of his head to the soles of his feet, alone in a six-by-ten-foot room, unable to walk a step," lamenting that he "is left entirely alone, sometimes for three days." Griffing discussed many other homeless, destitute elderly, and dis/abled freedpeople. As she explained, "At this moment, at least one hundred and fifty broken-down [former] slaves are at this office, covering all the porches, sitting on all the stairs, forming an almost impassable barrier to the entrances—all with a story of want in their faces … and all eager to say 'We has nobody to go'pon.'" (reprinted in Stanton et al. 1889, pp. 870–873).

In her personal and public writing, Griffing expressed a deep frustration with the erosion of the Freedmen's Bureau. She argued that it only focused on "the able-bodied freed people" for a short period and once education and suffrage were secured it was "no longer a necessary department." The government, she continued, dissolved the agency "without a substitute for the aged and worn-out slaves, though they were … [even] older and more infirm." Griffing cared for over a thousand freedpeople—"the crippled, blind, and broken-down … not one of whom is able to earn for himself the necessaries of life"—and worked hard to keep their plight in the public eye (Stanton et al. 1889). Her male counterparts chastised her for engaging in a type of "emotional" reform, unlike the more rational, efficient relief work they envisioned. Some "accused [her] of manufacturing images of poverty that damaged the reputation of the freedpeople and the freedman's aid movement" by not depicting them as self-reliant (Faulkner 2004). The approaches of northern relief workers began to splinter along gendered lines, particularly with regard to how they portrayed freedpeople—as woefully dis/abled and suffering or as robust, able-bodied laborers capable of self-sufficiency. Male relief workers' attitudes more closely aligned with those of Freedmen's Bureau agents, in contrast to female aid workers like Griffing. At the same time, another group of people invested in the South's recovery, former slaveholders, also evoked the rhetoric and realities of dis/ability to depict freedpeople in ways that supported their very different interests.

## The politics of pity and fear: dis/ability and the roots of lost cause ideology

In their discussions of freedpeople, many northern reformers initially echoed the dis/ability rhetoric once used by abolitionists, inadvertently creating opportunities for former slaveholders to answer them with similar discursive strategies that supported different claims. Throughout the Reconstruction years, southern whites emphasized the experiences of elderly and dis/abled freedpeople to cast emancipation as harmful to former slaves who "needed" their former slaveholders and to attack the ineptitude of the Freedmen's Bureau and northerner reformers. They also drew on more sinister ideas about dis/ability to stoke fears about interracial relationships, racial equality, and black citizenship among white southerners.

Decrying the "cruelty" of emancipation, white southerners weaponized the experiences of elderly and dis/abled freedpeople, using them to express their supposed concern. The poor health and poverty that some experienced "buttressed white Southerners' claims that ex-slaves could not lead independent lives and would go extinct" without the goodwill and care of their former slaveholders (Downs 2012). Before the war, the notion that slavery was a "positive good" was widespread. The southern intellectual George Fitzhugh mastered this argument by contrasting the purported benevolence of slaveholders toward elderly and dis/abled slaves with northern capitalists' ruthless abandonment of unproductive laborers. In an 1866 *DeBow's Review* article, Fitzhugh recalibrated this argument and responded to the question: "What's to be done with the negro?" Troubled by the influx of northerners to the South, the role of the federal government in Reconstruction, and the issue of financial responsibility for the support of aged and dis/abled freedpeople, he asserted that former slaveholders possessed the wisdom to guide the South through the changes wrought by freedom.

Claiming that a myopic and "peculiar monomania" afflicted northerners about Reconstruction that blinded them to the harm they heaped onto helpless freedpeople, Fitzhugh argued that former slaveholders were "guided by the lights of experience and the teachings of history" and should be responsible for the postwar South. Under their watch, former slaves would be put to "coarse manual labor," punished when they failed to live up to their obligations, and transformed into "useful, productive" paid laborers. Former slaveholders would also:

> Take care of, in the most ample and humane manner, those unable to provide for and take care of themselves; but they should be no charge on the whites. By a tax on the labor of the strong and healthy negroes we would raise a sufficient fund to provide comfortable subsistence for the weak, infirm, and aged negroes (Fitzhugh 1866, p. 578).

In Fitzhugh's vision, the South's racial hierarchy remained unchanged through a tax on able-bodied black laborers to provide for dis/abled and aged freedpeople. This would shift the perceived financial burden of their care off of whites and render the federal government obsolete in postwar reform efforts.

In "Justice to the Negro," another writer made a similar argument in *DeBow's Review* by framing blackness with dis/ability and weakness. Counseling white southerners to wait out the "maniacal" rule of congressional radicals, the author asserted that they should treat freedpeople "as fellow being[s] whose very weakness and inferiority strengthen his claims on our tutelary aid and assistance, and on our charity when needed and deserved" (De Bow 1866, p. 91). The author advised freedpeople to shun direct agitation for rights and, instead, leverage their "passive weakness and subordination" to ensure that whites, the "strong and healthy" of society, would not oppress them (De Bow 1866, p. 92). This perspective, coupled with the belief that the Freedmen's Bureau, northern carpetbaggers, and pro-Union southern "scalawags" were infinitely corrupt, allowed southern whites to further mobilize dis/ability behind their denunciations of federal intervention into the postwar South.

Another article in *DeBow's Review*, "The Atrocities of the Freedmen's Bureau," targeted the agency through a government report commissioned in spring 1866 and the imagery of downtrodden freedpeople, especially those who were dis/abled and elderly. Written by Generals John Steedman and Joseph Fullerton, the report documented progress in Virginia and North Carolina, but also highlighted tensions between Bureau agents, freedpeople, and planters. The *DeBow's* article strategically interpreted Steedmen and Fullerton's report to depict federal officials as corrupt tyrants who trampled the rights of white southerners and abused vulnerable freedpeople. After emphasizing the report's discussion of how federal agents in Virginia inflamed labor disputes between freedpeople and planters and "arbitrarily" punished former Confederates, the article reproduces a lengthy excerpt about North Carolina's dis/abled and elderly freedpeople. According to the report's "sad commentary," freedpeople complained to Steedmen and Fullerton about their poor treatment at the Trent River settlement near Newburn, with one man pleading for them to inspect it and "save me from my friends." According to the article's interpretation of the report, the "decrepit and helpless" lived off the government at the settlement and everyone else eked by in misery. Likewise, or so it was argued, the Superintendent, former Army chaplain Edward S. Fitz, oppressed freedpeople through unfair imprisonment, physical torture, and fines for trivial offenses ("The Atrocities of the Freemen's Bureau" 1866). In this case, a Freedmen's Bureau official abused innocent freedpeople, forced the able-bodied into dependency on the government, and provided only minimal care to the neediest of all freedpeople—the aged and dis/abled. A harbinger of Lost Cause mythology, the article conveys the message that all freedpeople, especially the aged and dis/abled, were happier and better cared for under slavery. Manufactured pity for elderly and dis/abled freedpeople, however, was only one rhetorical tactic southern whites employed to stir discontent.

White anxieties about interracial sexual relationships, social equality, and black citizenship emerged in the midst of the Civil War and often intersected with fears of dis/ability and "degeneration" (Baynton 2001; Hodes 1997). Josiah Nott, a physician who studied "mulattoes" in the antebellum years and discursively framed blackness as a marker of innate dis/ability, doubled down on this premise after emancipation (Barclay 2021). In "The negro problem" (1868), Nott decried racial equality and claimed it would cause Americans to degenerate into a physically, intellectually, and morally defective people, neither white nor black but perpetually inferior. Faced with this "legacy of increasing misery and degradation," he argued, no man "possessed of true manhood ... would not say death would be more preferable" ("The Negro problem" 1868, p. 252). Later in the 19th century, these anxieties culminated into tales of insatiable black men who lusted after white women, but in the Reconstruction years whites only "began to put forth the idea that such a crime was becoming more frequent" (Hodes 1997, p. 157). The postwar arguments of southerners like Nott bridged antebellum "degeneracy theory" to the later emergence of social Darwinism and eugenics, reflecting how anxieties about inheritable physical and mental dis/abilities overlaid growing fears of racial equality and interracial encounters.

The politics of fear also sometimes surrounded specific groups of dis/abled freedpeople and worked to white southerners' advantage. Freedwomen, for instance, were sometimes "displaced from the labor force" and compelled to migrate from "town to town in search of temporary employment and shelter" (Downs 2012, p. 149). Because of their precarity, mobility, and independence, whites often deemed the women insane, which presented a problem for the Freedmen's Bureau and an opportunity for white southerners. Lacking the resources to treat insane freedwomen in federal hospitals, the Freedmen's Bureau turned to state asylums and hospitals. Administrators, however, refused to admit freedwomen because of their race, despite the 1866 Civil Rights Act that outlawed racial discrimination (Downs 2012). Negotiating with local politicians, Bureau officials eventually pressured state institutions to accept patients like freedwomen who were labeled insane. This forced local healthcare providers to recognize former slaves' newly acquired citizenship rights and provide access to healthcare. Yet this process also began "transferring responsibility of dependent freedpeople ... to the state" and brought the Freedmen's Bureau closer "to dismantling its systems of care and leaving the Reconstruction South" (Downs 2012, p. 147). Freedmen's Bureau officials argued that cases of insanity among freedwomen were best handled by local physicians and state asylums, stressing the frightening prospect of dangerous insane freedpeople roaming through local neighborhoods to compel state and local administrators into action. By doing so, they opened the door to the beginning of the end of Reconstruction and legitimized racial anxieties and fears of dis/ability. Reconstruction and its demise, then, was not only and primarily about able-bodied freedpeople. Assumptions and fears about people with physical, sensory, and psychological dis/abilities profoundly shaped policy decisions, allowing white southerners to cast themselves as freedpeople's best caregivers, wrest control over Reconstruction efforts, and eventually return to "home rule."

## Conclusion

During and in the years immediately following the Civil War, whites both North and South deployed dis/ability as a discursive tool as they reckoned with the changing status of black people in the nation. Various groups, from military officials and Freedmen's Bureau agents to northern aid workers and former slaveholders, constructed competing representations of freedpeople that informed national conversations about race, the meaning of freedom, and the contours of black citizenship. While the "language of relationships" long used to stigmatize blackness through imagined associations with dis/ability was already entrenched in American society, new concerns emerged in the tumultuous context of the Civil War and Reconstruction that reveal the pliability of dis/ability rhetoric (Goffman 1963). Whites often debated vexed issues like black military service and the treatment of black veterans and freedpeople by re-imagining and redefining dis/ability in whatever ways best suited their various arguments. For freedpeople with dis/abilities, whether veterans or not, everyday life was shaped by the dramatic changes they lived through, the shifting and contested discursive terrain of black dis/ability, and the racialized and gendered particularities of their embodied experiences of dis/ability. This confluence of factors underscores the constant interplay between the reality and the rhetoric of dis/ability, the mutually constitutive dynamic between social constructivism and embodiment, that often emerges most clearly in moments of profound historical rupture and change.

## Notes

1 Black feminist scholars like Kimberlé Crenshaw (1989) and Patricia Hill Collins (2000) articulated intersectionality, a theory rooted in experiential knowledge of multiple, simultaneous forms of oppression.
2 See Blight (2001) on how white Americans reunited around a shared sense of whiteness after the Civil War.
3 To complicate the "savant" narrative, see Straus (2014).
4 For another example of a slaveholder's eviction of dis/abled slaves, see Berlin et al. (1993).

5 Downs (2012) notes that reformers and agents of the federal government found it difficult to ascertain whether freedpeople's dis/abilities resulted from enslavement or emancipation.
6 On northern benevolent societies and the education of freedpeople, see Butchart (2010). For African Americans' long fight to secure education, see Williams (2005).
7 Downs maps the inability of the Freedmen's Bureau Medical Division to provide for dependent bondpeople and its initial attempts to solicit the local support for the care of orphaned children and ill, dis/abled, and elderly freedpeople. Many refused, citing a lack of resources (instead of a desire for segregation). Thus, the Freedmen's Bureau established over 50 asylums from 1866 to 1870 for dependent freedpeople but was ultimately unable to care for all in need.
8 Downs (2012) further clarifies that the drought and resultant famine exacerbated southern poverty and impacted freedpeople's health, but federal policies left these concerns to local organizations. See also Foner (1988).

## References

"A Superintendent" letter, Beaufort, North Carolina, (1867). *American Missionary*. **11**, 272.

Barclay, J. L., (2021). *The mark of slavery: disability, race, and gender in Antebellum America*. Chicago: University of Illinois Press.

Baynton, D., (2001). Disability and the justification of inequality in American history. In: P. Longmore and L. Umansky, eds. *The new disability history: American perspectives*. New York: New York University Press. pp. 33–57.

Bederman, G., (1995). *Manliness and civilization: a cultural study of gender and race in the United States, 1880–1917*. Chicago: University of Chicago Press.

Bentley, G. R., (1955). *A history of the Freedmen's Bureau*. Philadelphia, PA: University of Pennsylvania Press.

Berlin, I. et al. eds., (1993). *Freedom: a documentary history of emancipation, Series 1, Volume II: The wartime genesis of free labor: the Upper South*. Cambridge: Cambridge University Press.

Blight, D., (2001). *Race and reunion: the Civil War in American memory*. Cambridge, MA: Harvard University Press.

Butchart, R. E., (2010). *Schooling the Freedpeople: teaching, learning and the struggle for Black Freedom, 1861–1876*. Chapel Hill, NC: University of North Carolina Press.

Clarke, F., (2002). 'Honorable scars': Northern amputees and the meaning of Civil War injuries. In: P. Cimbala and R. Miller, eds. *Union soldiers and the Northern homefront: wartime experiences, postwar adjustments*. New York: Fordham University Press.

Collins, P. H., (2000). *Black feminist thought: knowledge, consciousness and the politics of empowerment*. New York: Routledge.

Crenshaw, K., (1989). Mapping the margins: intersectionality, identity politics, and violence against women of color. *Stanford Law Review*. **43**(60), 1241–1299.

De Bow, J. D. B., (1866). Justice to the Negro. *De Bow's Review*. **2**, 91–92.

Downs, J., (2008). The continuation of slavery: the experience of disabled slaves during emancipation. *Disability Studies Quarterly*. **28**(3). Available from: https://dsq-sds.org/article/view/112/112

Downs, J., (2012). *Sick from freedom: African American illness and suffering during the Civil War and reconstruction*. New York: Oxford University Press.

Eaton, J., (1907). *Grant, Lincoln, and the freedmen: reminiscences of the Civil War with special reference to the work for the contrabands and Freedmen of the Mississippi Valley*. New York: Longmans, Green, and Co.
Emberton, C., (2012). 'Only murder makes men': reconsidering the black military experience. *Journal of the Civil War Era*. **2**(2), 369–393.
Faulkner, C., (2004). *Women's radical reconstruction: the Freedmen's aid movement*. Philadelphia, PA: University of Pennsylvania Press.
Fitzhugh, G., (1866). What's to be done with the negroes? *DeBow's Review*. **1**(6), 577–581.
Foner, E., (1988). *Reconstruction: America's unfinished revolution*. New York: Harper Collins.
Genovese, E., (1972). *"Roll, Jordan, Roll": the world the slaves made*. New York: Pantheon.
Gerteis, L. S., (1973). *From contraband to Freedman: federal policy toward Southern Blacks, 1861–1865*. Westport, CT: Greenwood Press.
Goffman, E., (1963). *Stigma: notes on the management of spoiled identity*. Englewood Cliffs, NJ: Prentice Hall.
Griffing, J., (1865). Appeal on behalf of the Freedmen of Washington, D.C. *The Liberator*. **3**, 174–175.
Hacker, J. D., (2011). A census-based count of the Civil War dead. *Civil War History*. **57**(4), 307–348.
Handley-Cousins, S., (2019). *Bodies in blue: disability in the Civil War North*. Athens, GA: University of Georgia Press.
Hodes, M., (1997). *White women, black men: illicit sex in the nineteenth century South*. New Haven, CT: Yale University Press.
Holmes, O. W., (1863). The human wheel, its spokes and felloes. *Atlantic Monthly*. **11**(67), 3–15.
Kelley, W. D., (1863). Addresses at a mass meeting held at National Hall, Philadelphia, July 6, 1863, for the promotion of colored enlistments. Library of Congress, Frederick Douglass Papers, Series: Speech, Article, and Book File A.
Logue, L. M. and Blanck, P., (2010). *Race, ethnicity, and disability: veterans and benefits in post–Civil War America*. Cambridge: Cambridge University Press.
Nielsen, K., (2012). *A disability history of the United States*. Boston: Beacon Press.
Nott, J., (1868). The Negro problem. *De Bow's Review*. **5**(3), 249–264.
Rules and regulations for leasing abandoned plantations and employing freedmen, (1864). American Missionary Society, Broadside.
Schweik, S. M., (2009). *The ugly laws: disability in public*. New York: New York University Press.
Siebers, B., (2008). *Disability theory*. Ann Arbor, MI: University of Michigan Press.
Southall, G. H., (1999). *Blind Tom, the black pianist-composer (1849–1908): continually enslaved*. Lanham, MD: Scarecrow.
Stanton, E. C., Anthony, S. B. and Gage, M. J., eds., (1889). *History of woman suffrage, Volume II, 1861–1876*. New York: Charles Mann.
Straus, J., (2014). Idiots savants, retarded savants, talented aments, mono-savants, autistic savants, just plain savants, people with savant syndrome, and autistic people who are good at things: a view from Disability Studies. *Disability Studies Quarterly*. **34**(3). Available from: https://dsq-sds.org/article/view/3407.

Tate, E. O., (1867). Chattanooga, Tennessee. *American Missionary*. **11**(6), 136.

The Atrocities of the Freedmen's Bureau, (1866). *De Bow's Review*. **2**(1), 98.

Welter, B., (1966). The cult of true womanhood, 1820–1860. *American Quarterly*. **18**(2), 151–174.

Williams, H., (2005). *Self-taught: African American education in slavery and freedom*. Chapel Hill, NC: University of North Carolina Press.

Yeatman, J. E., (1864). *Report to the Western Sanitary Commission, in regard to leasing abandoned plantations, with rules and regulations governing the same*. St. Louis, MO: WSC Rooms, 7.

# 13 Bending the Laws of Nature: DNA Literacy and the Coding of the Perfect Human Being

*Raphaela Tkotzyk and Kim Carina Hebben*

## Introduction

The world of film and television has long showcased perfect humans in the forms of clones,[1] genetically modified organism (GMO) babies,[2] cyborgs,[3] and humans with superpowers. They embody society's eternal preoccupation with human perfection. Documentaries such as *Unnatural Selection* (2019) or *Explained* (2018) have discovered this topic for themselves. At the moment, this goal is beyond reach; however, the discovery of deoxyribonucleic acid (DNA) in 1953 has brought it closer to us. Today, it is possible to alter genomes and identify and replace DNA before a baby is born. The mapping of the human genome can reveal the secrets of more than 3000 genetic diseases, but in the wrong hands, DNA-coding could lead to the unethical and questionable selection and production of humans. The result would be diversity cleansing, as the Netflix documentary series *Unnatural Selection* (2019) shows us in its depiction of the costs and benefits of genetic engineering technology. As the Netflix show indicates, the reading, (de-)coding, and programming of DNA to eradicate diseases and disabilities not only is carried out in laboratories but is also accomplished by untrained actors, the so-called biohackers. They bend the laws of nature by performing DNA experiments at home and on their own person, creating new species such as animals that glow in the dark. It is fair to say that the power over life and death and health and disease is in the hands of those who are able to read and rewrite DNA.

This leads to questions of who will decide what bodies are desirable and which are not, and how artificially "constructed" or modified bodies will fit into and shape our society and future generations of genetically altered individuals. The importance of these questions is clearly demonstrated in the Netflix documentary series *Unnatural Selection*, thus elevating the discourse from a niche group of experts to a mass audience. We are at risk of creating a world in which only healthy people live and people and animals are susceptible to reengineering by a select few. Underlying these possibilities is eugenics as the Netflix series *Explained* argues (Season 1, Episode 2, 0:15:59).

There is the danger that the power to create a new society will be held only by those with the requisite education and financial means. For example, already it

DOI: 10.4324/9781003257196-17

is possible to "order" so-called designer babies. Equally worrying, prenatal tests and procedures aimed at identifying non-normative and imperfect bodies could lead to their termination. In vitro fertilization and prenatal interventions already have an impact on the way bodies are evaluated and are able to set new standards.

Another level of creating a new society can be seen in the work of biohackers. Biohackers seeking to democratize the use of the gene-editing technology Clustered Regularly Interspaced Short Palindromic Repeats (CRISPR) have disseminated it via the Internet, their goals being to raise public awareness of genetic engineering and to dilute the power of the few over DNA modification. These developments have raised the stakes for those who fear the worst possible outcomes of these processes.

This chapter will address the matter of DNA literacy, defined as the ability to read and rewrite the human body in order to meet two goals. First, the analysis investigates the relationship between media practices, the dis/abled body, and its perception and meaning in society. Second, it will also open up a critical discussion of the responsibility and impact of mass media regarding this, as the aforementioned docuseries and most importantly the Internet play a significant role in distributing access to tools and knowledge that enable anybody who wishes to experiment with genomes. This ability, which we will present as biohacking, has its origin as a media practice, namely computer hacking. It therefore highlights the human body as an editable medium. With our current tools and knowledge, computer hacking skills can be transferred to edit (human) bodies, which ultimately impacts society. In addition to that, media portrayal of our understanding of genetically modified beings has power to influence fictional narratives, newscasts, and documentaries.

## The idea of the perfect human being and its link to eugenics: a historical overview

The desire for a so-called healthy society is almost as old as the history of humankind. In fact, this aspiration can be traced to ancient Greece, but here we will focus on the modern era. It was Charles Darwin, the English naturalist, geologist, and biologist who laid the foundations for distinguishing between positive selection by nature—or what he called "natural selection"—and its modification by culture and civilization (Darwin 1859). He wrote that the struggle for existence is inevitable because of the exponential growth in populations. Only those variants of individuals who are best able to meet the demands of the struggle for existence can thrive and reproduce unlike their less well-adapted counterparts. Inspired by Charles Darwin's theory of evolution and Gregor Mendel's theory of heredity, the British anthropologist and natural philosopher Francis Galton defined eugenics in 1883 as the "science of human improvement" (Galton 1883). From Great Britain, an international eugenic movement was formed, through which Galton's idea was spread. In concrete terms, this meant promoting the reproduction of supposedly superior individuals and preventing the reproduction of individuals deemed unfit for society (Schenk 2020). It was then Ernst Haeckel, a German physician, zoologist, and philosopher who formulated a detailed embryological argumentation for Darwin's "Theory of Descent with Modification" (Breidbach 2005). From this, Haeckel derived the "Biogenetic Fundamental Law" (Haeckel 1866). The thesis states that there is a certain connection between the development of the individual living being (ontogenesis) and its phylum development (phylogenesis). In the context of his discussions of the transferability of racial categories to the social development of humankind, Haeckel is one of the decisive representatives of "eugenic" social policy (Grimm 2012) and an inventor of eugenics and racial hygiene in Germany. In his work *Lebenswunder* (*Miracle of Life*), he postulates without any ethical concerns,

> Even the killing of crippled newborn children, as was practiced by the Spartans for the purpose of selecting the most capable, cannot reasonably be considered a 'murder,' as [it] still happens in our modern codes of law. Rather, we must approve the same as an expedient measure useful to both parties and society (Haeckel 1904, p. 23).

Later in the work, Haeckel speaks out against "keeping mentally ill, lepers or cancer patients artificially alive" (Haeckel 1904, p. 134) in order to create a healthy and mentally strong society.

Approximately 10 years before Haeckel, Alexander Tille discussed the "positive impact" of the limiting of the reproduction of 'unfit' people in order to create a healthier society (Harten et al. 2009). Alfred Ploetz later interpreted Tille's eugenicist reasoning as a call for "racial hygiene." In 1895, the same year in which the first eugenics law in the United States was passed in Connecticut, Ploetz asserted in his "Basic Lines of Racial Hygiene" that society should develop according to scientific principles. Accordingly, only racially superior couples would receive state permission to marry, and pregnancies would be monitored by so-called reproductive physicians. His ideas in combination with the eugenics movement in the United States were foundational to the eugenics programs of the National Socialists in Nazi Germany. A byproduct of these programs was the "Law for the Prevention of Offspring with Hereditary Diseases" which mandated the forced sterilization of individuals with physical and mental disabilities (Benzenhöfer 2006). This law allowed a self-proclaimed master race to implement the "destruction of li[ves] unworthy [of] living" between 1933 and 1945 (Mueller & Beddies 2006). Between 1940 and 1941, the Nazis inaugurated The Euthanasia Program, known as Aktion T4, which resulted in the murder of 70,000 individuals deemed emotionally and mentally unfit (Aly 1989). At much the same time, the German government launched the "Child Euthanasia," to which about 5,000 children fell victim (Klee 2004).

Despite the unprecedented political implementation under the Nazi regime, eugenic ideas and practices are an international phenomenon that existed in democratic states long before 1933 and continued unfortunately after 1945

(Bashford & Levine 2010). In fact, despite widespread horror over the most condemnable genocides in history, eugenical movements survived in many countries through the 1980s. These focused mainly on the forced sterilization on people deemed "confused" or "stupid" (Clees 1997), or as "dangerous to the public and unfit to produce" (Pitzke 2012).

Forced sterilization occurred for example in both Sweden and the United States. Already in 1922, the Swedish Institute of Racial Biology in Uppsala identified benchmarks for racial hygiene intended to preserve the "pure Swedish Breed" and to eliminate racial mixing (Clees 1997). These ideas had staying power as can be seen by Sweden's forcible sterilization of approximately 62,000 people during the years from 1935 to 1976 in service to "racial hygiene" (Clees 1997). Most victims were women and less than 10% were men (Orth 1997). Additionally, from 1934 to 1941, Sweden enacted laws that followed those adopted by Nazi Germany. The result was that Sweden was the world leader in forced sterilization by 1946.

In the United States, more than 60,000 Americans were forcibly sterilized between 1907 and 1981. According to state and federal authorities, this population was mentally ill and consequently, dangerous to the public and unfit to reproduce. At the height of the so-called eugenics movement, 32 American states enacted sterilization laws (Pitzke 2012). Many sterilizations were performed without the knowledge or consent of those affected (Corinth 2005). Because the procedures were often performed carelessly, 5,000–6,000 women and about 600 men died (Pitzke 2012).

Even in countries where there were no sterilization laws, as in Austria, legal gray areas were used to perform such sterilizations, in some cases until the 2000s. The main victims were women and girls with mental disabilities, as shown, for example, by otherwise scarcely available figures from Belgium and France (Ernst 2009, pp. 255–256). As research shows, after 1945 in Western countries, these practices were mainly performed on (mentally) ill girls and women. Therefore, these practices had both a gender-specific and a dis/ability-specific component (Schenk 2020).

The aforementioned sterilization practices can be seen as a bridge between racial cleansing campaigns of the past and certain ideas and the risks of today's gene selection and editing. The survival of eugenic movements after World War II shows in a very frightening way that not enough work had been done to educate the public about the atrocities of Naziism. Also needed is public discussion of ethically reprehensible interventions on what human life is. Moreover, eradicating eugenics depends on binding laws rather than ethical guidelines outlined in the "Nuremberg Codex" or the "Helsinki Declaration."

Given the history of eugenics discussed earlier, it is worrisome that only in 2008 did the Convention on the Rights of Persons with Disabilities (CRPD) come into force. CRPD rejects characterizations of them as "sick" and instead describes them as equal members of society with equal human rights. The Convention also recognizes that dis/ability is more likely to be caused by an inaccessible built world. This international treaty affects about 650 million people worldwide; however, despite this law, many people seek to genetically (de-)code and alter DNA in order to create the "perfect" human being (or animal), whatever this might mean to them.

In the next section, we will explore what exactly is meant by de/coding and thereby editing human genomes. We will then discuss and analyze media practices regarding genetic engineering by examining the Netflix documentary series *Unnatural Selection* (2019).

## DNA literacy or the capacity to read and edit human genomes

While it is true that humans have engineered life for thousands of years through selective breeding, it was not until the discovery of DNA, the code of life, that it became possible to experiment with altering the genetic code which guides the growth, development, function, and reproduction of all living things. If we change the information the code carries, we change the being (animal, plant, human) carrying it. At first, scientists radiated plants to cause random variations in the genetic code and to change a plant's appearance. Then, in 1974, the first genetically modified animal was born. Later in the 1980s, the first patent was given for a microbe engineered to absorb oil. Then, in 1994 the first modified food was available, the "flavr-savr-tomato" with a much longer life due to an extra gene that would suppress the rotting enzyme. At the same time, the first experiments with human genomes started. To treat maternal infertility, babies were created that carried genetic information from three different humans. Today, scientists are able to create super muscled cows, fast-growing salmon or glowing fish, and many chemicals such as growth hormones or insulin.

Until recently gene editing was very expensive, complicated, and took a long time to do. This has changed with the revolutionary new technology called CRISPR. CRISPR can be used in gene therapy as well as gene editing. However, altering genomes generally requires one to be DNA literate. In the history of humankind, those who could read were among the powerful; and today, those who can read DNA have the power to change it. The reference to literacy underscores the idea that those who understand genetics are able to participate in the production of cultural and scientific knowledge. Knowledge is always coded in a certain way, and decoding it requires us to understand the symbol systems in use and to apply our knowledge productively. For example, arithmetic is based on information encoded as numbers, and the (re)production of music is based on the notations of sound (Weidenmann 1997). Reading and (re)writing DNA refers to (de)coding genomes by using the technique of CRISPR, hereinafter referred to as DNA literacy.

## Designer babies

CRISPR is not only a tool to resolve maternal infertility or to cure genetic diseases prenatally, but it also makes possible the editing of embryos in vitro. Genetic trait prediction (GTP) allows fertility experts to foretell genetic attributes, e.g., the likelihood for genetic diseases, eye color, or the sex of the baby, even before an embryo is selected and implanted. Even though the embryo's DNA is not altered, there is a process of selection.

In genetic engineering as in medicine generally, we must distinguish between somatic or germline alterations. Altering genomes on a somatic level means to cure a disease, it is therapeutic. Changes to the genomes end with the patient. Germline alterations change the DNA of an organism and the resulting changes are inherited by offspring, In this way, genetic germline alterations ultimately change the human population and impact society.

There is a fine line between therapy and enhancement. Therapy cures diseases, whereas enhancement benefits people who are healthy. To date, and according to experts, CRISPR has not been used on germline DNA cells. But GTP already makes possible the modification of undesirable traits. For example, germline editing can be used to remove genetic diseases before a baby is born. However, this treatment is unavailable to those who cannot afford IVF or GTP. Because there is already unequal access to healthcare and germline therapy, the wealthy enjoy an extra genetic advantage. This inequity engenders the social risks that can arise from germline enhancement. Sociologist John Evans cautions in Season 1, Episode 19 of *Explained*,

> The Immigration Act in America of the 1920s was based upon an entirely faulty scientific premise, that the genes of the Nordic countries were superior to the other races. It doesn't even need to be true, gene editing doesn't actually even have to work, to have social effects (00:15:53-00:16-11).

Germline selection and editing resulting in, say, the creation of so-called designer babies, hold the (bio)power[4] to foster a new, irreversible, mode of eugenics.

Forestalling the worst possible effects of DNA editing requires us to consider important ethical questions. First, what conditions need to be cured? Who should hold the power to make such decisions? Second, should there be rules, ethics, guidelines, or procedures as with other medical treatments? Third, should CRISPR and gene therapy be institutionalized, and thus available selectively, or should there be open access to the technology? The answers to these questions are crucial for people with non-normative bodies. There already is a risk of narrowing the range of the human population through individual choices about prenatal testing that result in the termination of pregnancies. DNA editing could eradicate conditions like dwarfism or down syndrome in the near future. In this regard, Frank Stephens, Quincy Jones Advocate for the Global Down Syndrome Foundation, condemned this possibility while testifying before the USCongress in October 2017. He asked on C-SPAN, "Is there really no place for us in the whole world?" (Down Syndrome Research 2017). People with dwarfism or other dis/abilities do not regard themselves as impaired or as having a disease that should be cured. As Elizabeth Barnes (2016) has argued, "To be disabled is to have a minority body, but not to have a broken or defective body" (p. 6). She argues that dis/abilities are are socially "constructed" and should not be subject to genetic engineering.

The increasing accessibility of DNA editing among biohackers has created additional problems. Scientists fear that people will start tinkering with DNA. Editing genes means editing the body. Terms like decoding, programming, or editing DNA imply that bodies are medium and that modifying them is in fact a media practice because it entails reading and rewriting its code. Therefore, another media practice that unfolds in the context of DNA editing is (computer) *hacking*.

## *Un/natural Selection* (2019)

Hacking is a form of manipulation. The hacker as a conceptual figure acts between the margin of hidden virtual terrorism and understated tech-expert heroism (Pias 2002). They almost always operate from a secret hideout, a basement, or a garage. Alessandro Delfanti, a scholar of digital media, has argued, "Garage biology, biohacking, and citizen biology are all expressions that describe a new and emerging movement of amateurs conducting life sciences outside of traditional professional settings such as university and corporate labs" (Delfanti 2012, p. 163). Accordingly, biohacking "can be interpreted as an example of a direct transposition of free software and hacking practices into the realm of cells, genes, and labs" (Delfanti 2012, p. 163).

The Netflix docuseries *Unnatural Selection* (2019) addresses biohacking practices and their actors, amateurs as well as professional scientists such as former NASA biophysicist Dr. Josiah Zayner and emphasizes how gene editing has become a do-it-yourself practice. Zayner promotes CRISPR as open-source technology and teaches others how to use it. His credo aligns with the so-called "hacker ethic," which contains among others that there should be "unlimited and complete access" (Delfanti 2012, p. 164) to computers, all information should be free but at the same time authorities cannot be trusted. Furthermore, the "hacker ethic" suggests that hackers should only be judged by their ability of hacking (Delfanti 2012).

Zayner demands not only access to the CRISPR technology, but knowledge and education on DNA literacy while acknowledging the attendant risks. He asks, "What if that [biohacking] was democratized? What happens if somebody came up with an easy method to use it so that anybody could?" (*Unnatural Selection*, Episode 1 [00:19:07–00:19:19]). He answers these questions, asserting, "If we can give access to everybody it could completely change the balance of power" (*Unnatural Selection*, Episode 1 [00:21:27–00:21:36]). Zayner recognizes that "[o]ne big thing that everybody is afraid of is that only the rich and powerful will be able to use genetic engineering" (*Unnatural Selection*, Episode 1 [00:21:18–00:21:24]). Zayner argues against regulating biohacking by asking if computer programming should not be taught because it also can be used in a destructive or criminal manner.

To enable individuals to increase their knowledge of genetic engineering and to perform it, Zayner launched The ODIN organization which promotes online classes such as "genetic engineering and consumer genetic design."[5] The organization runs an online shop that sells DIY "kits and tools that allow anyone to make unique and usable organisms at home or in a lab or anywhere" (ibid.). Moreover, The ODIN offers video lectures and classes, for example, "Bioengineering 101," "Human Tissue Culture and Engineering," or "How To Grow Mushrooms."[6]

According to the Netflix docuseries, the better part of the biohacking community experiments without a specific goal. Their purpose is to learn how to use CRISPR technology through trial and error. For example, David Ishee, a biohacker who breeds and trains protection dogs, experiments on his own animals by trying to blend their germline cells (sperm) with jellyfish DNA. Ishee uses CRISPR to modify the sperm so that it is luminescent under the microscope, his goal being to breed dogs that glow in the dark. What is more, Ishee fits the profile of a (bio)hacker. He says of himself:

> I'm a dog breeder. I knew a little bit about genetics, but not about genetic engineering. I'm not a PhD, or I have no degree, actually. I have a GED. I had assumed that getting DNA and making changes and stuff cost millions of dollars and that you needed a huge lab and research team and all this sort of stuff, but you'd be surprised what there is on YouTube (*Unnatural Selection*, Episode 1 [00:01:18–00:01:34]).

Developmental biologist Professor Juan Belmonte shares Zayner and Ishee's enthusiasm for biohacking, stating, "CRISPR is a technology that has opened up our imagination," (*Unnatural Selection*, Episode 1 [00:14:15–00:14:20]). He continues, "We are learning to copy, edit, paste DNA, the same thing you will do in a word processor. That means rewriting the book of life" (*Unnatural Selection*, Episode 1 [00:15:01–00:15:14]).

In contrast, Dana Perls, the Senior Food and Technology Campaigner with Friends of Earth[7] strongly cautions against genetic engineering at home: "To allow people to play and experiment with profoundly risky technologies is incredibly problematic, and can put, not just individuals, but entire environments and other people in very dangerous situations" (*Unnatural Selection*, Episode 1 [00:29:44–00:29:59]). She adds that biohacking impacts not just humans, animals, and foods but also bioweapons and pharmaceuticals. In short, biohacking is potentially unethical and a threat to national security and economies.

As this discussion of biohackers suggests, gene editing is a media practice that depends on literacy competences. And similar to the development of media and technology, CRISPR is easily accessible, it is fast, relatively cheap "and can cut and paste genetic code with great precision" (*Unnatural Selection*, Episode 1 [00:12:24–00:12:21]). In 2000, after a significant discovery on reading DNA, then President of the United States of America Bill Clinton underscored the literacy competencies associated with genetic editing, writing, "Today, we are learning the language in which God created life. This is the most important, most wondrous map ever produced by humankind" ("Text of the White House Statements" 2000). In 2000, this experimentation was reserved for a small circle of scientists; today, it is openly available to all for use at home. In this context, CRISPR is advertised as a tool for "correct[ing] diseases" and "edit[ing] genetic mistakes" (*Unnatural Selection*, Episode 1 [00:05:26–00:05:52]). Left unexamined are the questions of what condition should be labeled a disease or dis/ability and how these categorizations inform the construction of (dis/abled) bodies.

The question of what counts as a disease, a condition, an experiment, or enhancement is raised by the documentary reporting of the medical history and treatment of 10-year-old Jackson Kennedy. The boy is missing both copies of the RPE65 gene and is "suffering" from a genetic disease that slowly causes blindness. The docuseries highlights his mother's battle with insurance companies and doctors to get Jackson the appropriate testing and treatment. She reports, "They said that there was no benefit for a young child to have genetic testing." But is it not one of the promises that genetic engineering holds, to "cure" humans even before they are born? In the case of Jackson, who took part in an experimental trial where the eye is directly injected with modified genes, gene therapy worked and significantly improved his vision (Lopez 2020). Again, this means there has to be a discussion on what counts as a disease, a condition, an experiment, or enhancement.

So, is CRISPR a kind of remedy for society? What if a genetic disease like Jackson Kennedy's is detected in vitro and parents can decide whether they continue the pregnancy? How does this decision-making accord with laws that protect people with dis/abilities? How does this manipulation of the unborn baby differ from the goals of past eugenic movements in which a few decided which bodies were healthy and which were not?

We have seen that there is an observable paradigm change. What was a huge breakthrough 21 years ago is now a do-it-yourself practice, performed by autodidacts using as try-out kits at home and without any specific objective. But this development has implications for society insofar as there is greater possibility to understand how the human body works and to alter it. Unquestionably, DNA literacy, which aims to educate and enable humankind to perform gene editing, is a Pandora's box. For example, DNA literacy has the potential to alter society and to create new hierarchies of fit and unfit. We live in a time when technology is ever more user-optimized and can be controlled through voice recognition and one-word commands. AIs and algorithms enable genetic engineering whether by a computer or human beings. Once the work and research are done, anybody can exercise a specific practice or application without being able to reconstruct the process that lies beneath it.

Media attention has increased public interest in genetic engineering and accelerated the rates of biohacking, as is showcased in Netflix's *Unnatural Selection*. Both are discussed in the news, in docuseries, and on late night shows. Comedian and talk show host John Oliver among others has questioned thinking by biohackers such as Zayner. Of him Oliver notes, "He makes some pretty wild statements. He argued that using CRISPR should ideally be like downloading an app" (*Unnatural Selection*, Episode 1 [00:47:49–00:47:54]).

Social changes are deeply interconnected with digital media practices and technological innovations as seen by the transference of digital literacy, including knowledge of programming and computer hacking, to re-engineering the human body in form of gene editing. Therefore, genetic experiments are a close reminder of the radical ideas that were executed within the eugenics movement.

## Conclusion

This chapter has outlined the interrelationships between DNA literacy, conceptions of the dis/abled body, and media practices through an interrogation of biohacking and its presentation in the Netflix docuseries *Unnatural Selection* (2019) and other media texts. With this analysis, we considered the potentially questionable ethics of gene editing and their antecedents in the eugenic movements.

As has been argued, DNA literacy can be used as a tool to create new bodies and a new society by those having the requisite power and ability to read DNA. In fact, with the help of CRISPR, one single individual can now shape society to his or her own imagination without regard for social and evolutionary processes. People who are DNA literate may also create a new balance of power some but not all are able to alter society. Further, reading and (de-)coding DNA may become a new cultural technique such as reading letters or symbols, which will be accessible to everyone. Thus, we conceive of the human body as a medium that can be edited. More importantly, the manipulation of the body via biohacking transforms into an easy approachable practice that can be taught and executed at home.

Conceivably, passing along congenital dis/abilities could become a conscious decision, one where a person decides whether to pass their genes or alter them in order to eradicate some conditions. But the question arises, who is allowed to make these decisions? Parents, professionals, or society? How would such decisions change our understanding of the embodiment of dis/ability? It could be seen as an opportunity to promote special needs conditions as chosen traits, and thereby, enable and empower the dis/abled by not marking them as unwanted.

It is also possible that access to the human genetic code can break the power over the many by a few and prevent atrocities like those committed under the Nazis. On the one hand, increasing public education about and knowledge of genetic engineering, achieved through media newscasting or documentaries might instill caution by sensitizing people to the risks of widespread DNA literacy and eugenics. On the other hand, we must anticipate the hazards of making bioengineering accessible to all. Will more experiments take place if everyone is able to perform them? Will people try to develop cures for their own diseases or the peculiarities of their bodies—those, which may not correspond to social norms? Will under-educated "DNA readers" try to offer their services to other people, as it was shown in *Unnatural Selection*? There is also a danger that the unscrupulous will exploit the hopes of sick or dis/abled people for a "normal" life for profit. This possibility calls into question the claim of biohackers that they seek only to provide people with complaint-free life through DNA editing. We must also address the legal and ethical dimensions of gene-editing on human beings for any reason. At what point does it reinvigorate the eugenics movement? How can we ensure that diversity cleansing does not occur again? Do we need stricter laws to prevent these possibilities from happening again, or are our current laws good enough? And last but not least, does society need to be educated about these matters more intensively? Media representation plays an important role within this discussion since it disseminates specific ideologies and discourse that can characterize biohacking as a DIY practice rather than as a continuation of past crimes against humanity. Further, media literacy is essential to obtain DNA literacy as the human body is a medium itself.

Equally important, we must deepen public understanding and acceptance of a diverse society; equality at law does not translate automatically as social equality. Related to this, we should consider and discuss the wishes of people with disabilities since as the Netflix documentary has shown, there might be people with certain kinds of health problems who wish to modify their bodies no matter what. Likewise, we must determine the responsibility of the media for disseminating information that previously fell within the purview of experts. In fact, "DNA narratives in television series broaden the spectrum of questions about an investigation or even transformation of the body" (Stollfuß 2017, p. 79), and thus the responsibilities of the media increase at the same time. This inevitably leads to the question of a critical and reflective approach as well as the meaning of these TV formats because it is not entirely clear what is intended with shows like the aforementioned analyzed ones. Do producers want to sensitize their viewers and make them aware of these ethical highly questionable approaches or are they just interested in viewer numbers. It would be desirable if the educational character of such formats would be stressed more. With this in mind, we will close with a 400-year-old warning discussed by Theodor Adorno with reference to the Holocaust: what once was real remains eternally possible.

## Notes

1 One example is the TV show *Orphan Black* (BBC 2013-2017, CA/ USA.) .
2 For example in GATTACA (USA 1997).
3 See for example the Russian series *Better Than Us* (Netflix 2018-2019, RU).
4 The terms "biopower" and "biopolitics" were used by Foucault (1978) to describe social, political, or cultural imbalances of power which go hand in hand with the use of regulations in order to achieve optimization.
5 Available from: https://www.the-odin.com/about-us/ [viewed on September 15, 2021].
6 Available from: https://www.the-odin.com/science-classes/ [viewed on September 15, 2021].
7 Available from: https://foe.org/about-us/ [viewed on September 15, 2021].

## References


Aly, G., ed., (1989). *Aktion T4 1939–1945. Die "Euthanasie"-Zentrale in der Tiergartenstraße 4*. Berlon: Edition Hentrich.

Barnes, E., (2016). *The minority body: a theory of disability*. Oxford: Oxford University Press.

Bashford, A. and Levine, P., eds., (2010). *The Oxford handbook of eugenics*. Oxford: Oxford University Press.

Benzenhöfer, U., (2006). *Zur Genese des Gesetzes zur Verhütung erbkranken Nachwuchses*. Münster: Klemm & Oelschläger.

Bolter, J. D. and Grusin, R., (1998). *Remediation: understanding new media*. Cambridge, MA: MIT Press.

Breidbach, O., (2005). *Bilder des Wissens: Zur Kulturgeschichte der wissenschaftlichen Wahrnehmung*. Paderborn, Germany: Fink.

Clees, E., (1997). Zwangssterilisationen in Skandinavien: Weitverbreitete Ideologie der Eugenik. *Aerzteblatt.de* [online]. Available from: https://www.aerzteblatt.de/archiv/7893/Zwangssterilisationen-in-Skandinavien-Weitverbreitete-Ideologie-der-Eugenik.

Corinth, E., (2005). Noch vor 30 Jahren wurden in den USA Menschen zwangssterilisiert. *Heise Online* [online]. 16 May. Available from: https://www.heise.de/tp/features/Noch-vor-30-Jahren-wurden-in-den-USA-Menschen-zwangssterilisiert-3400979.html.

Darwin, C., (1859). *On the origin of species by means of natural selection, or the preservation of favoured races in the struggle for life*. London: John Murray.

Delfanti, A., (2012). Tweaking genes in your garage: biohacking between activism and entrepreneurship. In: W. Sützl and T. Hug, eds. *Activist media and biopolitics: critical media interventions in the age of biopower*. Innsbruck, Austria: Innsbruck University Press. pp. 163–177.

Down Syndrome Research, (2017). C-SPAN [online]. 25 October, 01:06:01–01:06:10. Available from: https://www.c-span.org/video/?436266-1/frank-stephens-shares-experience-living-syndrome-research-hearing

Ernst, J.-P., (2009). Zwangssterilisation – Ein aktuelles medizinisches Thema. In: St. Westermann, R. Kühl and D. Groß eds. Medizin im Dienst der "Erbgesundheit". Ein Beitrag zur Geschichte der Eugenik und "Rassenhygiene". Berlin: LIT Verlag, pp. 253–285.

Foucault, M., (1978). *The history of sexuality. Vol 1: an introduction*. New York: Pantheon.

Galton, F., (1883). *Inquiries into human faculty and its development*. New York: Macmillan.

Grimm, C., (2012). *Netzwerke der Forschung. Die historische Eugenikbewegung und die moderne Humangenomik im Vergleich*. Berlin: Logos Verlag.

Grotlüschen, A. and Linde, A., (2006). *Literalität, Grundbildung oder Lesekompetenz?* Kornwestheim: Waxmann.

Haeckel, E., (1866). *Generelle Morphologie der Organismen. 2 Bände*. Available from: https://archive.org/details/generellemorphol01haec

Haeckel, E., (1904). *Die lebenswunder; gemeinverständliche studien über biologische philosophie*. Ann Arbor: University of Michigan Press.

Harten, H.-C., Neirich, U. and Schwerendt, M. (2009). *Rassenhygiene als Erziehungsideologie des Dritten Reichs*. Berlin: De Gruyter.

Juchler, I., (2010). *Die Zumutung der Demokratie und Political Literacy*. Berlin: Springer.

Klee, E., (2004). "Euthanasie" im NS-Staat. 11 Edition, Frankfurt a.M.: Fischer Taschenbuch Verlag.

Lopez, K. C., (2020). Altering the human genome, changing local lives. WLVT.org [online]. 15 January. Available from: https://www.wlvt.org/blogs/warren/altering-the-human-genome-changing-local-lives/.

Mueller, T. and Beddies, T., (2006). "The destruction of life unworthy living" in National Socialist Germany. *International Journal of Mental Health*. **35(3)**, 94–104.

Orth, S., (1997). "Minderwertige Elemente". In: Der Spiegel 36/1997. https://www.spiegel.de/spiegel/print/d-8777129.html.

Peter, J., (2008). *Der Einbruch der Rassenhygiene in die Medizin. Auswirkungen rassenhygienischen Denkens auf Denkkollektive und medizinische Fachgebiete von 1918 bis 1934*. Frankfurt: Mabuse-Verlag.

Pias, C., (2002). Der Hacker. In: E. Horn, S. Kaufmann and U. Bröckling, eds. *Grenzverletzer. Von Schmugglern, Spionen und anderen subversiven Gestalten*. Berlin: Kulturverlag Kadmos. pp. 248–270.

Pitzke, M., (2012). Die verdrängte Schande. *Spiegel* [online]. 5, 2012. Available from: https://www.spiegel.de/panorama/zwangssterilisation-in-den-usa-die-verdraengte-schande-a-806709.html.

Schenk, B.-M., (2020). Eugenik. In: S. Hartwig, ed. *Behinderung*. Stuttgart: J.B. Metzler. Available from: 10.1007/978-3-476-05738-9_12.

Stollfuß, S., (2017). *Cyborg-TV. Genetik und Kybernetik in Fernsehserien*. Wiesbaden: Springer VS.

Text of the White House statements on the Human Genome Project, (2000). *The New York Times*. 27 June. Available from: https://archive.nytimes.com/www.nytimes.com/library/national/science/062700sci-genome-text.html.

*Unnatural Selection*, Episode 1, Cut, Paste, Life, (2019). Netflix [online]. 18 October. Available from: Netflix.

Weidenmann, B., (1997). "Multimedia": Mehrere Medien, mehrere Codes, mehrere Sinneskanäle? In: Unterrichtswissenschaft. 25 (1997) 3. pp. 197–206.

# 14 Deconstructing Rules for Proof of Cognitive Impairments

*Tom Lininger*

This chapter explores the rules that apply in legal proceedings to determine whether a person lacks mental capacity. Of particular concern are the rules that the prosecution and defense counsel must follow when offering proof of the defendant's capacity or incapacity to form the state of mind required for a criminal offense. Statutes, jurisprudence, and ethical rules in this area show an alarming inconsistency, and recent decisions by the US Supreme Court have further undermined the cohesiveness of the law.

Why study these rules closely? They indicate the extent to which society accords respect to its citizens who are experiencing cognitive impairments. If proceedings relating to mental capacity stray too far from the normal rights-based approach taken in US courts, this divergence requires careful consideration. Advocates for neurodivergent people need to hold the law accountable for prioritizing any considerations more highly than the basic humanity of all people.

The chapter seeks to answer three questions. First, what are the theoretical underpinnings of the rules for proving mental incapacity? Second, how do the current rules operate to the detriment of neurodivergent litigants and witnesses, particularly in criminal cases? Third, what reforms would improve the law in this area?

At the outset, it is necessary to define the term "mental incapacity." This term refers to the legal sufficiency of a defendant's cognitive abilities. A person who lacks capacity cannot form the mens rea, or culpable mental state, necessary to commit a crime. One version of the capacity test is the insanity defense, which could provide an excuse for criminal conduct (at least in some jurisdictions). In addition to scrutinizing the defendant's capacity at the time of the alleged offense, a court also must consider the defendant's capacity at the time of trial and sentencing. Capacity to understand judicial proceedings—an ability that courts usually refer to as "competence"—is crucial for the defendant to make strategic decisions, advise counsel, and comprehend any punishment imposed at the end of trial.

As the following analysis indicates, the law's taxonomy of mental states necessarily implicates judgments about dignity, autonomy, and personhood.

DOI: 10.4324/9781003257196-18

A close analysis of this law exposes deep-seated prejudice against neurodivergent people.

## Theoretical underpinnings of rules governing proof of mental capacity

As a general matter, there are two possible approaches that the evidence rules can take to the proof of a person's character or mental state. First, the rules can set bright-line boundaries and insist upon consistent procedures. Evidence rules taking this approach reflect deontological notions that the people whose character is under discussion have intrinsic worth, and that the law should not treat these people instrumentally to further some utilitarian goal. A second possible approach to the proof of character is to set forth more general, malleable standards that bend according to judicial determinations of expediency in each particular case. When applying the second approach, a judge weighs the probative value of evidence against the risk of prejudice, confusion, or waste of time.[1] The evidence rules reserve this second approach as a default for situations in which more specific rules do not apply—for example, when a party offers physical evidence as opposed to witness testimony or an out-of-court statement by a human being. In sum, evidence consisting of speech, writing, or assertive conduct by a human being is generally subject to per se rules with predictable outcomes,[2] while judges have great discretion to admit or exclude other categories of evidence, including nonhuman evidence.

Examples of the first approach—bright-line rules with clear procedural requirements—abound in the Federal Rules of Evidence and most states' evidentiary codes. For instance, the rules impose limits on the ability of attorneys to impeach testifying witnesses' character for truthfulness,[3] and one purpose of these rules is to respect the dignity of the witnesses (Weinstein & Berger 1994).[4] The rules also limit evidence of propensity for violence, recklessness, and other blameworthy conduct[5] because such evidence conflicts with the presumption that all human beings have free will and moral autonomy (Friedland 1997; Kim 2000).[6] In rape cases, the rules generally forbid defense attorneys from attempting to show the sexual predisposition of complainants,[7] because such evidence could besmirch the dignity of complainants and mistreat them in a way that might discourage others from filing rape complaints in the future (Lininger 2005; Luban 1990).[8]

By contrast, statutes and jurisprudence have conspicuously exempted the proof of mental capacity from the categorical treatment normally accorded to proof of human character.[9] There could be several explanations for this exemption, but one that is relevant for present purposes is the law's long history of regarding insane people as less than human.

Over 700 years of Anglo-American jurisprudence, leading legal theorists have characterized the insane as "wild beasts." This conception took hold in 13th-century England (Fahey et al. 2020; Platt and Diamond 1965)[10] and came with the British colonists to North America, where it has persisted to modern times.

Within the last few decades, Professor Sanford Kadish has written that insanity should excuse criminal conduct because the insane actor is more like an animal or thing than a human being: "We may become angry with an object or animal that thwarts us, but we can't blame it" (Kadish 1987, p. 280).[11] Similarly, Professor Michael Moore has suggested that the insane lack "personhood," and the law should treat them as if they were "animals, or even stones" (Moore 1985, p. 1037).[12]

Stripped of their rationality and denied their basic humanity in this conceptual framework, the insane do not seem deserving of any meaningful moral autonomy (Garvey 2018).[13] While Kant generally insists that every human has intrinsic value, and cannot merely be a means to an end (Kant 2002),[14] such instrumentalism may be tolerable for the insane when the law treats them as essentially nonhuman due to their lack of rationality (Fischette 2004).[15] Foucault (2006) has written that society's history of subordinating, excluding, and confining the mentally ill has exemplified the biopolitical model of power.[16]

It is no surprise, then, that the rules governing proof of mental incapacity have their foundations in the shifting sands of expediency. These rules do not provide firm protections and are incapable of consistent, predictable interpretation. The elasticity of the rules allows courts to adapt them to utilitarian goals in particular circumstances, unconstrained by deontological obligations to autonomous moral agents. By contrast, fully "human" witnesses and parties are subject to clear, readily discernible rules that courts enforce consistently.

## Current rules for proving mental incapacity cause hardship for neurodivergent litigants and witnesses, particularly in criminal cases

There are two ways in which the law's utilitarian approach to proof of mental incapacity has disadvantaged neurodivergent people. First, the standards for the required showing—i.e., what constitutes adequate proof of incapacity—are onerous and unpredictable. Second, the procedural rules for proving mental incapacity are inconsistent and unfair. Each of these two problems receives separate consideration later.

### *Standards of proof for mental incapacity*

For the most part, the Supreme Court has deferred to the legislative branch, at both the federal and state levels, to determine what proof is sufficient to demonstrate mental incapacity in a criminal case. Because legislatures have the power to define criminal offenses, and mens rea is an offense element, the Court has yielded to legislative control in this area,[17] except in unusual cases that seem to implicate fundamental constitutional protections such as the Eight Amendment's guarantee against cruel and unusual punishment.[18] Accordingly, there is wide variation in the standards of proof for mental incapacity. Some states have exploited the Court's indulgence and have adapted their standards of proof to suit utilitarian goals such as limiting public expenditures for the treatment of offenders deemed insane. The Supreme Court has exacerbated the problem with a series of rulings in recent years that undermined both cohesion and fairness.

One example is the Court's 2020 ruling in Kahler v. Kansas.[19] There, a defendant raised a constitutional challenge to a law greatly limiting the scope of the insanity defense. Kansas had previously allowed a defendant to prove insanity either by showing an inability to understand the nature of his acts (the "cognitive capacity prong" of the insanity defense) or an inability to understand the wrongfulness of his acts (the "moral capacity prong"). Kansas adopted a new law eliminating the "moral capacity prong" and insisting that only proof sufficing under the "cognitive capacity prong" could establish insanity.[20] The defendant argued that this strict approach to proof of insanity violated the Due Process Clause of the Fourteenth Amendment because it ran contrary to fundamental principles of justice. The Supreme Court disagreed, holding that due process does not require a state to accept moral incapacity as adequate proof of insanity.[21] The Court expressly noted the wide variation among states in setting standards of proof for insanity, and the Court deemed this inconsistency to be expedient for the criminal justice systems.[22]

Another example is the 2019 ruling in Madison v. Alabama.[23] In that case, a defendant on death row had suffered a stroke prior to the scheduled date of his execution and could no longer remember the details of the offense he had committed. The Supreme Court had to decide whether he was "competent to be executed"—in other words, whether his mental capacity was sufficient for him to comprehend the reason for his execution, which the Court had previously held to be a condition for the death penalty to withstand an Eighth Amendment challenge.[24] The Court somehow determined that memory of one's offense is not necessary for mental capacity to be adequate. So long as a defendant on death row knows the general reason why he faces execution, he cannot claim cruel and unusual treatment within the meaning of the Eighth Amendment.[25] The Court cited utilitarian concerns in dispensing with the defendant's arguments concerning procedural fairness.[26]

In 2021, the Supreme Court once again accepted inconsistent standards of proof in a case involving mental illness. In Francois v. Wilkerson,[27] an immigrant from Haiti faced deportation on the ground that the United States had not lawfully admitted him. He had been in the United States since 1979, and two of his children had served in the US Army, but the government nonetheless sought to deport him nearly four decades after his arrival.[28] He invoked a statute that prevents the government from removing a noncitizen to a country where it is more likely than not that the noncitizen's "life or freedom would be threatened" on account of a protected ground.[29] The law made clear, and no party disputed, that mental illness could qualify as a protected ground. The immigration judge hearing this case decided to block removal after finding that Francois had presented adequate proof of severe mental illness, including schizophrenia, bipolar disorder, and psychosis, as well as proof that he would suffer cruel and dehumanizing treatment if deported to Haiti.[30] Francois lost an administrative appeal, however, even though the government did not challenge the facts in the record. When Francois petitioned the Supreme Court for a stay his removal, only Justice Sotomayor voted to grant the stay, and the rest of the justices let his removal proceed. The Court majority seemed more concerned with promoting efficiency in the immigration system than with applying well-settled law to avert what Justice Sotomayor characterized as an "unnecessary tragedy."[31]

### *Procedural rules for proof of mental incapacity*

Not only do the above-listed substantive rules forsake consistency for expediency, but the procedural rules also prioritize instrumental concerns over the need to treat all people with respect and dignity. As seen later, the rules of evidence, criminal procedure, and legal ethics include provisions that complicate the proof of mental capacity or incapacity, and that significantly weaken procedural protections for neurodivergent people.

One of the most conspicuous examples is Federal Rule of Evidence 704(b). This rule prohibits any party in a criminal prosecution from offering expert testimony on the defendant's mens rea. By contrast, experts may freely opine about any issue, including a person's mental state, in all other categories of cases.[32] The plain purpose of 704(b) is to limit the use of expert testimony by defendants seeking to win verdicts of not guilty by reason of insanity. Congress adopted Rule 704(b) as part of the Insanity Defense Reform Act, which passed with overwhelming support following the successful use of the insanity defense by John Hinckley, Jr., who had attempted to assassinate President Ronald Reagan (Capra 2001; Fahey et al. 2020; Riley 2015–16).[33] The disparate treatment of expert testimony in Rule 704, and the prohibition of such expert testimony on the issue of mental capacity in a criminal case, has drawn criticism on the ground that this approach advanced political goals at the expense of a principled, consistent approach to the regulation of evidence.[34] Indeed, Congress decided not to involve the Federal Rules Advisory Committee in reviewing the draft of Rule 704(b)—an implicit concession that the new rule would be incongruous with the rest of the evidence code.[35]

Other evidence rules are similarly problematic. The hearsay rules generally exclude out-of-court statements offered for their truth, but these rules do not exclude statements offered to show the insanity of the speaker,[36] and the rules provide for several exceptions in the event that the speaker becomes "mentally ill."[37] The impeachment rules usually exclude evidence regarding religious beliefs,[38] but such evidence is admissible to show mental illness when the beliefs are so aberrant that they appear to indicate mental infirmity (Park & Lininger 2021).[39] As in the case of Rule 704(b), the rationale for exempting proof of mental incapacity from the typical rules for evidentiary proof seems to rest on utilitarian considerations, such as the assumption that mentally ill people lack value as trial witnesses and would interfere with judicial efficiency if permitted to testify.

Even a procedural protection as fundamental as the right against double jeopardy yields to policy concerns about controlling neurodivergent people. Normally, when the prosecution has utilized certain proof to obtain a conviction, that same proof cannot provide the basis for a second punishment of the defendant in a different proceeding.[40] But proof indicating a dangerous mental defect could provide the basis for deprivation of a defendant's freedom in two successive proceedings notwithstanding the protection against double jeopardy.[41] Involuntary civil commitment is in many respects indistinguishable from incarceration in prison or jail—and is arguably a worse ordeal (Caspar & Joukov 2020)[42]—but courts and legislatures deem involuntary civil commitment to be "nonpunitive," so that it is not cognizable under the test for double jeopardy.[43] The practical reality is that a neurodivergent defendant could be subject to consecutive terms of incarceration based on the government's presentation of identical proof in two separate proceedings—a hardship that no other category of defendant must endure.

Finally, it is noteworthy that an attorney's ethical duty of deference to a client disappears upon the attorney's subjective assessment that the client is suffering from diminished capacity.[44] Remarkably, the ethics rules do not specify any means by which attorneys are to assess their clients' capacity. Of course, law schools provide no training in psychology, and state bars do not require such training at any point after admission to practice. Critics have pointed out that an attorney tend to raise concerns about a client's lack of capacity to the extent that the client's judgment about a particular course of action diverges from an attorney's judgment (Rhode 2020).[45] In effect, an attorney's unilateral and dubious judgment as to a client's capacity can provide a basis for overriding one of the most fundamental ethical duties for any lawyer: the duty to let the client determine the objectives of the representation.[46] Once again, the inconsistency in procedural rules for proof of incapacity redounds to the detriment of neurodivergent people in the legal system. The rationale appears to be a utilitarian concern that deference to such people would result in strategic decisions that would misuse judicial resources and contravene paternalist notions of what is best for mentally ill clients.[47]

## Reforms to provide consistent protections for neurodivergent people

Of course, some of the problems relating to proof of mental incapacity are attributable to bias among judges and attorneys and would be difficult to correct through law reform. Yet several changes to statutes and rules would help to remedy the presently inconsistent and unfair rules governing proof of mental incapacity. The proposals set forth below are only a starting point; further action would almost certainly be necessary to create a level playing field for all litigants and witnesses irrespective of the cognitive challenges they may face.

First, it is time to revise the insanity defense and other defenses for diminished capacity. The standard of proof for all such defenses should be expansive.[48] It should also be uniform so that judicial rulings and jury instructions are predictable. The Supreme Court would help to promote uniformity by recognizing that certain basic elements of capacity defenses are indeed fundamental to well-established principles of liberty, and therefore are enforceable as constitutional guarantees. Legislatures should go further by codifying precisely what state of mind is sufficient for each offense, and by making clear that people with diminished capacity are not subject to strict liability in criminal law for any crime. Statutes should also clarify that the "competence to be executed" (a strange term coined by the Supreme Court)[49] is lacking when a defendant experiences any significant problem with mental health while on death row, including lost memory of committing the offense at issue.

Second, evidence codes should eliminate or curtail insanity-related exceptions to the baseline rules for the admissibility of evidence. The ability of expert witnesses to opine on the "ultimate issue" should not depend on whether a defense attorney is asking questions about the defendant's sanity; the rules should apply uniformly to expert testimony on any subject. Hearsay rules should not freely admit out-of-court statements offered to show lack of cognitive ability; when a judge deems such statements admissible on the ground that they are plainly absurd, and therefore not offered for truth, the judge is denying fair treatment to out-of-court declarants with cognitive impairments, and is allowing attorneys to evade the hearsay ban simply by invoking a convenient label for their evidence. Moreover, evidence codes should not weaken the protection against hearsay by deeming declarants suffering mental illness to be unavailable so that their statements are admissible under hearsay under several exceptions. Evidence of a person's religious views should be off-limits to prove insanity, just as this evidence is currently off-limits to undermine the credibility of a witness. Closing loopholes in the evidentiary rules governing proof of mental incapacity would be consistent with the Supreme Court's guidance: the Court has held that inadmissible evidence does not magically become admissible merely because its proponent seeks to prove mental incapacity.[50]

Third, the Supreme Court should recognize that involuntarily civil commitment is not meaningfully different from incarceration. The Court should abandon the fiction that such civil commitment is "nonpunitive," and the Court should clarify that any confinement of a defendant based on a particular offense must be part of a single prosecution in which the defendant will be able to invoke all constitutional protections including the Double Jeopardy Clause. Such an approach would ensure that when the government seeks to prove mental incapacity for the purpose of incarcerating an offender, the government's proof will be subject to the rigorous screening commensurate with the gravity of the consequences at stake. The characterization of involuntary civil commitment as punitive would represent a significant break from the Court's past jurisprudence but is not beyond the realm of possibility. Indeed, the Court recently approved such a break in the context of civil forfeiture proceedings, which are less analogous to punishment than is the deprivation of freedom entailed in involuntary civil commitment.[51]

Fourth, the ethical rules for lawyers should set forth careful protocols for any evaluation of clients' cognitive capacities. The rules should not permit lawyers to discredit clients' capacity merely because lawyers feel that clients' preferences are unreasonable.[52] The rules should insist that lawyers must receive training in order to make determinations about clients' capacity, or lawyers must involve third-party professionals who have appropriate credentials to make such evaluations. State bars should employ such professionals so that lawyers will have easy access to their services. As a result of such reforms, the procedures for proving clients' mental incapacity would be much more methodical and reliable.

Most fundamentally, society must shift its overall approach to the challenge posed by mental impairments. The current policy relies too much on criminal and quasi-criminal sanctions, streamlined procedures that curtail the rights of people who experience mental illness, and nontherapeutic confinement in lieu of meaningful treatment and rehabilitation.[53] The Foucauldian conception of biopower seems to describe aptly our society's prioritization of warehousing over welfare in responding to the mental health crisis (Foucault 2006). A better strategy would be to reserve the criminal justice system for offenders who are both culpable and dangerous, and to divert as many mentally ill people as possible to alternative avenues such as mental health courts (Stefan & Winick 2005)[54] and noncoercive treatment settings, which are more likely to respond humanely, appropriately, and productively.

## Notes

1 Fed. R. Evid. 403 (setting forth default balancing test for evaluating admissibility of evidence).

2 E.g., Fed. R. Evid. 801(c) (specifying that definition of hearsay includes verbal statements, writing, and assertive nonverbal conduct by human beings if offered to prove truth of matter asserted); Fed. R. Evid. 803–807 (listing various circumstances under which hearsay could be admissible).

3 E.g., Fed. R. Evid. 608–10 (limiting categories of evidence that attorneys can use to impeach testifying witnesses).

4 Fed. R. Evid. 611(a)(3) (authorizing judges to constrain examination of witnesses where necessary to "protect witnesses from harassment or undue embarrassment"); Weinstein and Berger (1994) suggested that purpose of Fed. R. Evid. 611 is to promote "ascertainment of truth without unnecessarily sacrificing the dignity of the individual witness" (p. 611).

5 E.g., Fed. R. Evid. 404(a) (limiting use of character evidence to prove propensity of accused or victim in criminal prosecution under certain circumstances); Fed. R. Evid. 404(b) (limiting admissibility of uncharged misconduct or other extrinsic acts when offered to support inference of propensity).

6 Kim (2000) discusses Kantian "human autonomy rationale for the character evidence ban" based on the "intrinsic value that human beings have as ends in themselves"; "respect for human dignity and autonomy requires the exclusion of prior bad acts" pursuant to Fed. R. Evid. 404(b); Friedland (1997–98) characterizes Fed. R. Evid. 404 as repudiating notions of "deterministic behavior."

7 Fed. R. Evid. 412 (setting forth various protections referred to collectively as "rape shield law," whereby attorneys generally may not seek to discredit or otherwise embarrass accusers with general evidence of promiscuity, unchaste predisposition, or prior consensual sexual relations with partners other than the defendants on trial).
8 Luban (1990) explains that, except under limited circumstances, both legal ethics and morality require defense counsel to forbear from "brutal cross-examination" that would "humiliate and browbeat the prosecutrix" by attempting to discredit her chastity; *accord* Lininger (2005) who discusses asperity of cross-examination faced by accusers in rape prosecutions, and noting that widespread knowledge of accusers' ordeal on the witness stand discourages future reporting by other rape survivors.
9 For example, see Part II, *infra*.
10 Platt and Diamond (1965) chronicle the evolution of the "wild beast" theory over several centuries in England; *see*Fahey, Groschadl and Weaver 2020 discuss the early history of insanity defense noting the significance of the "wild beast" theory.
11 Kadish (1987) argues that a "[n]o blaming system would be coherent if it imposed blame without regard to moral agency" (p. 280) and suggesting that punishment of the insane for their crimes would be akin to "blaming a rock for falling or blaming a dog for barking" (p. 280).
12 Moore (1985) contends that "human beings who are insane are no more proper subjects of moral evaluation than are ... animals, or even stones" (p. 1037).
13 Garvey (2018) suggests that "blame presupposes moral agency, and calling someone insane is just another way of saying she's not a moral agent at all" (p. 145).
14 Kant (1785/2002) applies the principle that humanity must always be an end unto itself while stressing the need to respect the autonomy and dignity of other human beings due to their rationality.
15 Fischette (2004) collects authors who argue that a person lacking rationality stands outside the Kantian framework.
16 Foucault (2006) discusses the societal shift to confinement and exclusion of the mentally ill.
17 E.g. Montana v. Egelhoff, 518 U.S. 37, 56–61 (1996) (Ginsburg, J. concurring) (determining, in a concurrence that was the crucial fifth vote for upholding the defendant's conviction, that a state legislature could redefine the mens rea for a crime so that mental incapacity due to voluntary intoxication would not be a valid defense, but if a state did not redefine substantive elements in this manner, it would need to admit evidence of voluntary intoxication as a matter of procedural fairness).
18 E.g. Atkins v. Virginia, 536 U.S. 304, 321 (2002) (holding that the execution of a defendant who suffered from a significant mental impairment at the time of his offense would violate the Eighth Amendment's ban on cruel and unusual punishment).
19 140 S. Ct. 1021 (2020).
20 *Id.* at 1025–26.
21 *Id.* at 1027, 1032, 1037.
22 *Id.* at 1028 (citing value of states' "experimentation" with different versions of insanity defense).
23 130 S. Ct. 718 (2019).
24 Panetti v. Quarterman, 551 U.S. 930, 959 (2007) (holding that the Eighth Amendment prohibits the execution of a prisoner whose mental illness prevents him from "rational[ly] understanding" why the government is imposing this punishment).
25 *Madison*, 130 S. Ct. at 726–30 (upholding lower court's determination that defendant had failed to meet strict test for proving his inability to understand the rationale for his punishment).
26 *Id.* at 725, 727 (noting deferential standards of review for petitions seeking post-conviction relief – which present efficient concerns that Congress addressed in the

Antiterrorism and Effective Death Penalty Act of 1996 – and dismissing the idea of exempting the "simply forgetful" from punishment).

27 *Rehaif*, 139 S. Ct. at 2207 (Alito, J., dissenting). 141 S. Ct. 652 (2021) (Mem.)

28 *Id.* at 653 (Sotomayor, J. dissenting).

29 8 U.S.C. § 1231(b)(3)(A).

30 141 S. Ct. at 652 (Sotomayor, J. dissenting) (repeating finding of immigration judge, based on expert testimony, that Francois would likely be subject to "physical punishment, torture and isolation" in Haiti due to his mental illness and criminal record).

31 *Id.* at 655.

32 *Compare* Fed. R. Evid. 704(a) (allowing expert witnesses to give opinions on the "ultimate issue"—e.g., an element of a claim or defense—with no limitation on the use of such evidence concerning the mental state of any person) with Fed. R. Evid. 704(b) (forbidding expert opinions on mens rea in a criminal prosecution).

33 Riley (2015–16) traces impetus for Fed. R. Evid. 704(b) to congressional outrage over verdict in Hinckley prosecution; Capra (2001) recounts abrupt passage of Fed. R. Evid. 704(b) by Congress in reaction to Hinckley verdict.

34 Riley, *supra* n. 33, at 116–26 (criticizing Fed. R. Evid. 704(b) on various grounds); Capra, supra n. 33, at 692 (characterizing Rule 704(b) as a "fiasco").

35 Professor Daniel Capra, who has chaired the Federal Rules Advisory Committee, has noted the danger of this approach and the impropriety of its use to pass Fed. R. Evid. 704(b). *Supra* n. 33, at 691–93.

36 Under Fed. R. Evid. 801 and its state analogs, the definition of hearsay only extends to out-of-court statements offered to prove the truth of the matter asserted. This definition excludes a statement that the court deems absurd, and that a party offers to prove the mental infirmity of the declarant (as opposed to proving the truth of the statement).

37 Fed. R. Evid. 804(a)(4) (allowing a party to use any of the five hearsay exceptions set forth in Fed. R. Evid. 804(b) if the party has shown to the court's satisfaction that a witness is "unavailable" due to mental illness).

38 Fed. R. Evid. 610 ("Evidence of a witness's religious beliefs or opinions is not admissible to attack or support the witness's credibility").

39 Park and Lininger (2021) reviews reviewing case law and determining that Fed. R. Evid. and its state counterparts "do not impede the use of religious evidence to prove insanity" (§ 7.4).

40 To be more precise, the most common test for determining whether the Double Jeopardy Clause applies to successive prosecutions or multiple punishments is the "Blockburger test," which focuses on whether the elements of offenses charged in successive prosecutions are co-extensive. Under this test, successive prosecutions or multiple punishments are impermissible unless two distinct offenses are at issue, and each requires proof of an element that the other does not. United States v. Dixon, 509 U.S. 688, 696 (1993) (explaining "same elements" test in Blockburger, and noting that this test applies in "both the multiple punishment multiple prosecution contexts").

41 Kansas v. Hendricks, 521 U.S. 346, 360–70 (1997) (upholding as "nonpunitive" Kansas law providing for involuntary civil commitment of mentally ill defendants upon their release from prison if they pose a danger to public safety).

42 Caspar and Joukov (2020) contended that involuntary civil commitment can be a "worse punishment than incarceration" (p. 503).

43 *Hendricks*, 521 U.S. at 363 ("The State may take measures to restrict the freedom of the dangerously mentally ill. This is a legitimate nonpunitive governmental objective and has been historically so regarded.").

44 A.B.A. Model Rule 1.14 (providing that, under certain circumstances, a lawyer may substitute his or her own judgment for that of a client whose "capacity to make adequately considered decisions in connection with a representation is diminished").

45 Rhode et al. (2020) raised concern about "circular reasoning that bases judgments of incompetency based solely on a person's 'eccentric' choices, and then overrules those choices because the person is incompetent" (internal citations omitted).

46 A.B.A. Model Rule 1.2(a) (requiring lawyers to heed clients' preferences regarding objectives of legal representation); *cf*. Rhode, *supra* n. 45, at 215 ("Experts generally agree that mental illness should not be equated with incompetence").

47 See, e.g., United States v. Kaczynski, 239 F.3d 1108, 1126 (9th Cir. 2001) (Reinhardt, J. dissenting) (in high-profile trial of alleged "Unabomber," trial court resorted too easily to incapacity theory in approving defense counsel's decision to override defendant's preferences for objectives of representation; trial court had understandable concern about "impugning the integrity of our criminal justice system" if defendant made unorthodox decisions, but these paternalistic and utilitarian concerns could not outweigh defendant's right to self-determination).

48 An example of an expansive standard of proof is Section 4.01 of the American Law Institute's Model Penal Code (MPC), which provides as follows: "A person is not responsible for criminal conduct if at the time of such conduct as a result of mental disease of defect he lacks substantial capacity either to appreciate the criminality [wrongfulness] of his conduct or to conform his conduct to the requirements of the law." An even better version of this standard of proof would include three separate, independently sufficient grounds: cognitive incapacity, moral incapacity, and volitional incapacity. The first two of these grounds were at issue in *Kahler*, 140 S. Ct. at 1025–26, and the third is the last element in the MPC test quoted above.

49 E.g., *Madison*, 130 S. Ct. at 729 (discussing standards for determining "competency to be executed").

50 For example, the Court has refused to create an exception to the general rule that silence following Miranda warnings will not be admissible to impeach a testifying witness. Wainwright v. Greenfield, 474 U.S. 284, 295 (1986) (rejecting government's argument that post-Miranda silence should be admissible in unique context of proving whether defendant was insane); Doyle v. Ohio, 426 U.S. 610, 618 (1976) (establishing general rule that post-Miranda silence is not admissible for the impeachment of testifying witnesses).

51 Timbs v. Indiana, 139 S. Ct. 682, 689–90 (2019) (deeming civil in rem forfeiture to be partially punitive in nature, and therefore subject to review under Eighth Amendment's Excessive Fines Clause, which Fourteenth Amendment applied to states).

52 Rhode, *supra* n. 45, at 215–16 (discussing danger that attorneys could sometimes assess clients' capacity based in part on attorneys' disagreement with clients' preferences for objectives of representation).

53 "For decades, this country has underfunded and undervalued mental health and substance use care with devastating results. Today, only 43% of all people living with mental illness receive treatment for their condition – although the numbers go up to 67% for serious mental illnesses …" The National Council Unite for Behavioral Health, 2019, available at thenationalcouncil.org.

54 Stefan and Winick (2005) noted advantages of mental health courts, particularly their ability to craft individualized solutions in keeping with principles of therapeutic jurisprudence, but also noting some of the potential drawbacks such as greater discretionary authority reposed in judges, and possibility of class-based disparities in treatment of mentally ill people.

## References

Caspar, S. M. and Joukov, A. R., (2020). Worse than punishment: how the involuntary commitment of persons with mental illness violates the United States Constitution. *Hastings Constitutional Law Quarterly*. **47**(4), 499–532.

Capra, D. J., (2001). A recipe for confusion: congress and the federal rules of evidence. *Miami Law Review*. **55**(4), 691–703.

Fahey, E. M., Groschadl, L. and Weaver, B., (2020). "The angels that surrounded my cradle": the history, evolution, and application of the insanity defense. *Buffalo Law Review*. **68**(3), 805–856.

Fischette, C., (2004). Psychopathy and responsibility. *Virginia Law Review*. **90**(5), 1424–1485. doi:10.2307/3202382.

Friedland S. I., (1997). The criminal law implications of the Human Genome Project: reimagining a genetically oriented criminal justice system. *Kentucky Law Journal*. **86**(2), 303–366.

Foucault, M., (2006). *History of madness* (J. Khalfa, ed.; J. Murphy and J. Khalfa, trans.). New York: Routledge. (Originally published in 1961).

Garvey, S. P., (2018). Agency and Insanity. *Buffalo Law Review*. **66**(1), 123–191.

Kadish, S., (1987). Excusing crime. *California Law Review*. **75**(1), 257–289. doi:10.2307/3480580.

Kant, I., (2002). *Groundwork of the metaphysics of morals* (A. W. Wood, trans.). New Haven, CT: Yale University Press. (Originally published in 1785).

Kim, S. M., (2000). Characteristics of soulless persons: the applicability of the character evidence rule to corporations. *University of Illinois Law Review*. **2000**(4), 763–811.

Lininger, T. (2005). Bearing the cross. *Fordham Law Review*. **74**(3), 1353–1423.

Luban, D., (1990). Partisanship, betrayal and autonomy in the lawyer-client relationship: a reply to Stephen Ellmann. *Columbia Law Review*. **90**(4), 1004–1043. doi:10.2307/1122923.

Moore, S. M., (1985). Causation and the excuses. *California Law Review*. **73**, 1091–1149.

Park, R. and Lininger, T., (2021). *The new Wigmore: a treatise of evidence: impeachment and examination of witnesses*. New York: Wolters Kluwer Legal.

Platt, A. M. and Diamond, B. L., (1965). The origins and development of the "wild beast" concept of mental illness and its relation to theories of criminal responsibility. *Journal of Historical Behaviorial Science*. **1**(4), 355–367.

Rhode, D. et al. (2020). *Legal ethics*. 8th ed. St. Paul, MN: Foundation Press.

Riley, S. P., (2015). Federal rule of evidence 704(b): a remedy in need of a cure. *Regent University Law Review*. **28**(1), 111–136.

Stefan, S. and Winick, B. J., (2005). A dialogue on mental health courts. *Psychology, Public Policy, and Law*. **11**(4), 507–526. doi:10.1037/1076-8971.11.4.507

Weinstein J. B. and Berger, M. A., (1994). *Weinstein's evidence*. New York: LEXIS.

# 15 So That Playing to Win Is Not Playing to Die: Constructing Legal Recourse for Athletes with Sickle Cell Trait Laboring in the Actor-Networks of the Brown Commons

*Madeleine M. Plasencia*

Historians and legal scholars sometimes engage in what I have called "narrative-in-reverse"—a process of inferring facts about the world outside the record based on the way our understanding of the world makes sense of facts in the record.[1] In this chapter, I employ narrative-in-reverse to demonstrate how intersectional systems of socially constructed inequalities of race, class, and dis/ability converge to create a field of oppression for athletes of color with sickle cell trait (SCT), for whom the existing frameworks of dis/ability law offer a much too narrow path of protection and relief. To ground this analysis, first I turn to Cuban queer and critical theorist Professor José Esteban Muñoz (2020), who has theorized race or brownness as a commons, a "brown commons."

> "Brown commons" is meant to signify at least two things. One is the commons of brown people, places, feelings, sounds, animals, minerals, flora, and other objects. How these things are brown, or what makes them brown, is partially the way in which they suffer and strive together but also the commonality of their ability to flourish under duress and pressure. They are brown in part because they have been devalued by the world outside their commons. Their brownness can be known by tracking the ways through which global and local forces constantly attempt to degrade their value and diminish their verve. But they are also brown insofar as they smolder with a life and persistence: they are brown because brown is a common color shared by a commons that is of and for the multitude (p. 1).

Muñoz adds a Latinx perspective to the social constructivist theory of race, which argues that race is a socio-historical *concept*, whose *unstable* meaning is a proper target of political struggle precisely because it was invented to be used opportunistically to construct hierarchical categories of social groups and to legitimate the differential distribution of legal, financial, and property rights and statuses among the groups it constructs (Omi & Winant 2015). According to Muñoz, one is rendered brown through subordinating processes and interactions.

DOI: 10.4324/9781003257196-19

Being rendered brown means constantly having one's linguistic orientations and accents challenged, one's right to residency contested, one's customs and styles of living deemed *illegitimate*. Muñoz explains that brownness indexes multiple and concurrent vulnerabilities, from the contempt and scorn of xenophobes and racists, to racial profiling and the many other forms of subordination imposed both by private and state act actors under color of law. Being rendered brown engenders a sense of the world that elicits certain performances, such that brown humans "radiate a different kind of affect" (Muñoz 2020, p. 3).

Muñoz's formulation provides a powerful means of understanding the subjective experiences of young athletes in the Brown commons, whose psychic, educational, financial, and physical well-being are affected by the dynamics of the brown commons. In this chapter, I seek to extend the generative potential of Muñoz's formulation by drawing on "Actor Network Theory (ANT)" to further specify the objective structures of the brown commons.[2]

On the one hand, these athletes are exhilarated to be picked to join a team of cohorts, of similarly exceptional young people. In the brown commons of athleticism, they are feted with respect, support, admiration, encouragement and flourish; yet, there is the simultaneous specter/threat of expulsion, and dis/inclusion. I deliberately coin the word dis/inclusion with a forward slash to foreground the nature of discrimination athletes with SCT experience; it is not that they are excluded, but rather having been initially included, discovery of their dis/ability results in their dis/inclusion. Their inclusion is always provisional because for athletes in the brown commons, dis/ability = dis/inclusion. This threat of expulsion is itself best understood using ANT as the operation of power constituted by political assemblages that include networks of scientists, medical professionals, coaches, scouts, directors, and trustees—that is, the (white) sports-financial complex, whose interests are "against the poverty and educational disadvantage of African-Americans more generally, against the interests of those with either SCT or those with SCD, and in favor of a white, rich, sport-business elite, especially in the US South" (Carter & Dyson 2015, p. 62).[3] Athletes in the brown commons thus confront a complex constellation of subjective aspirations, incentives, and imaginings, and objective networks, and differentials of informational and economic power that often conspire to dissuade young athletes with SCT from complaining or notifying team staff or coaches that they are experiencing symptoms associated with exertional sickling.

As Muñoz theorized, "brownness is a kind of uncanny persistence in the face of distressed conditions of possibility" (Muñoz 2020, p. 1). In "The Life of the Undead," Antonio Viego wryly observed that Latinx people appear in the public health and epidemiological research as an "epidemiological paradox." Epidemiologists find Latinx people possessing "a body too brutally alive in the face of social and material inequalities … [of] poverty, lack of education and death" (Viego 2009, p. 131). They describe Latinx people as living longer than endured socioeconomic conditions would forecast, prompting Muñoz to remark that "Latinos live long deaths" (Muńoz 2020, p. 5).

For brown people coming from Caribbean nations and cultures, race is even further complexified. Speaking of Dominican racialization, Lorgia Garcia-Peña observed that in the Dominican Republic imaginary, race exists as an amalgam of social injustices and inequalities that are the consequence of the exploitation by *international* corporations, enabled by *local* governments (García-Peña 2015). Similarly, the brown commons of the athletic field reproduces in microcosm the structure and relations of power of the dominant culture that makes exertion on the field the fraught pathway from poverty to fortune by way of pain and blood, and sometimes death.

In 1906, sociologist William Edward Burghardt (W.E.B.) Du Bois presided as secretary and edited the collection of scientific research papers submitted to the "Eleventh Conference for the Study of the Negro Problems." The research challenged the scientific community, reaching what were then "heretical" conclusions. "There is no single European or white race," and there is no such thing as a "pure" race. Instead, African-Americans "represent a very wide and thorough blending of … European and African blood" (Du Bois 1906, p. 28). In addition, Professor Du Bois's study concretely linked disparate mortality rates and impact of disease on African-Americans to social and economic conditions such as unequal access to improved education and better economic opportunities. In other words, diseases were not racial diseases, but social diseases.

As it turns out, on all counts, Du Bois was right. Genomic experts caution against the peril of designating socially constructed racial and ethnic identities as biological constructs in genomic research. The danger is of producing genetic essentialism. This is because race and ethnicity are socially constructed identities that obscure the fact that the "boundaries" between social groups are in fact very fluid. Compounding this error, genetic information tends to have great public authority (Nelkin & Lindee 1995). Consequently, genetic markers linked to race can reify socially constructed racial and ethnic identities. Within the last 20 years, genome pioneers have called for an end to the use of racial and ethnic categories as a proxy for biological heterogeneity (Foster & Sharp 2002; Yudell 2016). Nearly all geneticists today reject the idea that there are such things as "Indian" or "African" genes (Yudell, 2016).

In the 1990s, scientists found that SCT is not uncommon in Whites (Shafer and Lorey, 1996). Misrepresentation of SCT as "exclusively or primordially African" illustrates how genetic essentialism is implicated in the construction of race. Playing its role in the actor-network of the sports industry's brown commons, it enables SCT to more readily be cast, not as an avoidable risk of injury from overexertion, but rather as marking "a genetically flawed 'black body'" (Carter & Dyson 2015, p. 69). The athlete carrying the SCT gene is in a double-bind, occupying polarizing binaries—good and bad , strong and weak, superior and inferior—regarded at once as athletically gifted but flawed by a "black" gene.[4] For young athletes in the brown commons, who view their future prospects as tied up in their status as "studs," the stigma of dis/ability not surprisingly induces avoidance of interactions which would cast them as dis/abled. Thus, the first step to secure the well-being of student athletes living with SCT is to understand the unique risks it poses, in the lived experience of bodies in the brown commons. The second step is to articulate the intersectional reality and imagine a corresponding legal regime that will de-pathologize "the pathologies of non-disablement" (Hughes 2007, p. 673).

## What is SCT?

The term sickle cell disease has been used in the scientific literature to describe "a group of genetic conditions in which pathology results from the inheritance of the sickle cell gene either homozygously or as a double heterozygote with another interacting gene" (Serjeant, 2013, p. n/a). Sports medicine specialists have relied heavily on the important work of Dr Felix I D. Konotey-Ahulu, who focused on African-Americans in the diaspora. Dr. Konotey-Ahulu's decades-long and comprehensive study of sickle cell disease formed the canon of the subject of sickle cell disease in the Archives of Internal Medicine (Buchanan 1978). It is now understood that SCT is widespread in equatorial Africa, Saudi Arabia, and India, reaching a trait frequency as high as 40% in certain parts of sub-Saharan Africa, eastern Saudi Arabia, and central India (Serjeant 2013, para. 1). Persons with SCT have been found to resist falciparum malaria, parasites, and have a high survival rate, if infected (Serjeant 2013, para. 2). The prevalence of SCT has been established in populations throughout the world, and is not confined to any specific geographic place or ethnic group.[5]

The most common genotype is homozygous sickle cell (SS) disease. People with this genotype possess two abnormal genes for hemoglobin formation, and at least one of these (or both) are the sickle cell gene (Buchanan 1978). These genes morph the red cells from a round or doughnut shape to the signature crescent or sickle shape that blocks blood flow, resulting in acute rhabdomyolysis, renal failure, and death ("Consensus Statement" n/a). Sickle cell anemia is the more severe and debilitating disease, and is characterized by two abnormal genes. In these cases, the person is homozygous SS, is permanently anemic, and as a result is unlikely to perform or achieve at high levels in athletics (Buchanan 1978).

SCT is not sickle cell disease. A person with SCT has inherited the sickle cell hemoglobin gene (S) from one parent and one normal hemoglobin gene (A) from the other parent. Thus, this person has the genotype AS (Buchanan 1978). SCT has been found to be common, and may be relatively benign. However, increased attention has been given to SCT because athletes, especially young athletes with SCT have developed a syndrome that can be quite serious and even fatal—fulminant exertional rhabdomyolysis (Anzalone et al. 2010).

## Dis/ability is socially constructed

As McGinley and Cooper (2020) have argued, dis/ability can also be understood as a social construction. Like race, dis/ability has been defined by the effects of structural, economic, and cultural exclusion. Persons labeled dis/abled have been devalued, treated as biologically deficient, burdens or non-contributing members of society, and labeled welfare cases (Goodley 2013).

Building on prior conceptual work to establish a transdisciplinary space for dis/ability studies, a number of scholars assert that dis/ability studies is *the* space in which to theorize political, theoretical, and practical issues relevant to all socially constructed inequalities (Goodley 2013). For example, McRuer expressly channels Adrienne Rich's "compulsory heterosexuality" (which produces queerness) to forward a theory of "compulsory able-bodiedness" (which produces dis/ability) (McRuer 2006). Goodley (2014) notes that "[d]isabled people, women, children, queer, people of colour and poor people share an Other space to that of the dominant same that is founded upon ableist, heteronormative, adult, white European and North American, high-income nation's values" (p. 637). In Campbell's formulation of ableism, dis/ability (through the lens of Bruno Latour's *We Have Never Been Modern*) is the site where identities, performances, and processes as "co-relationally constitutive" converge to maintain what she terms "ableist normativity," which coercively enforces a presumption of human sameness (Campbell 2009).

Severing dis/ability from the body has its complications. Dis/ability studies theorists in the social construction model have been critiqued for failing to recognize that the body does matter, and that the experiential realities of an impairment do present challenges (Davis 2017; Siebers 2008). Still, the meaning of those challenges is what is fundamentally at issue.

More recently, DisCrit theorists study the intersectionality of race and dis/ability, in order to understand how ableism and racism construct "interlocking oppressions" in the lives of students of color with dis/abilities (Annamma et al. 2013, 2018; Connor et al. 2016). This intersectional approach can advance critical analysis of dis/ability law by further specifying the conversion of oppressions that bear down upon athletes laboring with SCT in the brown commons of the athletic field.

## Dis/ability as ambiguous

In SCT cases, the necessary impairment for legal protection may be elusive. Discussions of the body in medical research addressing SCT coalesce around the *risks* of a somatic manifestation. For example, a recent study found no relationship between SCT and adverse changes in cognitive function or pathological changes in the brain that lead to cognitive impairment (unlike patients with sickle cell disease) (Cahill et al. 2019). The organs however are a different matter. SCT carriers were found to have *increased risk* of kidney disease (Naik et al. 2016), venous thromboembolism (Austin et al., 2007), and stroke (Golomb 2005).

Leading theorists argue for a break from thinking about dis/ability under the medical model (Thomas 2007). On the social fluidity and ambiguity of the dis/abled body, Anne McGuire has noted that

> [d]isability marks the body in ambiguous ways—it appears and disappears, is noticed and is hidden … . It's also critical to consider how dis/ability marks different bodies in different and relational ways; systems of ableism come into contact with racialized bodies, queer bodies, classed bodies, gendered bodies, bodies that already have been touched by other (and perhaps multiple) systems of oppression (McGuire 2010, p. 30).

The shifting meaning of dis/ability depends on this "interactional process—a 'living-with'" (McGuire 2010, p. 30).

In our case, even as athletes with SCT may risk their lives to participate in certain team sport activities, they simultaneously risk becoming paradoxically quite visible (and stigmatized) when sidelined or dis/included precisely because of that risk. On the practice field, and in the training rooms, athletes with SCT routinely find themselves in a constructed insider/outsider status, as able-bodied players linger around, bustle by, and surround their sidelined teammates.

The challenge of imagining and constructing a de-pathologized brown commons requires the affirmation and embrace of human difference. Rather than expecting the athletes and the parents, elders, and leaders in the community to attempt to emulate the ableist norm, the flourishing of all human beings can only come after we have imagined humans differently. As in Tom Shakespeare's formulation, "rather than interrogating the other, let us de-construct the 'normality-which-is-to-be-assumed'" (quoted in Campbell 2008).

Dis/ability jurisprudence reflects the idea that defining dis/ability is a moving target, even as the Court has attempted to stabilize the ambiguous terms of the ADA in ways that implicate the transformation or reiteration of dominant structures of oppression.[6] As I demonstrate in the next two sections, the lived reality of athletes with SCT in the brown commons provides a meaningful framework through which to critique (and expand) the jurisprudence of dis/ability.

## The Bragdon Framework

Civil rights litigation begins with the threshold challenge of successfully establishing dis/ability. Ironically, in order to secure justice—through compensation or accommodation—for a person who has experienced discrimination at the hands of a society that has refused to appropriately recognize difference, the task at hand involves "marking" the individual as having an "impairment." Once the claim is made that a person has a dis/ability within the meaning of the law, the person has now collaborated in the assignment of a label that, by definition, renders them less than the norm.

Federal disability statutes only protect individuals who have a "disability." Under the Americans with Disabilities Act, "disability" means (A) a physical or mental impairment that substantially limits one or more … major life activities; (B) a record of such an impairment; or (C) being "regarded as" having such an impairment (42 U.S.C. § 12102). Like persons living with human immunodeficiency virus (HIV), a person living with SCT may be asymptomatic, but is nonetheless living with a dis/ability and should be entitled to protection under the ADA and other civil rights statutes protecting persons with dis/abilities.

There are sufficient theoretical similarities between SCT and HIV to warrant SCT's legal classification as a dis/ability under the Court's reasoning in *Bragdon v. Abbott*, 524 U.S. 624 (1998). In *Bragdon*, the Court focused on the risks presented by the HIV virus, not to the person who carried the virus, but to the children she might have. Sidney Abbott was found to have been "substantially limited" in her major life activity of reproduction. The "substantial limitation" did not require that one show a complete inability to engage in reproductive activity, to bear or conceive children. The risk of passing HIV to a conceived child was sufficient to dissuade many people from assuming that risk. The state of living with the fear of, and acting or rather not acting, based on the risk of passing HIV to one's children, satisfied the substantial limitation requirement.[7]

For young athletes competing for a future in and beyond the brown commons, participating in sports is a major life activity. In Division I football, 45%, and 25% of deaths from 2004 to 2008 were attributable to sports-related cardiac, and SCT, respectively (Harmon et al. 2012). From 2000 to 2017, overexertion has been linked to the deaths of 35 college football players, and thirteen football players were hospitalized with rhabdomyolysis (Anderson 2017; Fain 2017). Athletes with SCT, and especially football players, live with the heightened risk of hospitalization or worse, and having to act or not act based on this actual risk should satisfy the substantial limitation requirement, thus warranting its recognition as a dis/ability.

The *Bragdon* Court found that the mere presence of HIV in the body caused bodily harm, and that its presence constituted an impairment: "In light of the immediacy with which the [HIV] virus begins to damage the infected person's white blood cells and the severity of the disease, we hold it is an impairment from the moment of infection."[8] Similarly, SCT causes damage to the red blood cells. It is not as severe as the damage caused by sickle cell anemia, but for athletes in the brown commons, SCT has resulted in exertional sickling on the athletic field, resulting in sudden death.

In *Sutton v. United Airlines*, the Court restricted the reach of the ADA's protections in cases of uncorrected vision by ruling that a "disability" determination does not include untreated or unmitigated conditions. The proper inquiry was whether the condition substantially limits life activities, *after* the use of mitigating measures, for example, wearing corrective lenses.[9] Notably, this portion of *Sutton*'s ruling was reversed in the ADAAA. Congress expressly rejected the formulation that "whether an impairment substantially limits a major life activity is to be determined with reference to the ameliorative effects of mitigating measures."[10]

A person who has SCT has no "treatment" per se to correct the condition. In fact, the only "treatment" is to take precaution not to develop *exercise collapse associated with sickle cell trait (ECAST)* through screening, prevention, and detection. The National Athletic Trainers Association recommends prevention and treatment by hydrating, allowing players to set their own pace, to rest longer between repetitions, to adjust their activity in extreme heat, and to *be excluded from certain tests such as mile runs and serial sprints* (Casa et al. 2012). Legal protections might be extended by establishing a rule of tort law holding schools negligent for failure to keep all of the athletes, including those with SCT, adequately hydrated, and otherwise bar *all* intense exercise in extreme conditions.

Once "treated" by being singled out for special support, and dis/inclusion from some of the team training, student athletes with SCT might very well be placed beyond the reach of ECAST, but not beyond the reach of discrimination. Like HIV, SCT has been highly stigmatized. Unlike people wearing glasses, which can readily be observed in every segment of society, the diagnosis that an athlete has SCT is likely to end the athlete's opportunity to compete absent appropriate [non-stigmatized] accommodations not likely to be forthcoming in the brown commons. Indeed, stigma and dis/inclusion have flowed from the media's sensationalistic narratives of SCT as the "monster within" and "college football's serial murderer" (Carter & Dyson 2015). In anti-discrimination law, stigmatic harm is as legally significant as economic harm, as it comes from being evaluated by a process that treats people as inferior.[11] Barring athletes with SCT from participation, when universal measures could accommodate them, reiterates unlawful exclusionary and oppressive structures.[12]

Unsurprisingly, players who test positive for SCT report being made the object of "good-natured ribbing" on and off the field, especially when singled out during wind sprints or conditioning workouts with teammates.[13] For example, off the field, Pryce Macon, an Oklahoma defensive end remarked that his roommates call him "Sickle" (Thomas & Zarda 2010). As Dr. Lanetta Jordan, chief medical officer for the Sickle Cell Disease Association of America, has queried, "Does it now slide from protection of the athlete who has SCT by sitting them out, to maybe losing a scholarship, to maybe not being recruited at all" (Thomas & Zarda 2010, p. n/a). Adding to the pressures of the brown commons are the realities for some of living in poverty. In 2015, the percentage of African-American and Latinx people living *below* the poverty line was 26% and 24%, respectively, compared to 10% of Whites (DeNavas-Walt & Proctor 2015).

Currently, the spectrum of legal recognition of SCT as a dis/ability ranges from clear and unimpeachable to possibly uncertain and malleable. For example, in 1997, Louisiana's anti-discrimination law (La. RS § 23:352) specifically prohibited discrimination against persons with SCT in any way which would deprive any individual of employment opportunities or union membership.[14] Florida and North Carolina have enacted similar laws that prohibit discrimination in the workplace against people with SCT.[15] Less clear on the spectrum is the federal view. The Genetic Information Nondiscrimination Act of 2008 was enacted to prohibit discrimination on the basis of genetic information with respect to health insurance and employment.[16] Nevertheless, under the leadership of Nancy Berryhill, the Social Security Administration

(SSA) ruled in 2017 that SCT alone is not defined as an impairment. Instead, Berryhill's SSA provided this guidance:

> As defined by the Social Security Act, an impairment must result from anatomical, physiological, or psychological abnormalities that can be shown by medically acceptable clinical and laboratory diagnostic techniques. To establish an impairment ... we require objective medical evidence (medical signs and laboratory findings) from an acceptable medical source of complications from sickle cell trait. In addition, a person's complications from sickle cell trait must meet the statutory duration requirement, i.e., be expected to result in death or last or be expected to last for a continuous period of not less than 12 months. Therefore, we cannot find a person disabled due to sickle cell trait if there are no medical signs or laboratory findings of complications from sickle cell trait and the complications from sickle cell trait do not meet the duration requirement.[17]

Under this guidance, only at the moment of death or following year-long complications resulting from SCT would a student athlete living with SCT be recognized as dis/abled by the SSA.

## The athletes

From 2000 to 2011, at least 17 high school and college student athletes suffered sudden death on the training field, attributable to SCT (Limón 2011). Many of these athletes were the children of recent Caribbean immigrants. Many were football players (Tanier 2017).[18] Between 2004 and 2008, all deaths directly attributable to SCT occurred among *African-American* Division I football athletes, and the risk of exertional death was found to be 37 times higher than in players without SCT (Harmon et al. 2012).

Two examples are given: on September 24, 2006, Dale Lloyd, a 19-year-old Rice University football player, took the college football field in Texas for the fatal workout of his life. He ran 16 consecutive 100-yard sprints before collapsing on the field. His coach refused to allow his teammates to help him. Lloyd lost and never regained consciousness, dying from complications of SCT triggered by his exertions on the field. His autopsy reported that the cause of death was acute exertional rhabdomyolysis secondary to SCT. On September 23, 2008, his parents brought a wrongful death lawsuit against Rice University, the National Collegiate Athletic Association (NCAA), the head football coach, two school doctors, and nutritional supplement companies who were alleged to have a role in his death. As a result of the subsequent settlement on June 19, 2009, the NCAA revised its bylaws to require testing for SCT, and on August 1, 2010, implemented mandatory screening of all Division I NCAA athletes. By 2013, the requirement had been extended to Division II and Division III schools ("NCAA, Div. II School Sued over Sickle Cell Death" 2013).

In March 2008, UCF wide receiver Ereck Plancher collapsed to his death after an offseason workout. A Florida jury found the UCF Athletics Association negligent in Plancher's death and awarded his parents $10 million. However, in 2015, the Florida Supreme Court overturned the UCFAA's liability for payment of this award to $200,000, under principles of limited sovereign immunity.[19]

There are likely nearly 670 players competing at the highest levels of collegiate football who have SCT (Limón 2011). It has been estimated that universal screening would identify over 2000 NCAA Division I student athletes with SCT, and that without intervention over a 10-year period, approximately eight student athletes would die suddenly from complications associated with SCT. Several commercially available blood tests to screen for the trait cost as low as $2–4.00 per sample with high reliability (Bonham et al. 2010). Many university doctors and athletic trainers supported compulsory testing, but opponents fear that athletes determined to have the trait could be denied the chance to compete (Bonham et al. 2010). In the absence of accommodations, such as aggressive hydration and temperature monitoring, universal screening would only prevent death from SCT complications by dis/including athletes who tested positive (Kark et al., 2008; Tarini et al., 2012).

Examples of SCT screening programs that have done more harm than good abound. In the 1970s, 10 states with the largest African-American population passed mandatory screening laws, effectively compelling more than 40% of the total African-American population of the United States to submit to mandatory sickle cell screening (Rutkow & Lipton 1974). The state of Virginia, as an example, expressly mandated compulsory screening for SCT. Section 32–112.10 of the Code of Virginia provided:

> In order to protect and preserve the health and welfare of the citizens of the Commonwealth, every parent, guardian, or other person in the Commonwealth having control or charge of any child who has reached his sixth birthday shall present the child to a duly licensed physician for sickle cell trait test [sic] and such physician shall perform or cause such sickle trait tests to be performed as he, in his professional judgment and discretion, deems necessary or required.[20]

The General Assembly of Virginia thus accomplished several aims with this statute. First, it established a mandate that appeared to apply race neutrally to *every* child in the Commonwealth even as it deputized and empowered the local (male) physician to act, as an actant or *entelechy* within this network, to inscribe and measure, as *he*, in *his* discretion, determined, thus opening space and providing cover for racial essentialism to distinguish children for whom screening is/not "necessary or required" (regardless of the substantial stigmatizing effects of such a screening, and with little or no evidence in support of the medical value of detecting SCT in preadolescent children—other than race); and second, it raised the legal scaffolding for the professional networks of scientists and medical professionals to bridge, influence and connect with (as "chains of translation" in Latour's terms) the networks of the state, school, and other public entities down below, and adopt the interests and concerns of those networks (Joyce 2012; Latour 1993).[21] Following an extensive campaign by the Nixon administration, on May 16, 1972, Congress enacted the National Sickle Cell Anemia Control Act, which implemented mass screenings to identify individuals with sickle cell. Although the federal statute indicated that participation would be voluntary, persons found to be carrying SCT could be denied life insurance, health insurance, and discriminated against at work (Lappé et al. 1972; Rutkow & Lipton 1974). Additionally, 22 state health departments reportedly favored premarital screening procedures as a prerequisite to obtaining a marriage license, with no or poor counseling, prompting an outcry from the African-American community "voices have already been heard charging that this (genetic counseling) is simply another white plot aimed at carrying out genocide against the blacks" (Rutkow & Lipton 1974).[22]

This painful and abusive history of mandatory and/or prejudicial screening programs reflects its own actor-network of state and federal governments, health departments, insurance companies, but it also constitutes part of the broader context that informs the brown commons of the athletic field, where the subjective experiences, suspicions, fears, and vulnerabilities of athletes with SCT respond to the deployment of power by actors networked in and through the incentives of the sports-financial complex. In Latour-speak, the relationship between these networks reveals a *technological process* within the ANT enabled by law, in which the racial interests circulating and inscribed within each network easily move between and among linked networks of government-medico-sports complexes, each actor-network enlisting and translating the (racial) interests of the other, which can then be deployed to allow discrimination against children in the brown commons of that actor network (Latour 1996, 2000; Latour & Woolgar 1979). In order to design and enforce meaningful solutions, dis/ability law must understand how discrimination operates in the subjective experiences and objective (and interlinked) actor-networks of power in the brown commons.

## Conclusion

This chapter focuses on the subjective aspirations and vulnerabilities of student athletes who labor with SCT under the burden of the objective networks of differential power in the brown commons of the sports industry. Neither these subjective nor objective dimensions of the brown commons appear in jurisprudence of dis/ability law that defines the limits of accommodation and protects against discrimination. By the time these players are ready to play at the professional level, overt discrimination by the teams is quite open. As former Pittsburgh Steelers safety Ryan Clark has said, "of course they'll bring those things up because they're trying to get players as cheap as possible" (Thomas & Zarda 2010). While young African-American and Latinx players drafted into professional leagues may be understandably grateful for the opportunity

(Srikanth 2021), expanding the framework of dis/ability jurisprudence to incorporate this narrative-in-reverse is critical to articulating meaningful legal protections for at-risk athletes driven to overexert until they suffer exertional death on the field.

## Acknowledgement

I am greatly indebted to the editors Frank Rudy Cooper, Micky Lee, and Patricia A. Reeve, for including me, and who brought this project to a successful on deadline completion despite the coronavirus disease (COVID-19) pandemic. I would like to acknowledge commenters on my work, Mary Crossley, Eric Miller, Kim Hebben, and Raphaela Tkotzyk for their invigorating conversations. I also thank John W. Murphy for discussing an early draft of this chapter. Without the support of Robin C. Schard and Barbara Cuadras at the University of Miami School of Law Library access to hard to find sources and materials would not have been possible. Finally, I am eternally and deeply grateful to my wife, Elizabeth M. Iglesias, for her enduring support and wisdom.

## Notes

1 For my original articulation of "narrative-in-reverse" as interpretative methodology, see Plasencia (2014).

2 The works of Bruno Latour pioneered the theory of ANT, especially in the social sciences. Latour reveals the connections between structure, framework, and what he calls "the Wolf of Context" as these relate to all interactions. See, e.g., Latour (1996, 2005). Latour's notions of "modality" and "splitting" in the context of natural entities (human and non-human alike) eerily made me think of the COVID-19 coronavirus, as these entities are at play, escape the laboratory setting, and are severed from their origins (Latour & Woolgar 1979). Latour's earlier works set the stage for describing society as social in the sense that things are *associated* with one another, and as a way of assembling or tying heterogeneous bundles, *translating* entities into another, explaining how subjects (such as microbes) are recalcitrant to compliance, and "strike back" (Latour 2000).

3 In expressly following Latour's theory of ANT, Carter and Dyson theorize that the sickle cell gene *itself* has agency and power to do things, including the power to influence the character of the networks into which it has been assembled. Thus, within ANT, sickle cell trait eludes being exclusively cabined as a genetic condition, a political project, or an artifact of racism.

4 Anthropologist Melbourne Tapper (1999) argues that since 1910, sickle cell anemia has been used to promote and construct white superiority and identity hierarchies in public health and medical science discourses where, for example, "[s]ickling was presented not only as a flaw within the constitution of the black body, but also, more important, as a particular threat to urban black communities" (p. 104). Campbell discusses desire and dis/ability, and the long history of people with dis/abilities in association with carnivals and *freak* shows (Campbell, 2009). I also wish to acknowledge and thank Eric Miller for specifically introducing notions of the "freak-athlete" in our lively exchanges during the book-related symposium.

5 As mounting evidence pointed to the global prevalence of the sickle cell gene, the medical and scientific literature endorsed expanding newborn universal screening for

sickle cell. During the period spanning from 1990 to 1994, the state of California Newborn Screening Program identified 6,921 non-African-American infants with sickle cell trait among the 2 million infants screened (Ballas & Park 1996; Hayeems et al. about the experience in Canada; Shafer et al., 1996).

6 Krieger (2003) discusses dis/ability under the ADA, e.g., "Murphy v. United Parcel Serv., Inc., 527 U.S. 516, 119 S. Ct. 2133 (1999) (high blood pressure controllable by medication does not constitute a disability under the ADA); Sutton v. United Airlines, Inc., 527 U.S. 471, 119 S. Ct. 2139 (1999) (correctable myopia does not constitute a disability under the ADA); and Albertson's, Inc. v. Kirkingburg, 527 U.S. 516, 119 S. Ct. 2162 (1999) (individuals with monocular vision are not per se "disabled" within the meaning of the ADA, but must prove on a case-by-case basis that their conditions substantially limit a major life activity)."

7 *Bragdon v. Abbott*, 524 U.S. 624, 641 (1998).

8 *Bragdon v. Abbott*, 524 U.S. at 637.

9 *Sutton v. United Air Lines*, 527 U.S. 471, 488–89 (1999).

10 The ADA Amendments Act of 2008, 110 P.L. § 325 (2008).

11 *Price Waterhouse v. Hopkins*, 490 U.S. 228, 265 (1989) (O'Connor, J., concurring).

12 *Automobile Workers v. Johnson Controls, Inc.*, 499 U.S. 187 (1991) (exclusionary policy in battery manufacturing factory barring the participation of potentially fertile and pregnant women in occupations that could be detrimental to their reproductive capacities constituted sexual discrimination in violation of Title VII of the 1964 Civil Rights Act). I wish to acknowledge Mary Crossley for pointing out this case.

13 On September 15, 2004, Aaron Richardson, an 18-year-old who aspired to be a non-scholarship "walk-on" defensive back for Bowling Green State University, showed up for the 3 PM practice, and participated in "gassers," a conditioning exercise involving interval sprints from sideline to sideline in 85 degrees. The walk-ons ran these gassers on a different field from the scholarship players. Finishing the gassers, Aaron, and the other third-string and walk-on players moved to yet another field for a stretching regimen. Aaron began to complain that he was cramping, and a student coach attempted to assist him by stretching Aaron's calves as Aaron lay on his back. Then the assistant coach cautioned Aaron to "get out of the sun and go inside," further warning Aaron that he might "not be cut out for football." The student coach testified that the defensive coordinator and coach who supervised the other coaches, then yelled at Aaron to "get the fuck off the field!" *Estate of Richardson v. Bowling Green State Univ.*, No. 2005-10179, slip op. 3475, 1, 5–6 (Ohio Ct. Cl. 2010).

14 Prohibition of sickle cell trait discrimination; exceptions, LA. STAT. ANN. § 23:352 (La. 1997).

15 Employment discrimination on basis of sickle-cell trait prohibited, FLA. STAT. § 448.075-76 (1978); Discrimination against any person possessing sickle cell trait or hemoglobin C trait prohibited, 95-28.1 N.C. Gen. Stat. (1975).

16 Genetic Information Nondiscrimination Act of 2008, 42 U.S.C. §§ 2000ff-1 (2008).

17 Titles II and XVI of the Social Security Act: Evaluating Cases Involving Sickle Cell Disease (SCD), 82 F.R. § 43442 (2017).

18 These are some of the players who collapsed to their deaths on the football field. Many were Caribbean immigrants, including 15-year-old high schooler Olivier Louis – September 7, 2010; Preston Birdsong - Tennessee Tech - August 13, 2000; Devaughn Darling – Florida State – February 26, 2001; Aaron Richardson – Bowling Green – September 15, 2004; Aaron O'Neal – Missouri – July 12, 2005; Dale Lloyd II – Rice – September 25, 2006; Ereck Plancher – Central Florida – March 18, 2008; Chad Wiley – North Carolina A&T – May 28, 2008; Ja'Quayvin Smalls – Western Carolina – July 8, 2009.

19 *Enock Plancher v. UCF Athletics Association, Inc.*, 175 So. 3d 724 (Fla. 2015).

20 1972 Va. Acts 1141.

21 I am reiterating and extending Latour's notions of translation or network, and have benefitted from and wish to acknowledge specifically the formulations of ANT as explained by Campbell (2009) and Carter and Dyson (2015).
22 Quoting Schwartz, H. Resentment Complicates the Case. N.Y. Times, November 5, 1972.

## References

Anderson, S., (2017). NCAA football off-season training: unanswered prayers … a prayer answered. *Journal of Athletic Training*. **52**(2), 145–148. doi:10.4085/1062-6050-52.3.02

Annamma, S. A., Connor, D. and Beth, F., (2013). Dis/ability critical race studies (DisCrit): theorizing at the intersections of race and dis/ability. *Race Ethnicity and Education*. **16**(1), 1–31. doi:10.1080/13613324.2012.730511

Annamma, S. A., Ferri, B. A. and Connor, D. J., (2018). Disability critical race theory: exploring the intersectional lineage, emergence, and potential futures of DisCrit in education. *Review of Research in Education*. **42**(1), 46–71. doi:10.3102/0091732X18759041

Anzalone, M. L. et al., (2010). Sickle cell trait and fatal rhabdomyolysis in football training: a case study. *Medicine and science in sports and exercise*. **42**(1), 3–7. doi:10.1249/MSS.0b013e3181ae0700

Austin, H. et al., (2007). Sickle cell trait and the risk of venous thromboembolism among blacks. *Blood*. **110**(3), 908–912. doi:10.1182/blood-2006-11-057604

Ballas, S. K. and Park D., (1996). Newborn screening for Sickle Cell Disease. *Journal of Pediatric Hematology/Oncology*. **18**(4), 418.

Bonham, V. L., Dover, G. J. and Brody, L. C., (2010). Screening student athletes for sickle cell trait – a social and clinical experiment. *The New England Journal of Medicine*. **363**(11), 997–999. doi:10.1056/NEJMp1007639.

Buchanan, D. J., (1978). Genes of sickle cell disease. *British Journal of Sports Medicine*. **12**(2), 107. doi:10.1136/bjsm.12.2.107.

Cahill, C. R., Leach, J. M., McClure, L. A., Irvin, M. R., Zakai, N. A., Naik, R., Unverzagt, F., Wadley, V. G., Hyacinth, H. I., Manly, J., Judd, S. E., Winkler, C. and Cushman, M., (2019). Sickle cell trait and risk of cognitive impairment in African-Americans: the REGARDS cohort. *EClinicalMedicine*. **11**, 27–33. doi: 10.1016/j.eclinm.2019.05.003

Campbell, F. K., (2008). Refusing able(ness): a preliminary conversation about ableism. *M/C Journal*. **11**(3). doi:10.5204/mcj.46

Campbell, F. K., (2009). *Contours of ableism: the production of disability and abledness*. New York: Palgrave Macmillan.

Carter, B. and Dyson, S. M., (2015). Actor Network Theory, agency and racism: the case of Sickle Cell Trait and US athletics. *Social Theory & Health*. **13**(1), 62–77.

Casa, D. J. et al., (2012). National athletic trainers' association position statement: preventing sudden death in sports. *Journal of athletic training*. **47**(1), 96–118. doi:10.4085/1062-6050-47.1.96

Connor, D., Ferri, B. A., and Annamma, S. A. eds., (2016). DisCrit: *disability studies and critical race theory in education*. New York: Teachers College Press.

"Consensus statement: sickle cell trait and the athlete", (n/a). National Athletic Trainers' Association. Available from: https://www.nata.org/sites/default/files/sicklecelltraitandtheathlete.pdf

Davis, L. ed., (2017). *The disability studies reader*. 5th ed. New York: Routledge.

DeNavas-Walt, C. and Proctor, B. D., (2015). *Income and poverty in the United States: 2014*. Washington, DC: U.S. Government Printing Office. Available from: https://www.census.gov/content/dam/Census/library/publications/2015/demo/p60-252.pdf

DuBois, W. E. B., ed., (1906). The health and physique of the Negro American. *Report of a social study made under the direction of Atlanta University; together with the proceedings of the Eleventh Conference for the Study of the Negro Problems*, Held at Atlanta University, on May the 29th, 1906. Atlanta, GA: Atlanta University Press.

Fain, P., (2017). Deadly day for college football. *Inside Higher Ed* [online]. February. Available from: https://www.insidehighered.com/news/2017/09/21/two-college-football-players-die-after-games-last-weekend-another-paralyzed

Foster, M. W. and Sharp, R. R., (2002). Race, ethnicity, and genomics: social classifications as proxies of biological heterogeneity. *Genome Research*. **12**(6), 844–850. doi: 10.1101/gr.99202

García-Peña, L., (2015). Translating *Blackness*. *The Black Scholar*. **45**(2), 10–20. doi:10.1080/00064246.2015.1012993

Golomb, M. R., (2005). Sickle cell trait is a risk factor for early stroke. *Archives of Neurology*. **62**(11), 1778–1779. doi:10.1001/archneur.62.11.1778

Goodley, D., (2013). Dis/entangling critical disability studies. *Disability & Society*. **28**(5), 631–644. doi:10.1080/09687599.2012.717884

Goodley, D., (2014). *Dis/ability studies: theorising disablism and ableism*. New York: Routledge.

Harmon, K. G. et al., (2012). Sickle cell trait associated with a RR of death of 37 times in National Collegiate Athletic Association football athletes: a database with 2 million athlete-years as the denominator. *British Journal of Sports Medicine*. **46**(5), 325–330. doi:10.1136/bjsports-2011-090896

Hayeems, R. Z. et al., (2015). Expectations and values about expanded newborn screening: a public engagement study. *Health Expectations: An International Journal of Public Participation in Health Care and Health Policy*. **18**(3), 419–429. doi:10.1111/hex.12047

Hughes, B., (2007). Being disabled: towards a critical social ontology for disability studies. *Disability & Society*. **22**(7), 673–684. doi:10.1080/09687590701659527

Joyce, P., (2012). *The social in question: new bearings in history and the social sciences*. New York: Routledge.

Kark, J. A. et al., (2008). Sickle cell trait and fatal exertional heat illness: implications for exercise-related death of young adults. *American College of Sports Medicine (ACSM/DOD) Roundtable Conference*, October 22–23, 2008. Available from: https://apps.dtic.mil/sti/citations/ADA500648

Krieger, L. M., ed., 2003. *Backlash against the ADA: reinterpreting disability rights*. Ann Arbor: University f Michigan Press.

Lappé, M., Gustafson, J. M. and Roblin, R., (1972). Ethical and social issues in screening for genetic disease. *New England Journal of Medicine*. **286**, 1129–1132. doi:10.1056/NEJM197205252862104.

Latour, B., (1993). *We have never been modern*. Cambridge, MA: Harvard University Press.

Latour, B., (1996). *Aramis, or, the love of technology*. Cambridge, MA: Harvard University Press.

Latour, B., (2000). When things strike back: a possible contribution of 'science studies' to the social sciences. *The British Journal of Sociology*. **51**, 107–123. doi:10.1111/j.1468-4446.2000.00107.x

Latour, B., (2005). *Reassembling the social: an introduction to Actor-Network-Theory*. Oxford: Oxford University Press.

Latour, B. and Woolgar, S., (1979). *Laboratory life: the social construction of scientific facts*. New York: Sage.

Limón, I., (2011). MoreEducation Still Necessary Sickle Cell Trait Series: The Silent Killer, Part 3Great Strides Have Been Made, But There's Room For Progress. South Florida Sun-Sentinel. July 26. 1C. Retrieved from: https://infoweb.newsbank.com/apps/news/document-view?p=WORLDNEWS&docref=news/138C5893EDD55E30

McGinley, A. C. and Cooper, F. R., (2020). Intersectional cohorts, dis/ability, and class actions. *Fordham Urban Law Journal*. **47**, 293–341.

McGuire, A., (2010). Disability, non-disability and the politics of mourning: re-conceiving the "we". *Disability Studies Quarterly* [online], **30**(3/4). Available from: https://dsq-sds.org/article/view/1282/1309

McRuer, R., (2006). *Crip theory: cultural signs of queerness and disability*. New York: New York University Press.

Muñoz, J. E., (2020). *The sense of brown*. Durham, NC: Duke University Press.

Naik, R. P., Wilson, J. G., Ekunwe, L., Mwasongwe, S., Duan, Q., Li, Y., Correa, A. and Reiner, A. P., (2016). Elevated D-dimer levels in African Americans with sickle cell trait. *Blood*. **127**, 2261–2263. doi: 10.1182/blood-2016-01-694422

NCAA, Div. II School Sued over Sickle Cell Death, (2021). *USA Today* [online]. 9 September. Available from: https://www.usatoday.com/story/sports/ncaab/2013/09/09/slippery-rock-ncaa-sued-over-sickle-cell-death-of-jack-hill-jr/2787507/

Nelkin, D. and Lindee, M. S., (1995). *The DNA mystique: the gene as a cultural icon*. New York: W.H. Freeman.

Omi, M. and Winant, H., (2015). *Racial formation in the United States*. 3rd ed. New York: Routledge.

Plasencia, M. M., (2014). No right to lie, cheat or steal: public good v. private order. *University of Miami Law Review*. **68**(3), 678–761.

Rutkow, I. M. and Lipton, J. M., (1974). Some negative aspects of state health departments' policies related to screening for sickle cell anemia. *American Journal of Public Health*. **64**(3), 217–221. doi:10.2105/ajph.64.3.217

Serjeant, G. R., (2013). The natural history of sickle cell disease. *Cold Spring Harbor Perspectives in Medicine*. **3**(10), a011783. doi:10.1101/cshperspect.a011783

Shafer, F. E. and Lorey, F., (1996). Newborn screening for sickle cell disease: 4 years of experience from California's newborn screening program. *Journal of Pediatric Hematology/Oncology*. **18**(1), 36–41. doi:10.1097/00043426-199602000-00007

Siebers, T., (2008). *Disability theory*. Ann Arbor: The University of Michigan Press.

Srikanth, A., (2021). New NFL star throws draft party at homeless shelter where he and family once lived. *The Hill*. 30 April. Available from: https://thehill.com/changing-america/enrichment/arts-culture/551152-new-nfl-star-throws-draft-party-at-homeless-shelter

Tanier, M., (2017). Football's silent killer forces players and teams to make tough choices. *Bleacher Report*. 6 July. Available from: https://bleacherreport.com/articles/2716677-footballs-silent-killer-forces-players-and-teams-to-make-tough-choices

Tapper, M., (1999). *In the blood: sickle cell anemia and the politics of race*. Philadelphia: University of Pennsylvania Press.

Tarini, B. A., Brooks, M. A. and Bundy, D. G., (2012). A policy impact analysis of the mandatory NCAA sickle cell trait screening program. *Health Services Research*. **47**(1 Pt 2), 446–461. doi:10.1111/j.1475-6773.2011.01357.x

Thomas, C., (2007). *Sociologies of disability and illness: contested ideas in disability studies and medical sociology*. New York: Palgrave Macmillan.

Thomas, K. and Zarda, B., (2010). In N.C.A.A., question of bias over a test for a genetic trait. *The New York Times*. 12 April. p. 6.

Viego, A., (2009). The life of the undead: biopower, Latino anxiety and the epidemiological paradox. *Women & Performance: A Journal of Feminist Theory*. **19**(2), 31–147. doi:10.1080/07407700903034113

Yudell, M., Roberts, D., DeSalle, R. and Tishkoff, S., (2016). Taking race out of human genetics. *Science*. **351**(6273), 564–565. doi:10.1126/science.aac4951

# Index

For Product Safety Concerns and Information please contact our EU
representative GPSR@taylorandfrancis.com
Taylor & Francis Verlag GmbH, Kaufingerstraße 24, 80331 München, Germany

www.ingramcontent.com/pod-product-compliance
Ingram Content Group UK Ltd.
Pitfield, Milton Keynes, MK11 3LW, UK
UKHW020148200926
475702UK00016B/2608

*9781032189802*